JOEY PYLE

Notorious: The Changing Face of Organised Crime

JOEY PYLE

Notorious: The Changing Face of Organised Crime

Earl Davidson

This edition first published in Great Britain in 2005 by
Virgin Books Ltd
Thames Wharf Studios
Rainville Road
London
W6 9HA

First published in hardback in Great Britain in 2003 by
Virgin Books Ltd

6

A catalogue record for this book is available from the British Library.

ISBN 978 0 7535 0943 2

Typeset by TW Typesetting, Plymouth, Devon

The Random House Group Limited supports The Forest Stewardship
Council (FSC®), the leading international forest certification organisation.
Our books carrying the FSC label are printed on FSC® certified paper.
FSC is the only forest certification scheme endorsed by the leading
environmental organisations, including Greenpeace. Our
paper procurement policy can be found at
www.randomhouse.co.uk/environment

Printed and bound in Great Britain by Clays Ltd, St Ives PLC

CONTENTS

ACKNOWLEDGEMENTS

To the following:
My son Joe Pyle Jr, Julie, Roy Shaw, Craig, Mitch, Michelle, Ashley, Susan, Dave Fred, Paul and Wayne, Dave, Ted Pyle, Jean Pyle, Vic Park, Ajay and Brian Emmett.

Thanks for all your support.

To my pals:
Dave Thurston, Freddie Foreman, the Nash Family, Wally, Dave Courtney, Rod, Arthur, Braker, Tony Lambrianou, George Norris and Chris.

A big hello.

And to my pals in prison:
Charles Bronson, Big H, Charlie Smith, John McFadden and Jimmy Dowsett.

You should all have been let out years ago.

I dedicate this book to my mother, Cathleen, my brother-in-law Dennis and all my grandchildren.

INTRODUCTION

It was a traditional New York Mafia dinner and Joey Pyle was guest of honour.

The Londoner was one of fifteen men sitting around a large oak table in a lavishly decorated dining room at the corner of Howard and Bowery, the heart of Little Italy. The women knew better than to try to join in – they stayed in the kitchen, appearing only to serve up each new course.

The meal began with stuffed cannellonia in a rich *ragù* sauce made from braised beef, pork butt and veal shanks. This was followed by ziti with meat gravy, *maccheroni* with ricotta, flame-roasted red and orange peppers and string beans baked with olive oil and garlic. After that came steaming plates of pan-fried veal cutlets – golden brown on the outside, milky white within – rosti potatoes and heaps of rocket salad with pecorino and asparagus. Then, finally, zabaglioni with fresh fruit, and chocolate-dusted tiramisu with lashings of Marsala. Sorbets helped to cleanse the palate between courses and everything was washed down with gallons of fine Sicilian wine.

When it was all over and a few of the men had started lighting cigars, Danny, the eldest son, sidled over. 'Hey Joey,' he said, in his thick New York accent, 'the old man wants a word with you.'

Without hesitation, Joey got up and moved to the other end of the table where Joe Pagano, one of the leading lights in the Genovese family, the largest and most powerful of the five New York Mafia families, was holding court.

Pagano enjoyed an unequalled reputation following a life of distinguished service to the Mob. He had made his 'bones' during the early 1950s when he had been part of a team contracted to murder Eugenio Giannini, a gangster who had made the mistake of upsetting the legendary Charles 'Lucky' Luciano. Giannini was shot twice in the head with a .38 calibre handgun and his body was found lying face down in the gutter on Manhattan's 107th street by a deli owner opening up his shop.

Now in his seventies, Pagano was rhythmically tapping the side of his foot with his walking stick as Joey Pyle sat down beside him. The old man cleared his throat and then began to speak.

'Joe, can I help you in any way? Is there anything you would like me to do for you?'

'Nah, I'm OK thanks.'

'Are you sure? Do you need any money?'

'Nah, I got money, I got enough for now. There is one thing. I think I'm gonna head over to the West Coast – it's a bit warmer there – but if I come back to New York and my problems in London haven't gone away, I'd really appreciate it if you could get me a job or something.'

A mass of sharp creases appeared on Pagano's forehead. 'A job? What you talking about? A job? Why would you want a job? Forget about it. From this moment, from now on, you run with us.'

If there was nothing more to recount than the truly incredible saga of how one of London's most feared and respected gangsters came to be offered the hand of friendship by the New York Mafia, the story of Joey Pyle's life would be remarkable enough. But what quickly becomes clear the moment you sit down with Joey Pyle is that here is someone who has played a key role in virtually all of the seminal moments in British criminal history of the past forty years.

From the murder of Jack 'The Hat' McVitie by the Kray twins to the Great Train Robbery, from the police corruption scandals of the 1970s to the birth of unlicensed boxing, from the biggest Payola scam in the world to the unstoppable rise of the international drugs trade, Pyle has had a hand in it all.

The story of Joey Pyle's life is, in fact, the story of the changing face of professional organised crime.

Pyle first rose to prominence after a night of murder and bloody mayhem in a London drinking club. Sent to prison to await trial, with the threat of the hangman's noose hovering over him should he be found guilty, Pyle and his co-defendants quickly became some of the best-known criminals in the country.

A close friend of the Krays from the earliest days of the launch of their criminal empire, Pyle not only managed to maintain an equally close friendship with their sometime rivals, the Richardson brothers, but also escaped police swoops on both firms. By the end of the 1960s, with the Krays and Richardsons in prison and the Age of the Gangster at an end, Pyle was still at liberty and just getting into his stride.

It was a notoriety that did not escape the attention of the police. During the course of the next thirty years Pyle was arrested more than fifty times on charges ranging from robbery and firearms offences to murder and drug smuggling. He spent months in prison on remand but each and every time his case came to court, he would walk out a free man.

'The law have always hated me, fucking hated the sight of me. I've been their target more times than I care to think. I've been in police stations where the rooms have been full of files, wall to wall, and every single one has my name on it.

'But every time they put me through their washing machine, I came out clean. I don't care what they think. I've always said I'd rather they fucking hate me than love me. If they loved me, there would have to be something wrong with me. Once they like you, then you're a no good bastard in my book. That's how people like me see it.'

The end finally came courtesy of a controversial sting operation worthy of the FBI, involving undercover police officers, non-existent drug shipments, covert bugging devices and a liberal amount of economy with the truth.

'That night I was in my cell, just after I'd been sentenced to fourteen years and I was lying on my bed listening to the radio. Detective Chief Superintendent Coles, the man in charge of the investigation, came on and started talking about the case. "We are all celebrating down at the nick," he said. "And now that Mr Pyle is behind bars, the streets of London will be much safer." He made it sound as if I was running around with an axe like some kind of lunatic.'

Yet despite the years in prison, the violence and the hounding he has received from the police over the years, Pyle remains unrepentant and certain that, if he could live his life over, he would do it all again.

'Remorse? Regrets? Nah, there's none of that. If I had done anything in my life which I thought was wrong, then I would be sitting here wishing that I hadn't done it, that instead of what I did do, I'd taken some other path. But everything I have ever done, I did it because I thought it was right. And if I think something is right, then I couldn't care less what any of you people think. I wouldn't change a thing. Throughout my life, I've always gone with the grain in the wood. I've always done what I thought was right. I don't go against that grain. So why should I have any remorse?'

Earl Davidson

1. 'WHAT DO YOU WANT TO BE? A THIEF OR A FIGHTER?'

Joey Pyle's childhood was anything but conventional.

At the tender age of fourteen, while cycling home from his Saturday job in the local metal factory, Joey ran into his mother who was out looking for him. It was the start of an angry confrontation.

'Where's that fucking money Joey?'

'What money you talking about Mum?'

'Don't give me that. You know exactly what I'm talking about, you little git. You fucking went and robbed that place didn't you? Didn't you? The bloke's been round and told me everything. So where's the fucking money?'

Joey could hardly believe what he was hearing. It had only been nine, maybe ten hours since he had pulled off the biggest score of his life and already he had been grassed up. He got off his bike, reached into the saddlebag and pulled out a fat wad of notes. His mother took the bundle – more than five thousands pounds – and stuffed it down her bra. Then she clipped her son around the ear. 'The fucking police might be round the house tonight. They'd have easily found it there. What the fuck were you thinking of?'

Joey smiles at the memory. 'The thing is,' he explains, 'my mum wasn't angry about me doing the robbery – she didn't mind about that at all. She just didn't want me getting caught.'

The money had come from a TA centre in Hackbridge, close to Joey's home in Carshalton. 'They used to have a dance there one or two nights a week. They never had a safe or a till so they just used to stick all the money for wages in this big glass and lock it in the cloakroom. I found all this out because the caretaker decided to rob the place and wanted me to help. I'd been getting up to all sorts of petty thieving –

nicking lead from roofs and a bit of shoplifting, stuff like that – and the caretaker had heard about me through his son, who I was at school with.

'He got me a one-off job working in the cloakroom, hanging up coats and hats when there was a dance on, and the plan was that we'd do the robbery together that same night. But there was something about him that I didn't like so I decided to cut him out of the deal. Whenever I had a spare moment in the cloakroom I took out a screwdriver that I'd taken with me and used it to loosen all the putty around the main window. I didn't tell the caretaker about what I'd done, but later that night I went back with a mate of mine, popped out the window glass and nicked all the money.

'The next day the caretaker went straight round to my mum and told her everything. That's when she went out looking for me. There was no question of giving the money back. Both my parents felt I'd earned it. "Just as long as no one got hurt," my dad told me, "then you'll have no problem with us."'

The only person who did have a problem was the caretaker. He was furious because the job was his idea, but he'd been kept out of it.

'But that was nothing compared to how my dad felt about the fact that the man had gone and grassed me up. When he'd talked to my mum, he'd threatened to go to the police but there was no way he could without putting himself right in it. What he really wanted was a share of the loot. My dad was having none of it. That night he took me around to his house and knocked on the door until the bloke appeared. "You are a fucking dirty bastard and you ain't getting no money," he told him. "You can go and fuck yourself, you little grass." And then we left.

'That day I learned one of the most important lessons of my life: that the only thing worse than the police is a grass. It was a lesson I would never forget.

'As for the money, my mum kept hold of it and paid it out to me in bits and pieces, whenever I wanted to buy something. It was a fortune in those days and it must have lasted a good year. I bought whatever I wanted and, in those days, what I wanted most of all was clothes. Before long I was the best dressed kid in the neighbourhood. I was this little teenager going around in midnight blue Gabardine suits, orange crepe shoes, drapes and the lot. Up until then I'd only been dabbling in silly little things, but that was when I realised, for the first time, that not only did crime pay, but the hours were bloody good.'

Joey Pyle was born in the Angel, Islington in November 1937, the youngest of three children. His father, Arnie, had been a good thief in his day and had also dabbled with professional sports, showing promise as a boxer, footballer and cricketer. His mother, Cath – 'a game old girl who could fight like a man' – looked after Joey, his brother Ted and sister Jean.

Joey was just two when the Second World War broke out, and he spent the next six years in the Lancashire countryside. When he returned to London rationing was still in place, luxuries in short supply and petty crime had become a way of life for all those who wanted to do more than just get by.

The aftermath of the Blitz meant the streets of East London were the ultimate adventure playground for gangs of teenage boys, with unexploded bombs, condemned buildings and lumps of shrapnel by the score scattered all around.

As Pyle reached his teens, his family decided to relocate to Carshalton in south London. A bright and popular kid, Pyle soon made new friends, but the allure of the old East End never faded and Pyle made regular trips back to the Angel to hang out with his old pals.

'It's almost impossible to say how it happens – it just does. You meet one, you meet two, you build up and then suddenly you're part of a little gang. Only I had two gangs. When I was in Carshalton I used to hang out with a lad called Peter Marshall and another called Peter Tilley. Then there was a kid called Jack McVitie from Tooting – he became a pal. He'd lost his parents during the war and had been adopted by a local couple. Finally there was a half-Italian kid called Tony Baldessare. They were the main people, with a few others here and there. I also got to know this bloke called Charlie who lived up Wimbledon way.

'When I was up in Islington I was part of a different crowd. I'd got to know a kid called Johnny Nash, who was around my age. He was part of a big family – six brothers in all – and the whole lot of them lived on the City Road while I was round the corner on the Caledonian Road. I was at the Vernon school while Johnny, who was really bright, had won a scholarship to the Hugh Middleton School.

'Even though they were still young, Johnny and his brothers were getting pretty well known in the area. They could all look after themselves and because there were so many of them, they became a bit of a force to be reckoned with. They were a firm in themselves. I got very friendly with Johnny and then Jimmy Nash as well, but Billy was a lot older than me while the others, Ronnie, George and Roy were a bit younger. I'd hang out with Johnny and Jimmy whenever I got the chance but the only thing we got up to was kids stuff, just mucking about.'

Pyle had another reason to wish he had remained in Islington. Shortly before leaving the area he had taken up boxing, joining the Tiverton and Preedy Athletics and Boxing Club in Penton Street. Throughout the East End, boxing had long been seen as one of the best ways to break out of the ghetto, make a lot of money and still keep the respect of the people around you. But Pyle had another reason for pulling on the gloves.

'It was actually my mum who wanted me to do it, pushed me into it. It wasn't about the money – I was an amateur so I was just boxing for prizes – it was all about the love of the game. She and my dad both loved boxing and just wanted me to do it.'

From his earliest days in the ring, Pyle showed great promise. As his skills developed so the number of trophies on his mantelpiece began to grow. It helped that the club was an inspiring place to train. One of the highest profile boxers there was Terry Allen, at one time the World Flyweight Champion. Allen had begun his career using the name Edward Govier. After going AWOL from the British Navy during the war he swapped ID cards with a man named Terry Allen. He was eventually arrested and sent to Egypt for the remainder of the war, but he continued boxing throughout.

After the move Pyle joined a new boxing club in Carshalton and continued to build on his earlier success. He boxed his way through to the quarterfinals of the All England Championships, and a few months later he was awarded the much-prized title of 'most stylish boxer in Surrey'.

He left school at fifteen and worked briefly as a printer, but quickly realised the nine-to-five world was not for him. Word of his big payday from the TA centre job the year before had spread among his circle of friends; for all of them, the temptation to make a living from crime soon became overpowering – and addictive.

'Most kids after the war, they were all involved in some form of crime. Or at least all the ones I was hanging around with were. We'd all done a bit of nicking stuff out of shops when we were young and then just graduated into other things. Why did we turn out that way? There's no one you can pin the blame on, especially not our parents. It was just the ways things were. It was what I saw going on all around me and in the end you just fall in line with the way things are.

'When you planned out a robbery and then you saw it succeed, it gave you a real lift. It was good to see. And it was a hell of a lot better than going to work and sweeping a factory floor. It had to be. And even if you had a job that you quite liked, I realised that I'd much rather be sitting there cutting up a bag of money with my mates than waiting to get a cheque paid into my bank. It's a hell of a lot more exciting, even if it's the same money. Working never became a way of life, but crime did.

'We got up to all sorts but we had our standards and we had our codes. As far as we were concerned, a man who went and robbed someone of their watch or their wallet, well he was just a no-good bastard – you wouldn't have anything to do with someone like that. We were all proud of what we did and we would discuss our robberies with each other.'

As time went by, Pyle's south London gang, made up of the likes of Jack McVitie, Tony Baldessare and the two Peters, got better and better at what they did. They targeted mostly cigarette shops and wholesalers at first because the stuff was always easy to sell on. Some of them had alarms, large bells fixed on the front above the door. The team soon worked out how to get round those. They would drill a hole in the top, mix some plaster of Paris and pour it in. When it set it was rock hard and the bell wouldn't be able to ring.

A more sophisticated form of alarm was the silent bell, which would be linked directly to the nearest police station. Lesser villains who were unaware of the existence of such technology would often find the police waiting for them the moment they emerged from a robbery. Pyle was determined not to come a cropper in the same way.

The gang devised a system whereby they could check what sort of alarm was in place before going ahead with a robbery. The lock of the front door would be opened, either by force or with a skeleton key purchased from a bent security guard or locksmith. If a silent alarm was in place, that act alone would activate it. Once the lock was open Pyle and the others would retreat to a safe distance and keep the place under observation for a couple of hours. If no one turned up – either the owner or the police – it was safe to assume that there was no silent alarm in place. They would lock the shop once more, assemble a crew and go back to rob it.

Once Pyle reached the age of eighteen, everything stopped to make way for National Service. 'I knew the army would be a good place to keep my fitness going, so at first I signed up to do a Physical Training Instructor course. Then, as I found out more about it, I changed my mind. It was more than just PT, there was loads of army bullshit that went along with it and I wasn't interested. Then the corps wanted to know if they had any boxers. I put my hand up and ended up being transferred to Sandhurst as an instructor, training the officer cadets.

'I didn't have to do any army duties at all, just training in the gym, boxing and teaching boxing all day long. I was part of the Southern Command Team, fighting as a middleweight. The main heavyweight on the team was a bloke called Henry Cooper, later British champion, who went on to challenge Muhammad Ali for the world heavyweight title. His brother George was there too. I loved it. The team was worked hard and it was taken very seriously. We had loads of contests and I became army champion.'

Ironically, it was only when Joey gave up crime to join the army that he ended up getting his first criminal conviction.

'Me and a kid called Harris used to like to take girls out on the town. We didn't have cars so we used to borrow the ones belonging to the officers. We'd take a different car each week then bring it back at the end of the night and no one ever seemed to notice. But then one day we took a car without realising that it belonged to the brigadier. We were on our way back when we got spotted, dumped the car and ran for it. But we were caught down an alleyway. We both denied the car was anything to do with us but a week later Harris decided to own up. He told them he had stolen the car with me and that was it, I was up before the courts for the first time in my life.

'They decided to prosecute me criminally, rather than a court marshal, and I was found guilty of taking and driving away. At the time they had introduced a new system to replace Borstal. They called it the short sharp shock – a regime of hard physical exercise and touch discipline. It was a brutal place and I hated every minute of it. Everything had to be done on the double – you couldn't relax for a minute. And the screws were really nasty. If you didn't do what they said or didn't do it quick enough they would punch you full in the face. You just couldn't do anything about it, you just had to accept that it was gonna be like that.

'My first morning there I woke up and looked out of the window to see it was snowing outside, there were a good couple of inches of it on the ground. I knew that every morning was supposed to start off with PT and I pulled on this pair of grey flannel trousers, which were part of the kit, and then went out into the hall. That's when I noticed that everyone else was wearing shorts.

'The PT instructor came stomping over to me.

'"Where are your shorts?"

'"It's snowing outside."

'"I know, but that doesn't stop you doing your PT. Come here you."'

The instructor took Pyle by the scruff of the neck, made him change into his shorts and then fetched a large duck-board off the floor of the shower. 'He made me hold it in front of me like a snow plough and then made me clear a path in the yard. I was fucking freezing. Once I'd finished, all the others came out and we did our PT. I really hated it. Everything was hard in there and it was double up, double up all the time.'

When he finished serving his time, Pyle was kicked off the boxing team and thrown out of Sandhurst. He finished his time in the Pioneer Corps but the large amount of boxing success he had had in the army convinced Pyle that the thing to do was turn professional.

Pyle emerged from the army in the early part of the summer but, with most of the professional boxing circuit taking place in the winter, his trainer suggested he join a boxing-booth in the interim.

In the post-war, pre-television days, boxing-booths were big business and seen as the ideal training grounds for up-and-coming fighters. Freddie Mills, one time world light heavyweight champion, Dick and Randy Turpin and Tommy

Farr all served their time in the booths before going on to bigger and better things.

There were a hundred or so booths in existence at the time, each attached to a travelling fair and moving around the country during the summer. The boxers, usually wearing robes, would line up outside the tent, often jogging on the spot to keep their muscles warm. The MC would then start building up a crowd: 'If any one of you fancies your chance against any of our champions then step forward now.' Then he would pull a wad of notes from his pocket and count out five pounds. 'If you last three rounds, only three rounds, just six minutes, that's all, then these five notes are yours. Who wants to win a fiver? Come on up and show your girl what you are made of.'

What would almost always happen next is that someone from the crowd would make a derogatory comment directed towards one of the boxers. 'I saw him fight yesterday, he's useless, my mother could knock him out.' And so on. The boxer would say a few things in return and the insults would get more and more out of hand until the pair had to be held back from going at it there and then. That was when the MC would intervene: 'Gentlemen, gentlemen, why not come up and settle your differences the British way?'

Once the two men had agreed to battle it out under the Queensbury rules, the crowd would invariably cheer and the tickets to the tent where the bout would take place were almost always sold out within minutes.

The boxers were paid a paltry fifty shillings a week but if they put on a particularly good show, members of the audience would throw coins into the ring, or the manager would pass the hat round. But being at the booths wasn't about money; it was about training. All the top managers of the day would send their wannabe professional boxers off to the booths in order to learn the finer points of the noble art, claiming that one month on the booths would be worth at least three in the gym.

On busy days, the fighters could be in the ring five or six times against a wide range of opponents, though things were not always what they seemed. 'Most of the time the fights were fixed – the bloke in the crowd would be one of the fighters from the booth putting on an act. But every now and then you would get a genuine one, a straight – that was what they called it. It would happen when someone got up out of the crowd and pushed and pushed and pushed. If that happened, then the boss had to let them have a fight to stop people getting suspicious. There would be drunken louts out to impress their girlfriends, rock-hard dockers and farm boys who didn't care whether they got hurt or not, and old pros eager to have one last shot at a bit of ring glory.

'Trouble was, the straights were not good for business. If they were so drunk they were useless, which most of them were, then it was impossible to make them look good in the ring. The crowd would know right away that you were taking it easy. But on the other hand, if they were sober and out to kill you, then you had to knock them over straight away and the punters would go away thinking they had been cheated of their money.

'The best thing was to have two professionals having a proper fight. That way it would look good, last the distance and everyone would go home happy.'

By the time winter came around, Pyle felt he was primed and ready for his first professional fight. He was wrong. Losing the bout did little to put him off his chosen career. In fact, it only made him all the more determined. He stepped up his training routine, dedicating himself to the art. It paid off handsomely. Over the course of the next couple of years Pyle had a further 23 professional fights and won every single one, mostly by knockout or stoppage.

'I trained hard. I trained hard for every fight. I was still a bad boy but I never neglected my training. I went running every day, I was always down the gym. As far as I was concerned, I was a professional boxer – that was how I was making my living. Everything else was the icing on the cake.'

Still living at home, Pyle was working his way towards a long career as a boxer. But it was only a matter of time before his two chosen professions came to a head.

'It was pouring down with rain and I'd gone to bed just after nine, which had become part of my routine the night before a fight. I'd only been in bed for an hour or so when my father came upstairs. "Joe, there's two of your mates downstairs." It took me a few seconds to wake and ask what they wanted. "I don't know, they just asked me to wake you up."

'I went down and Peter Tilley and Peter Marshall were at the door.

' "What's the matter then?"

' "We've just turned a snout shop off, we want you to make one," said Marshall.

' "I can't, I'm fighting tomorrow."

' "How much are you making for that?"

' "About two hundred pounds."

' "Well you're gonna get a grand for this lot."

'Then I looked at the two Peters, standing there in the rain.

' "Ah fuck it, hang on a minute."

'I rushed upstairs and threw on a pair of trousers and an old raincoat. On the way down I passed my dad on the stairs.

' "What are you doing, Joey? Are you crazy? You're fighting tomorrow. You must be mad."

' "But Dad, I can get more money this way."

' "Look son, you've got to make a decision. What do you want to be – a thief or a fighter?"

' "Dad, I think I want to be a thief."

'I went straight out after that and got the stuff – a motherload of cigarettes. I drew the short straw and ended up being the one who sat with it. That was the way it worked, you didn't just leave it somewhere, you sat with it all night until you saw the buyer the next day. I didn't get a wink of sleep. The sale went smoothly – I met the buyer, gave him the stuff, got the money and went straight to the weigh-in for the fight. And did I ever look fucking terrible.

'I went home and got about three hours sleep then it was time to go to the fight. The guy was all over me. Every punch was like a hammer blow and I had nothing in response. In the third round, he stopped me. I wasn't happy that I'd lost but by then I'd already decided to give the fight game up.'

Instead Pyle turned his attention to bigger and better robberies. There were wages snatches, bank robberies and attacks on security vans, all carried out with military precision.

'When you're on a blag, it's like being part of a football team. Each person has their role and you count on the rest of them to pull their weight. We'd get tip-offs about likely targets and the normal percentage for that kind of information is ten per cent of whatever you get.

'Once you'd picked a day, you'd work on getting your tools together – skeleton keys, a gemmy for the door – getting a ringed car for the getaway and stuff like that. If you could go and have a look at the place you would, but most of the time you'd have to base your plans on what you had been told. You just take the information and hope for the best.

'I was working mostly with the two Peters and Tony Baldessare, but then we got into blowing safes and we needed to bring other people in. For that, you needed someone who knew what they were doing – it was a profession in itself. There was this bloke, George Medicine, and he was the best in the business and we used to work with him. You would find the safe and he would plug loads of gelignite around the keyhole, then put plasticine on top to hold it in place and then slip in a detonator. You didn't want to be in the room when the thing went off so what he used to do was take the light bulb out of the socket and run the wires to that. Then you'd all hide in the next room and he'd reach round, switch on the light and boom. That was that.

'When I used to tell people about it, they were always amazed that you could get away with it when you were making so much noise. Sometimes you used to try to muffle the thing with carpets or whatever you could find in there, but there was no real need.

'My old man, who had blown a few safes in his time, once said to me when I was a kid: "What do people do when they hear a bang? If they're lying in bed and they hear a bang? I'll tell you what they do. They wait for a second bang. If there's no second bang then they turn over and go back to sleep." And he was right. Any noise you hear, nine times out of ten people wonder what the noise is but, instead of jumping out of bed, they wait to hear it again. So when you blow a safe, you have your one big bang and then you stop. You don't move. You wait for everything to be sweet then you go in, get your money and get out of there.'

It wasn't always so straightforward. 'Sometimes it was almost comical. We had done a few snatches on the pavement and that had worked pretty well so we decided to do another. We saw this fella down in Clapham going in and out of betting shops, collecting all the money, and decided to follow him. We waited until he had made his very last collection and then jumped him. The idea was to take the bag and run off, but he put up a hell of a fight. Then we realised the bloody thing was a on a chain around his wrist. We had to smash him across the head a couple of times to let him know we were serious, but even then we couldn't get the chain off.

'We weren't panicking, but it was all taking much longer than we had planned. No one had brought any bolt cutters because we hadn't been expecting it. In the end we got it off but it took a hell of a lot of effort. After that, we always tried to be prepared for whatever might happen.

'Another time we got a tip about this safe in a factory up north. The tip we got said that the safe was about three feet high and that the place was completely unguarded at night. When we got there, we found there were a couple of security guards on patrol. We tried to sneak in without being seen but, as we were creeping along one of the corridors, one of them came round the corner. He never stood a chance. We got the other one as well, tied them up, put typewriter hoods over their heads and dragged them along with us as we went to find the safe.

'When we got to the room we were in for a bit of a shock. The safe was massive, at least eight foot high. We knew the only way we were going to blow it was to put a big load of gelignite into it, and that's what we did.

'When Georgie set it off, it was like a fucking atom bomb. The door flew off – I mean it really flew. It went right across the room, smashing everything in its path including the wall. I thought the fucking building was going to fall down. All our ears were ringing and everyone was shaking like leaves. I don't know what the two guys on the floor with the hoods on must have thought.

'The next day we all had a good laugh when we read the papers. They had interviewed one of the guards and he was talking about how he had put up a real fight and almost stopped the robbery. It was a load of rubbish. In fact, he'd been so little trouble that we'd actually stuffed a few quid into his top pocket on our way out.'

At the same time as Joey and his south London friends were getting involved in ever-more sophisticated robberies, so his north London friends were also expanding into new areas.

'I had made a lot of good friends on the booths. One guy, Johnny Read, became a real pal and once the season was finished, he moved into the spare room at my parents' house. He was a great fighter, rated number four in the world, a top middleweight. I was living in Carshalton but still going back into town all the time to see the Nash brothers and my other friends, and soon Johnny was part of that circle too.'

The Nash brothers had moved into the club business, offering a new form of protection to owners. At the time most of the 'security' being offered was nothing more than a cheap con trick. Gangs of heavies would invade a club and cause as much damage as possible. A few days later the same heavies would then approach the owners and offer them 'protection' from further damage in return for a rake-off. Once terms had been agreed the wrecking crew would install a 'tough' on the front door, not so much for the security of the club but to prevent any other gang from moving in on the patch. Along with Joey Pyle, the Nash Brothers operated differently. They would only enter a club on invitation and their reputation alone would be enough to ensure troublemakers stayed away. It didn't take long for the Nashes to realise just how much money some of the clubs were able to make, a revelation which led them to set up clubs of their own.

The activities of the Nash family were being duplicated by the Kray twins a little further east, who had opened up the Double R club in Bow. Ronnie Nash had opened his own club in Islington and a dozen or so other smaller gangs had places in-between. Gambling was still illegal and many villains saw a golden opportunity to establish themselves in business before the law changed.

Billy Nash, the brains behind the brothers, penned an extraordinary article for the now-defunct *Sunday Pictorial*, which summarised the state of London's gangland in the late 1950s and early 60s.

The trouble now is over the clubs. There are about ten or a dozen families in the club game running all that goes with it – the birds, the protection, the gambling and one new thing, the one-armed bandits.

If you want to find the basic cause it's the Street Offences Act of 1959. Everyone was pleased when the birds were run off the streets but now they are in the clubs. When the Act started the clubs suddenly became valuable property. Where a back street club was once taking thirty to fifty quid a week for its owner, all of a sudden the birds came in and the place was a goldmine.

A lot of the little club owners didn't want to be bothered so the gangs started taking over the clubs. Often the men who had been working for the little club owner, protecting him, either genuinely or on the racket, took over by force. The take-over bids being made for clubs these days are made in bullets instead of stocks and shares.

That's the way it goes. There are the have and the have-nots in the club game and the haves need muscles and guns to keep what they've got. Me and my brothers would quit the rackets if we could but how could we? I'm not a violent man by nature and you can believe that or not. But it's true I never wanted to join in any of these capes. But no one would let me get out of it now. We have to be on our guard day and night against people who want to do us harm. We have the toughest reputation in London. That means there are fools all over London who would try to take us and make their names. They include violent men of all kinds, clever crooks, moronic muscle men and silly little Teddy-boys who think they are tough. Remember, these people would only have to knock over a Nash and they would be famous among the gangs for years.

The Kray twins were getting involved in the same activity, and south of the river it was the Richardsons. But none were in the same league as the Nash brothers at the time. Says Joey: 'Although the Twins would ultimately become far more notorious, you would have been in a lot more trouble if you came up against the Nashes than the Krays in those days. But it was never a problem. We were all friends. I knew the Krays from the boxing circuit and we often used to hang out. They respected the Nashes. They'd all been working behind the scenes and their names and faces were known to only a handful of people in the country.'

All that changed when a young scaffolder called Ronald Marwood went out drinking to celebrate his first wedding anniversary, on 14 December 1958.

'I'd met Ronald a few times but always in company so I could never say that I knew him that well. Everything I'd seen and heard told me that he was a very nice fella, well respected among the people I was hanging out with and very well liked. He lived in Islington and was very pally with Jimmy and Johnny Nash. The Kray twins had a lot of time for him as well. In fact, no one had a bad word to say about him, which made it all the more tragic.'

Although it was their wedding anniversary, Marwood's wife had decided to stay at home and watch television, so Marwood met up with his friend, Mick Bloom, and a few others and went to their local pub. After drinking ten half-pints of brown ale, the group went on to the Double R where Marwood drank another nine or ten half-pints of brown ale. The group then went to Grays Dance club in Seven Sisters Road.

Outside Grays the group got involved in some scuffles with another group of youths. Marwood was right in the thick of the fighting when PC Ray Summers tried to break things up. Within seconds, the crowd had dispersed and PC Summers lay dead on the ground, blood pouring from a single stab wound to the chest.

Two years earlier the law on hanging had been revised. Instead of an automatic death sentence for the taking of a life, the offence of 'capital murder' was introduced. Hanging was applicable for deaths falling into one of five categories:

1. In furtherance of theft.
2. In resisting or avoiding arrest, or escaping from legal custody.
3. Killing prison officers and people assisting them.
4. Killing police officers and the people assisting them.
5. By shooting or causing explosions.

Everyone in London knew what had happened and what the consequences might be. It surprised no one that, after that same night, Ronald Marwood vanished from the face of the earth. The Kray twins tried to get in on the act with Reggie

(Ronnie was in prison at the time) taking the credit for hiding him and refusing to co-operate with the police. It was a boast that would eventually cost the Krays the Double R – police refused to grant a new licence because of their claims. But a boast is all it was.

'The twins never had anything to do with hiding Marwood; it was the Nash brothers. While he was on the run he stayed with Johnny Nash for a bit and then Doreen Masters, Jimmy's girlfriend, looked after him for a bit as well. I knew all about it because I was part of the Nash crowd.

'No one knew the exact detail of what had happened but it didn't seem to matter. The fact was that a copper had been killed and that someone was going to have to hang for it. I remember Ronald asking Johnny if there was anyone he wanted killed. "I've got nothing to lose now, not after what I've done, so if there's anyone you want done, let me know and I'll do it for you." Johnny turned him down.'

Realising that the police net was growing ever closer and that he simply couldn't stay on the run for ever, Marwood walked into City Road police station and gave himself up at the end of January 1959.

At the end of a marathon ten-hour interview, Marwood signed the following statement:

I saw Mick and one of the younger blokes go up to the door of the dance place to see somebody about some argument. The next thing I know is that a lot of people came running out of Grays. A few scuffles started on the pavement. Someone swung a chopper at my head. The blade hit my hand, cutting two of my fingers. I fell down and felt dizzy and sick.

I walked up the road away from Grays. I was putting a handkerchief around my hand. Mick was a couple of yards in front of me, being pushed by a copper. I walked up behind the policeman and as I got up to him he half turned around and said words to the effect of 'go away' or 'clear off'. He struck me with his fist, I think, in the region of my shoulder. I remember I had my hands in my pockets. I pulled out my hand intending to push him away. I must have had my hand on the knife in my right-hand pocket. I struck out with the intention of pushing him away from me. I had some idea of rescuing Mick. I thought I would just hit him about the arm – I remember striking him with the knife on the shoulder and the policeman fell down. There was never any intention on my part to use the knife. I must have been holding it in my hand. I would like to say when I struck him I didn't realise the knife was in my hand.

But when the case came to court, Marwood denied ever having made such a statement. He admitted punching the policeman but not to having a weapon. Marwood told the jury that the police had worn him out and forced him to sign the papers when he was exhausted and unable to think straight. The statement was the exact opposite of what he had actually said.

Summing up the case for the defence, Neil Lawson QC said: 'I would suggest to you, members of the jury, that unless you are convinced that Marwood made these statements freely and voluntarily and that what he said in relation to his possession and use of the knife was actually true, then you should answer "no" to the question of whether he did strike the final blow.

'If you think Marwood may have struck the fatal blow in the confusion and excitement of the moment, meaning to push away the police officer, and that at the moment the blow was struck, his mental state was fuddled by drink and confusion over the fighting in which he had been involved, then your verdict should be guilty of manslaughter.'

The jury deliberated for just under three hours. They returned with the verdict that Marwood was guilty of the capital murder of PC Summers. He was sentenced to death.

Feelings ran high. Despite their verdict the jury had recommended mercy, and Marwood believed to the last that he would be reprieved while at Pentonville prison waiting for the sentence to be carried out.

On the eve of the day he was due to be hanged, the prison erupted into a huge riot. While inmates smashed their furniture and banged their iron plates against the bars of their cells, the officers on death watch sat with Marwood in an attempt to ensure he came to no harm.

The following morning, a thousand-strong crowd waited outside the doors of the prison for news of the hanging, and it took dozens of mounted police officers working to disperse the crowd before officials from the prison managed to slip the death notice into the glass case on the door. For days afterwards booing took place in cinemas where newsreels of the incident were shown. Marwood's hanging became one of the key executions on which the abolitionists based their campaign to end capital punishment, Joey recalls.

'It affected me. It affected everyone, not just because it was someone that we all knew, but because none of us thought it was right. Everyone felt really sorry for the bloke and for his wife – she took it really badly. Everyone rallied round as much as they could, and for years afterwards all the Nash brothers would put wreaths on his grave on the anniversary of his death.

'For me personally the worst part was the fact that Ronald was around the same age as me, and hanging out in the same social circles. I'd been in a few rows and knew the same thing could easily happen to me or anyone else. I couldn't help thinking about what it must have been like for him sitting there in the prison, knowing what was going to happen to him. That really haunted me. I had no idea that before too long I'd be in exactly the same position.'

2. 'EVERYONE HAS TO DIE SOMEDAY. IF THEY SENTENCE US TO DEATH, THE ONLY DIFFERENCE BETWEEN US AND THEM IS THAT WE KNOW EXACTLY WHERE AND WHEN, THEY DON'T'

There were 36 people in the east London drinking den known as the Pen Club the night Joey Pyle stopped being a gangster and started on the journey towards gangland legend.

The fighting began just after 1 a.m. on Sunday, 7 February 1960. By the time the gun-smoke had cleared, one man lay dead and two others were badly wounded. In the time it took the police to arrive all but four of the club's customers had somehow suffered such catastrophic memory losses that they were unable to tell the detectives where they had been standing when it all kicked off, let alone what they might have seen.

In the weeks that followed, one of these four vital witnesses would be viciously attacked, and his girlfriend would be kidnapped, beaten and slashed with a blade on two separate occasions. Another witness would go missing, and yet another would suffer a bizarre family tragedy.

Three months later, the court case would prove to be no less eventful. Friends and acquaintances of the accused did their best to help out and the first jury were soon so thoroughly intimidated and terrified that the judge was forced to order a retrial. The second time around, things were little better: witnesses began to change their stories and contradict one another, while others were exposed as outright liars.

When it was over, the judicial system, the police force and London's underworld were irrevocably changed, yet the Pen Club killer or killers would be acquitted of all but the most minor charges. 'As far as the law is concerned,' one newspaper said of the man shot dead that night, 'all that happened is that he leaned on a bullet which happened to be passing.'

For Pyle, the evening began with little hint of what was to come. 'It was just an ordinary Saturday night on the town. Me and Johnny Read started out in a club run by Ronnie Nash in Penton Street in Islington. Jimmy Nash was in there with his girlfriend, Doreen, and we got chatting with them and a crowd of other fellas. Jimmy said he was going on to the Pen Club so me and Johnny decided to go with him. That was all there was to it. We never knew who was going to be there, nothing had been planned.

'I'd been to the Pen Club two or three times before and it had always been full of faces. It was set on the top two floors of a building in Duvall Street, just around the corner from Spitalfields Market. The story is that it was bought with the proceeds of a robbery on the Parker Pen Company and that they named it as a way of sticking two fingers up to the law.

'We came in the main door – me, Johnny, Jimmy and Doreen – and made our way to the bar on the top floor. I see this bloke Simons, Johnny Simons, who I know to say hello to but wouldn't call a pal. We nodded at each other then me and Jimmy and the others have a drink. Then we go down to the floor below for more drinks. That's when it happens. There was this bloke at the bar with his back to us, talking right loud. He was shouting out all sorts of stuff and banging the bar with his fist: "Fuck Ronnie Nash," he goes. "Fuck all the Nashes. If Ronnie or any of the Nash brothers want it, if they want to mess with me, they can have it any time."'

The man making the noise was one Selwyn Keith Cooney (aka Selwyn Neill, aka Jimmy Neill, aka Manchester Jimmy), who worked as manager of the Billy Hill's New Cabinet Club in Gerrard Street. A few weeks earlier his car had collided with one driven by Vicky James, a club hostess and close friend of Ronnie Nash. There hadn't been much damage but Cooney had sent his bill to the girl. When Cooney and Ronnie Nash ran into each other in a Notting Hill drinking club, the bill was still unpaid. Words were exchanged, a fight broke out and each man went away with a black eye.

'We're standing there and none of us can quite believe what we're hearing. None of us had ever seen the guy in our life. It takes a second to sink in, then Jimmy walks over, taps the bloke on the shoulder and says hey, my name is Jimmy Nash and you're talking about my brothers. Cooney turns around and puts his drink down on the bar. "I couldn't give a fuck what your name is," he says, and right then Jimmy goes bosh and hits him a couple of times. Cooney falls back against the bar, his nose is broken, bleeding, and two of his teeth have been knocked out, and then all fucking hell breaks loose.

'Everyone jumps in and goes for Jimmy, all of Cooney's crowd are after his blood. So Johnny and me jump in as well, he's our pal. So now they're not fighting Jimmy, they're fighting us. They're all trying to get Jimmy and we're trying to keep them all away. But there are only two of us and a fuck of a lot of them. It's all going off. There are fists and boots and chairs and bottles and all sorts flying around. I remember hitting someone – I don't know who it was – over the head with a soda siphon.

'It's chaos. Everyone's shouting and bawling and it's all happening in this really small space – there's only a yard and a half between the bar and the wall. There isn't room to swing a cat, let alone have a row. It's just a melee and you can't see who is trying to get who or do what or anything. Someone hits me, I grab some bloke from behind and I see it's Billy Ambrose, the owner of the club. Then I hear a couple of bangs and I see his leg jerk up, right up into the air like he's had an electric shock. I don't see any gun. Next thing some woman starts screaming and screaming that her old man's been shot. I push Ambrose away and keep fighting.

'We're heading for the exit, fighting and moving at the same time. And all the while Jimmy's trying to keep Doreen out of it and I'm watching Jimmy's back and Johnny's watching mine. We make it to the stairs and head down towards the door. When we get to the bottom Doreen's first, then Jimmy and then me. And then I turn around and see that Johnny isn't with us. So I start running back up the stairs. And Jimmy shouts out "Where you going, what are you doing?" and I tell him I'm going to get Johnny. So Jimmy leaves Doreen there and sprints up behind me. We get to the top, head for the bar and I run in first. Straight away I see Johnny. He's lying face down over a table and everyone is laying into him, beating the shit out of him. I see him take a bottle over the head and I start charging towards him.

'As I'm going forward I hear a couple more bangs, more screaming, and everything goes misty. But I haven't got time to worry about what's going on: I'm there to get my pal. I pick Johnny up and take him down the stairs and put him into Doreen's car. He's hurt pretty bad – the blood's pouring out of him – but he says he's OK. Doreen takes him straight to hospital where he gets some stitches and ends up with a big bandage wrapped around his head. In the meantime I take Jimmy round to one of his brothers and then head over to Doreen's place to catch up with Johnny.

'He'd been fixed up and was feeling a lot better, so we headed over to Notting Hill and holed up in this flat owned by a couple of girls that Johnny knew. We stayed there through the night, just drinking and talking, and that was when the news came on the telly that Cooney was dead, shot in the head at point-blank range.

'We didn't go home. We waited a few more hours and then made a meet with the Kray twins at The Regal, their snooker hall over in Eric Street, down Mile End way. They were friends, but they were also powerful and well connected enough to help out if we got into trouble. If it had been the other way round, we would have been the first people they would have turned to.

'When we arrived, Ronnie and Reggie were sitting up at the bar drinking coffee.

' "You've heard he's dead?" said Ronnie. I nodded.

' "So what do you want to do Joey? Do you want to get out of the country? We'll get you out if that's what you want."

'The three of us had already discussed it. We all felt that, what with the size of the place where the fight had happened and all the noise and confusion and chaos, there didn't seem much hope of the police getting any evidence about who had done what.

' "Nah. We're gonna stay."

'Jimmy nodded. "Yeah, we're gonna face the music."

'Ronnie looked at each of us in turn. "Are all three of you agreed on that?"

'We spoke as one: "Yeah."

'Jimmy headed off to his home while Johnny and I set off for Carshalton. When we got there the police were waiting and we let them take us in without any fuss.'

The pair spent that first night in Wimbledon police station, the local nick, before being transferred to City Road police station the following Monday morning, along with Doreen Masters who had also been picked up. It was only when the trio arrived at the station that they learned that Jimmy Nash had somehow managed to avoid arrest and was still at large. 'It wasn't a problem,' says Pyle, 'just the luck of the draw. We thought good luck to him. In fact, it would have been better for us if they'd never caught him.'

By now the story was all over the newspapers, with the tabloids in particular in a frenzy to find out the details and backgrounds of those involved. Many reported that Cooney had been carried down a flight of stairs and died on the pavement a few yards down from the club – a futile attempt by those there to disguise the scene of the crime. When the police and ambulance arrived a woman, Fay Sadler, manager of the Club and Cooney's mistress, was still by his side.

Sadler was running the club on behalf of two men, ex-boxer Billy Ambrose and Jeremiah Callaghan, a member of a well-known criminal family. They needed Sadler because they were both serving ten-year prison sentences, though they had managed to wangle weekends at home on parole. Thanks to their personal notoriety, the Pen Club soon became a popular hangout for villains, and police raids became a routine occurrence.

That same afternoon Joey Pyle was placed on a series of ID parades. At the first Joan Bending, a 21-year-old barmaid at the Pen Club, picked him out of the line-up without hesitation. Pyle eyed the young woman in front of him carefully.

'You didn't see me shoot anyone did you?'

Bending nodded slowly. 'No, I didn't see you shoot anyone.'

Second time round another witness, Johnny Simons, failed to pick out either Read or Pyle, but at the final ID parade, Pyle was surprised to find himself being picked out by none other than Fay Sadler. Otherwise known as the Black Widow, Sadler was a former prostitute from Stockport who moved to London and quickly established herself as the ultimate femme fatale. Neither strikingly beautiful nor irresistibly charming, Sadler somehow managed to attract a steady stream of London's most notorious villains, only to see them come to sticky ends. Cooney was the third of her boyfriends to have been murdered, while several others had received vicious beatings. No stranger to the codes of conduct that governed the underworld, Pyle and the others were astonished that she of all people had chosen to co-operate with the police.

That night Read and Pyle chatted through the walls of their cells. Police Constable Roland Spiers, listening in from the custody desk, grabbed a pen and paper and began scribbling down their words.

Pyle: I never knew what the row was about. He just walked in there. They can't say we were concerned in the matter can they?

Read: Nah. We never done any shooting. Three or four tried to get going into Nash. I said turn it up boys. It was a ruck and that was that.

Pyle: But it's horrible because you don't know what they are going to do you for.

Read: No, it's a worry.

Pyle: I think I'll lead a quiet life after this.

Read: You're telling me.

Pyle: I never knew they could do us for being concerned. Did you? This never happened with that stabbing at the Common.

Read: Yeah, it's all that gun business. It's silly isn't it. I mean, they were only having a ruck to start with.

The pair had good reason to be concerned. Although neither had shot anyone or known that there had been a gun at the club, they could still be found guilty of capital murder and therefore sentenced to hang. The principle had been underlined seven years earlier during the case of Christopher Craig and Derek Bentley.

Craig and Bentley had broken into a warehouse intent on robbery but were surprised by the police. The pair made it to the roof and Bentley surrendered. He shouted out 'Let him have it, Chris' to Craig, who immediately opened fired with a pistol, killing one policeman and injuring several others before he ran out of bullets. Craig was convicted of murder but, being just sixteen, was too young to hang. Bentley, however, was nineteen. The case hinged on the meaning of Bentley's words – were they a plea to hand over the gun or an incitement to kill? The jury decided on the latter and found him guilty. In the eyes of the law, despite never holding the gun or pulling the trigger, Bentley was every bit as guilty of murder as Craig.

The following afternoon, Pyle, Read and Masters found their worst nightmare had come true. The three were brought before Superintendent Rowland Millington and formally charged with the capital murder of Selwyn Cooney. Masters said nothing; Read said 'nothing to say', while Pyle shrugged his shoulders and whistled 'murder?' through his teeth.

Pyle and Read were remanded in custody and later that day the police issued the first of several appeals for information about the whereabouts of James Lawrence Nash. His profession was given as 'scaffolder' and he was described as being five feet ten inches tall, well-built, with a fresh complexion, round face, close-cropped sandy hair, blue eyes and scars on the back of the neck and left arm. Members of the public were urged not to approach him, as he was, without doubt, 'armed and dangerous'.

The description was sent out from Scotland Yard to every police station in the country, though in reality no one believed Nash had strayed far from his home patch, and almost as quickly as it had begun, the manhunt was over. True to his word, Nash decided to face the music, and walked in to City Road police station on the Friday morning with London's top underworld lawyer, Manny Fryde. Though qualified in his native South Africa, Fryde had never bothered to requalify in London. Officially he was a clerk, but he did all the duties that would normally fall to a solicitor, and had a hard-won reputation as a canny operator.

Fryde entered the station with Nash at his side, slapped his palms down on the counter to attract the attention of the desk sergeant, cleared his throat and then spoke. 'I understand you wish to see this man James Lawrence Nash in connection with a shooting affair last Sunday morning at Stepney, when a man was shot dead. I want you to understand that he denies the charge of any kind. He is not guilty and, acting on legal advice given, he is not making any verbal or written statement.'

With Nash and the others safely in custody, police quickly moved the case towards committal. Sadler was by far the most essential witness, but she vanished around the beginning of March. She had, it seemed, been scared off. Urgent appeals were launched asking her to come forward – she was the prosecution's best witness by far – and offering her all the police protection she would ever need. The total lack of any response led many officers to conclude that she had been killed to ensure her silence, and the Pen Club case immediately took on a more sinister air.

The notion that this case involved something more than just a group of hardmen involved in a bar brawl was confirmed a few days later, when Johnny Simons was attacked with a razor while sitting in a café in Paddington, leaving a gaping wound that needed 27 stitches to close it.

The assault was followed by two on his girlfriend, a 23-year-old model, Barbara Ibbotson. On the first occasion she was snatched in broad daylight in Soho and thrown into a car where her face was slashed four times. Three weeks later she was the victim of another attack, when three men broke into her flat while she was taking a bath, held her under water and slashed her again. This time she received wounds also requiring 27 stitches. In the light of the disappearance of Fay Sadler, the barmaid Joan Bending and Simons both accepted the police protection that had been offered to them.

Sadler was still missing on 14 March, when Pyle, Read, Nash and Masters appeared for committal at Thames Magistrate's Court. All four pleaded not guilty.

First to give evidence against the accused was Billy Ambrose, who explained that he was wounded when he tried to take a gun away from the man who was doing the shooting. 'I left the club, went home and found I had an injury on the head and a bullet wound in the stomach. I felt a bit of pain, but not a terrible lot.'

Along with the jury the magistrate gasped at the revelation. 'You are obviously a man of great guts and you aren't frightened of anybody, are you?'

'No Sir.'

Ambrose went on to explain that he was standing on the left of Cooney who was having a drink at the bar. There were around twenty people there and the jukebox was playing.

'I was talking to my wife when someone pulled Cooney round,' he said. 'There seemed to be a bit of a scuffle. When I turned round I saw blood on Cooney's nose and he was staggering. Someone cried out "He's got a gun" and I tried to get the gun from the man. I asked the man to give me the gun and I got pushed. I heard a bang and felt a burning pain in my stomach. I then got a blow on the head and it seemed to be a free for all. Five or six were fighting. A man pulled me round and that's when I saw Cooney on the floor. I went home and tried to patch myself up, then went by car to the London hospital.'

The only thing left out of Ambrose's detailed account was any clue about the identity of the man who had pulled the trigger. Asked by the magistrate to look around the court and see if he could see anyone who was in the club that night, Ambrose knew far better than to break the criminal code.

'The club was dimly lit,' he said firmly. 'I cannot see anyone. I would be unfair of me to say that I could.'

A shaky Johnny Simons then appeared on the witness stand. He said that although he recognised the men in court, he had not picked them out at the ID parade because he had been too scared. It was only now that he was under police protection that he felt safe enough to tell everything that he had seen.

It began, he said, when he saw a man pull Cooney around and hit him in the face saying: 'You are the bastard I've been looking for.'

'People then tried to attack Nash and Pyle and Read fought them off. Nash was shouting "come outside, come outside" then he opened his coat and took something from the top of his trousers. Then there were words between Ambrose and Nash and then Ambrose copped it in the guts. I heard the shot. Ambrose sort of fell back to the bar and his old woman screamed that he had been shot.

'Nash started to make his way along the room toward the door, and Cooney went towards him shouting, "Don't let him get away." All of a sudden Cooney slumped against the wall over a piece of furniture. Read and Pyle were fighting with the others, trying to keep them away from Nash. Cooney took a couple more steps and fell on his face and then Nash made for the door but then came back in again and said to someone: "Do you want some too? Get out of the fucking way."'

Simons also said that it was he who had hit Read over the head with a bottle.

Joey recalls: 'I was sitting there, listening to Simons give his evidence and I couldn't believe what I was hearing. Simons was no friend of mine but I knew him well enough to say hello to, and I remembered explicitly that when we had got to the Pen Club, he had been in the upstairs bar. A little while later we had gone downstairs and that's where the trouble started, but Simons was nowhere near it at the time.

'It didn't take us long to work out what the law had done. They had taken a statement made by Jerry Callaghan – one of the owners of the Pen Club – and given it to Simons, getting him to say that he was the one downstairs. They couldn't use Callaghan because he was on probation and wouldn't have been a credible witness, but we knew it was his statement because Read and I had seen it while we were in the cells.'

As the hearing went on, so Pyle began to fear that the whole case was going to escalate out of control. It's all very well saying that if you can't do the time, don't do the crime, but Pyle was doing the time for a crime he hadn't committed. He had always seen prison as an occupational hazard and, having got away with robberies and thefts for years, he knew he had some time in the boob coming – but not like this. Pyle hadn't shot anyone and he certainly hadn't killed anyone, but he was going to hang for it. Here he was on death row, waiting for the hangman's noose.

'I knew that if we were found guilty, we would have gone to the gallows. I guess I could have been well choked by now. But being so young in those days, I didn't really take it all that seriously. I remember one time I was walking around the prison yard with Jimmy. I'd got to know him much better by then and I realised that, though he was one of the soundest men you could ever hope to meet, he was also as fucking mad as a March hare.

'We were doing big circuits around the yard and passing this screw who was standing guard. Jimmy leaned over to me and said, "Keep doing neck exercises" as we approached him. We both started waving our necks around like crazy. The screw just looked at us as if we were crazy but never said a word. Then, about the fifth time we passed him, the screw couldn't bear it any more. "What the hell are you two up to?" Jimmy looked back at him. "We're doing neck exercises. We're trying to make our necks fatter than our heads so the rope will slip off." The screw shook her head: "You two are fucking mad."

'Jimmy was in one cell; I was in another. Jimmy used to send me stuff all the time, like a little noose made out of a shoelace. In those days you weren't allowed to shave yourself. No one had invented the safety razor and it was all cutthroats – there was no way they were going to let us get hold of those. Instead they had a con come in and shave us. The first time, I was sitting at the sink and when I looked up, Jimmy was pretending to be strangled. It made me laugh. I couldn't help it. To me, the whole thing was nothing more than an experience.

'Most of the time it didn't bother me. The only time I really worried about it was after lock up when I put my head on the pillow in my cell. I shared the place with a guy called Gypsy Jim Smith who was in for killing a copper. He'd killed a copper when the bloke fell off his car as he tried to make a getaway.

'He hadn't meant to do it. He'd stolen a load of scaffolding clips and was driving them away in his car, one of those old Ford Prefects that had the running board down the side. Halfway home to Plumsted he came to a crossroads and saw a copper standing there, directing traffic. Now this copper knew Smith and the kind of things that the old pikey got up to, and he also noticed that the car was well weighed down at the back.

'The copper ran over, jumped on the running board and shoved his hands in through the open window, trying the grab the steering wheel and move the car across to the kerb. But Smith panicked, put his foot down on the wrong pedal and the car shot forward. The copper fell off into the middle of the road and got run over by a bus going the other way. Killed instantly. But because it was a copper and it happened in the furtherance of theft, it counted as capital murder and Gypsy Jim was going to hang.

'One night he said to me: "Joey, are you afraid of hanging?" There was no need to lie. I had been up all night with the worry of it. I told him I was.

'"Look at that screw over there," he said to me. "Look at the copper, look at yourself in the mirror. Everybody has to die someday. If they sentence us to death, the only difference between us and them is that we know exactly where and when, they don't." After that I started looking at people, at the whole fucking world, differently. I would always remember what he said. I would repeat it to myself all the time. It became the answer to the problem that had been driving me crazy, the answer to the question that had been running round in my mind since that night in the Pen Club.'

Back in the early 1960s, British justice was a well-oiled machine and cases came to court within weeks rather than months. And so it was that less than four weeks after committal, the case of the Pen Club Murder opened at number one court of the Old Bailey.

The judge, Mr Justice Gorman, took pains to point out in simple terms what was at stake. If the jury decided that Pyle and Read knew that Nash had a gun and was going to use it, then they were guilty of capital murder and they would hang.

If, however, the jury felt they had not known about the gun but had kept others away from Nash in order to allow him to escape, then they were guilty of being accessories after the fact in Cooney's murder, which was still a serious charge carrying a substantial sentence.

The charges against Doreen Masters had been dropped a week or so earlier. She had initially denied being at the club at all, but her pale blue raincoat had spots of blood on it and a bloody towel was found hidden in her house. In a statement she admitted having Read in her car and using the towel to mop up his blood. She said she had lied before because she didn't want to get anyone into trouble or get into trouble herself. The police decided that the case against her didn't warrant pursuing any further and let her go.

Instead of being in the dock, Masters took her place in the public gallery, where she found herself in the company of some of the most notorious figures in London's gangland. The Nash family was there, of course, as were the Krays, Billy Hill and many others.

The prosecution opened with a summary of the evidence against the three men, based largely on the testimony of Ambrose, Bending and Simons. Bending had made a new statement saying that while in the downstairs bar, she heard someone say they had come for Cooney. She also said she had seen Nash shoot Cooney from just two feet away.

Victor Durand QC, acting for the defence, offered the jury an alternative scenario. He claimed that Cooney was shot long after Nash had left the room and that Ambrose had been shot while Nash was heading for the door. Using Ambrose's unwillingness to turn grass against him, Durand suggested the real reason he was keeping quiet about the identity of the gunman was because he had something to hide.

Despite Durand's best efforts, things were not looking that good for the defendants after four days of testimony, and the jokes Pyle and Nash had shared about going to the gallows started losing their appeal. But then came a miracle.

'I was at Brixton going through reception on my way to get supper along with Nash and Read when a little fella started staring at the three of us. "Are you the boys over at the Bailey, the ones up for that Pen Club murder?" It had been a long day at court and we were in no mood for small talk. We just looked at him like he was some kind of nutter.

The geezer gave a half smile and then pointed at each of us in turn. "Read, Pyle, Nash, you're all fucking guilty. That's why my old woman reckons. Made up her mind already she has. Told all the rest too. She's found you guilty and the others will too, no doubt about it."'

It soon transpired that the man, a remand prisoner at Brixton, was married to a woman sitting on the Pen Club jury. This was reported to the judge by both the prosecution and the defence, and it didn't take long before other problems with the members of the jury came to light.

One juror, who was later found to have a conviction for dishonesty when he had been a juvenile, had appeared to nod towards Billy Nash in the public gallery as he took his seat. Then there was a conversation overheard by two police officers that another juror was going to be nobbled. The man in question was kept under surveillance, and was seen being approached in his car by a suspicious looking young man.

The following day, the father of Joan Bending, the barmaid who had been placed under constant police protection, was found unconscious in his gas-filled kitchen. Whether he had been attacked or whether he was attempting to take his own life because of threats was never made clear. What was certain, however, is that neither the jury nor the witnesses seemed entirely beyond the reach of the underworld.

On 25 April, just four days after the trial had started, Mr Justice Gorman brought it to a halt. 'Certain information has been brought to my notice which makes it impossible for this case to be continued for trial before this jury,' he told the court. 'In these circumstances I discharge this jury from giving a verdict and send the case for trial at the next session opening here tomorrow.'

Two days into the second trial came another the surprise. The crown said they would be offering no evidence against either Pyle or Read for the charge of capital murder or being accessories after the fact. They had made the decision after listening carefully to the evidence of the first two witnesses, both of whom supported the notion that Pyle and Read were unaware that their friend was carrying a gun. They would, however, be charging both men with GBH and they would have to remain in custody.

When the defence case in the murder trial was reached, a surprise witness came forward. David Sammons had been drinking in the Pen Club on the night in question and had been following the case in the newspapers. What he had read had appalled him so much that he felt compelled to come forward and tell the truth.

He explained that at the time Cooney had been shot, Johnny Simons had been drinking in another bar, and that Joan Bending was so drunk she had to be helped out of the bar long before the fight had taken place.

On 3 May it was the turn of Jimmy Nash to enter the witness box. Speaking confidently and often directly at the jury, he explained that he never had a gun on the night in question and would not carry one, as he had always managed to defend himself with his fists.

'As for Cooney, I had never heard of him in my life, either by the name of Cooney of Neill. I was in the first floor bar when Cooney beckoned to me. I took no notice at first because I did not know him, but he beckoned to me again. I went over and he turned his back on me. I pulled his sleeve wondering what it was all about and he turned round and before I could say anything he started to have a go at me. He said: "So you are another one of those fucking Nashes?" I asked what it was all about. He said you are a lot of fucking jailbirds, you, Ronnie and the rest. Then he pointed to Doreen and said: "Who is that bird with you? A bit of easy money for you I suppose." By that I took it he was suggesting that I was living off her, so I hit him on the nose with my right hand.

'There was nothing in my hand. I didn't need anything. I have been a boxer in the army and I was pretty good. I won the Tripoli welterweight and I belong to two clubs now. I asked Cooney to come outside and fight, man to man, but then I was surrounded by five or six of Cooney's mates. I was blocking a lot of blows but I was really worried about Doreen. I think I heard someone say, "he's got a gun". There was a lot of shouting going on. I tried to make my way out. After I hit him, I didn't see Cooney any more. I reached the door and I was going downstairs when I heard another bang. I don't know if anyone got shot or anything. I just carried on down the stairs and I never looked back.'

The evidence of Jimmy Nash concluded the case for the defence and the following day the judge gave the jury his summing up speech.

'You may think there is no doubt that there was murder done in the Pen Club in the early morning of 7 February, and so the matter which you have to concentrate your mind is are you satisfied on all the evidence that it was Nash who did that dreadful deed. You may have felt as you listened to this story of witnesses disappearing, of what you may feel were surprising lapses of memory on the part of those who have been called, that there are sinister implications here, and that you have had a glimpse of an underworld which has its own code of loyalty, or its fear. But if you felt that you must not visit it on the accused. He is being tried for murder, not the company he keeps.'

After 100 minutes of deliberation, the jury came back with their verdict: Jimmy Nash was not guilty of the capital murder of Selwyn Cooney.

The public gallery, packed full of London's top faces, went wild but the celebrations were short lived. First Cooney's father, James, stood up and pointed at Nash, tears of rage pouring down his cheeks. 'He killed my son and I will kill him,' he screamed. 'That is a certainty. My son's death will not go unavenged.'

Then Nash was immediately charged with committing Grievous Bodily Harm on Cooney – the same charge laid against Pyle and Read – with the trial set to start exactly an hour later. This time Nash had no chance. He had already admitted on oath, as a key part of his defence, that he had hit Cooney on the nose at least once, and thus sealed his fate. He was found guilty almost instantly and all three men were then brought up into the dock to be dealt with one last time.

Sentencing Nash to five years, the judge told him: 'You have been found guilty on abundant evidence of a brutal assault upon a man who is now dead in a drinking club frequented by crooks. And as a result of the fight you started, there was much panic and two men were shot. An example must be made of people like you.'

The judge then turned to Pyle and Read. 'You have been professional boxers. You went to this drinking club, the resort of crooks, and when Nash made a brutal attack upon another man, you tried to prevent justice takings its course. You and your like have got to learn you cannot do that. I take into account that you have been in prison for three months and have had hanging over your head a capital charge. I sentence you to eighteen months.'

The moment the trial finished, Fay Sadler suddenly resurfaced. At first she claimed to have been ill but later she admitted the truth: that she could never do anything that would mark her out as a grass. 'I was just being faithful to the code,' she said.

A year later, Billy Nash elaborated to the *Sunday Pictorial* what had happened to her. 'I have been told but of course I can't say if it is true that Mrs Sadler was around in London the whole time.

'I think it is true to say that Mrs Sadler had a bit of a problem. Some people approached her, or so I understand, and suggested that if she did tell all to the judge and jury it would be a very disloyal thing to do. Disloyal, that is, to the code of behaviour which applies to the owners of drinking clubs and their friends. Indeed I am told the word grass was used to her. Now a grass is an informer. And grasses, it is well known, often end up having little accidents. She was never a captive. She may have been frightened, but no one put a scare into her. Let us say that she volunteered to remain absent.'

The Pen Club Murder case had been a watershed in that it led directly to the formation of the Criminal Intelligence Branch at Scotland Yard to co-ordinate information about organised crime. The case had highlighted a massive lack of intelligence on the key figures running London's gangland and the police were determined never to be caught out again.

From then on, young CID officers were encouraged to attend court on a regular basis. Wearing plain clothes and sitting in the public gallery, the idea was that they would learn the faces of the people they would eventually be pursuing.

The Pen Club case had also highlighted just how vulnerable juries were and led to formal rules being drawn up on how they should be protected. Until then few provisions were in place and during lunchtime breaks, members of the jury were allowed to dine alongside members of the public and court staff. The scandal reached the very highest levels: in Parliament there were calls to the Home Secretary to launch a public inquiry into the intimidation of witnesses, and juries have dined separately ever since.

But more than anything else, the case had made it clear that, along with the Nash brothers, Joey Pyle was a major force in the underworld, a man with sufficient clout and influence to encourage others to intimidate witnesses on his behalf in order to see him remain at liberty. To this day Pyle remains coy about the exact events that night. 'Who pulled the trigger? All I can say is that I was found not guilty, Jimmy was found not guilty and so was Read. People are just going to have to decide for themselves.'

But as far as the police were concerned, Pyle had had a lucky escape and in doing so had stuck two fingers up at the justice system: they would not rest until he was back behind bars.

3. 'ANOTHER BULLET WOULD BE CHEAPER'

When Joey Pyle emerged from prison one thing was certain: nothing in his life would ever be the same again.

'They sent me away as a kind of punishment, to try and teach me a lesson, but the only thing I learned was how to be a better criminal. When you're banged up the only thing you do the whole time you're there is talk about crime. You sit around with people chatting about what they did, how much they made and why they got caught and you try to work out ways of doing it all better.

'Everything changed after they dropped the murder charge. Up until then I'd been convinced that I was going to hang so my day-to-day life in prison had no real meaning, it was a just a stage I was going through on the way to the gallows. Afterwards, I had to face up to the fact that I was actually going to be stuck in the clink for a while and then at some time afterwards, I'd be getting back.

'Even though we had to slop out and things were pretty grim, I never found any of it too much of a hardship. When you choose to make your living from crime, getting nicked becomes an occupational hazard. Everyone has their own way of dealing with it and mine was to switch off, forget about the outside world and just get on with it. I remember saying to myself: "All right Joey, you're living another life now. Forget about going down the pub, forget about your night life, this is it from now on until they let you out."

'Some people brown nose their way through prison – try to make friends with the screws, that sort of thing. I never had any time for people like that, didn't respect them at all. If one of the screws called me Joe I'd have a real go at them. "Don't fucking call me Joe, I don't call you Bob do I? I ain't your friend and I don't want to be." I'd just get on with doing my bird and that's it. I guess a lot of people respected me for that.

'But respect is a funny thing. I don't know if I got more respect because of the whole Pen Club thing. That's for other people to answer, not me. It showed people that I wasn't a grass; that even though I was on death row I wasn't the sort of bloke who would try to put the blame on someone else to save my own neck. But personally I don't think any man in the world is entitled to respect just for that.

'If you go on a job and you get nicked and then another fella who was on the job with you doesn't grass you up, well then he's just done exactly what he's supposed to have done. It doesn't make him superman or anything like that. I'd never look at someone and think "Oh he didn't grass me up, what a lovely fella." I wouldn't be with him in the first place if I thought he was gonna turn grass on me. Grassing is a terrible, despicable thing. People like myself and my friends would rather fucking die than be a grass.

'More than respect, the Pen Club thing showed that I was someone who could be trusted. And for that reason alone, I made a lot of good friends in prison, friendships that have endured right up until today.

'I remember in particular being approached in the nick by this bloke called John Buggy, who everyone knew as Scotch Jack. He introduced himself and said that one of his mates on the outside, a fellow called Waggy Whitnall, had written to him and told him to look me up as I was a stand-up sort of guy.'

Charles 'Waggy' Whitnall was a well-known South London face. 'He and I had met in passing a few times but we'd never been properly introduced. We weren't pals, but we certainly weren't enemies either. He had a reputation as being a dangerous little fucker, but also as a very good money getter. I knew that if he had time for Scotch Jack, then the bloke was probably all right, and pretty soon we became good friends.

'Jack had been born in the States but had come to Britain with the US forces after the Second World War. After that he'd ended up working as a hard man for various gangs in Glasgow, which is how he'd come to pick up his nickname. I'd been inside when Jack had committed the crime that got him put away but he soon filled me in on the details.

'He had gone down to the Pigalle club with a friend called John, who at the time was going out with the singer Shirley Bassey. She had been on stage at the Pigalle that night, performing in front of rows of little tables while people ate their dinner, and when the show was over, John asked Jack to go backstage and fetch her so that they could go off somewhere and have a drink.

'The entrance to the dressing rooms was just on the side of the small stage and the club manger had put someone on guard there to stop Shirley getting harassed. Jack went over and the guard wouldn't let him get through, so Jack starts shouting and screaming at the bloke. This is all happening in full views of loads of people sitting down at tables and having drinks, including the actor Peter Finch who was out for the night with some woman.

'Finch starts complaining about the commotion and says that someone should throw Jack out because he's making such a row. But Jack hears him and goes rushing over and says: "Chuck me out, I'll fucking have you", and he hits Finch over the head with his own dinner. Then another guy, a wrestler called Charlie Reeder who was out of the East End, jumps up and tells Jack to pick on someone his own size. The two of them start grappling but they're smashing into tables and knocking things over and people are panicking and the club owners are shitting themselves. So then Reeder says: "All right, we'll have it outside."

'Then Jack says to Reeder: "Yeah, all right, we'll go outside. Get yourself a tool." Then he calls out to John to get a tool for him. I think he meant an iron bar or something. But John goes out to his Rolls Royce parked outside and pulls out a gun.

'So Jack and Reeder are squaring up to each other in Regent Street, just outside the Pigalle, and John passes over the gun.

Then Jack says: "Fuck me, you've put a gun in me hand." And after that there's only one thing he can do: he pulls the trigger and shoots Reeder in the stomach.

'Jack got nicked almost straight away. Reeder pulls through and Jack ends up getting done for shooting with intent to cause GBH and gets sent down for nine years. That was how we met, and by the time I got out we had become good prison pals, and I promised him that I'd keep in touch.

'Waggy Whitnall, the man who had introduced us, had been in to visit Jack a few times and towards the end of my sentence, he'd started visiting me too. Then, the day I got out, I had a little party at the Castle pub in Tooting. It was a good night and loads of faces turned up, including Waggy, and that was when we started getting to know each other properly.

'It was good to be out and catch up with all my old pals, but sometimes that meant going back into prison. Having spent just a year inside, I knew only too well how much it means to have a bit of contact with the outside world. Jimmy Nash still had four years of his own sentence to go so I used to go and see him quite regularly. Then there was Scotch Jack and a few other people I'd met in the nick, and also my old pal Tony Baldessare had been banged up over some robbery that he'd got caught for.

'With Jimmy Nash being away, I started to get much more friendly with his brother John. One of the things I liked most about John was his dry sense of humour. One time he had been involved in a lunchtime row with some Canadian bloke called Colin and had ended up shooting the geezer up the arse right in the middle of a pub. It wasn't a serious argument, I wasn't there at the time and I can't actually remember what it was about, but I knew it couldn't be a big deal because John had only used a .22, and you don't do that if you're trying to finish someone off.

'A couple of weeks later John and I were in the same pub and as we went up to get our drinks, the barman handed John a letter. It was from the bloke that John had shot: "Dear Mr

Nash. You shot me up the arse and ruined my suit. I am in a private nursing home and am also on the run from the Canadian army. I need money to pay for my treatment and would be grateful if you could send me £500. I think it is the least you could do for me as I have not grassed you up about the shooting. With thanks. Colin."

'John shook his head and sighed and then passed the letter over to me and asked what I thought. I told him the bloke had a real fucking cheek, asking for a new suit and everything. "Yeah, that's what I think too," he replied, then asked the barman if he had a piece of paper so he could write Colin a reply. He scribbled down what I thought was a blinding one-liner: "Dear Colin, another bullet would be cheaper."'

'Work-wise I didn't have any real firm plans when I got out of the nick. There was always the possibility of going back to doing jobs over the pavement, and I still knew enough people who were doing that to get offered bits of work, but I was looking for something a bit more steady.

'The Government had announced a series of relaxations to the laws on gambling that were to be introduced over the next couple of years, and a lot of people were trying to get on the bandwagon. The theory was that if you could set up an illegal club and make a name for yourself as a good operator, then you'd have the knowledge of how to make it all work and a ready-made customer base for when things went legit. The ministers were getting wind of this and were talking about making it the law that no one with a criminal record could own a casino, but we all knew there were still plenty of ways to get around that.

'Through Waggy I got to know a man called Billy Hill – probably the best organised criminal that Britain has ever had. He was a very clever man but also very powerful and enormously respected. He was around my dad's age by the time I got to know him, and I really looked up to him. The measure of his success is the fact that when he died, a decade or so later, he was a multimillionaire.'

Billy Hill had basically run the Docklands of London in the days after the War. When Reggie Kray was twenty, he wrote that the person he most wanted to be was Billy Hill. Hill made money from burglary and receiving stolen goods, but most of his fortune came from illegal drinking and gambling clubs.

'He was incredibly generous. He lived in a flat in Bayswater and whenever you went to see him, he would always give you something. Two or three hundred quid most of the time. It was through talking to Billy and Waggy and people like that that I decided to go into the illegal gambling business.

'I'd learned how to play dice growing up in Islington and Carshalton. Gambling was something I'd been interested in for a while and a big part of my social life. I'd seen a few illegal games that seemed to be pulling in a crowd over in East London but there was nothing happening down south, so I decided to start a game up.

'The first one I set up was a dice game at a pub called German Harry's in Balham. I made the table up myself. I took a big bit of board, around the size of a snooker table, and built up the sides with foam and then covered the lot with green felt and stapled it all down. I put the whole lot on some beer crates and then put some curtain around the side to hide the crates and make it look nice and neat.

'Anyone who has ever been to a modern casino will have seen how the dice table has loads of different printing on it for all different kinds of bets and combinations. Our tables were never like that, just plain green. It was as simple as you could make it: no betting on the field, no betting on the proposition. Just throw a dice and right away, you win or you lose. It's the same way that you see people playing dice on the pavement or in army barracks where they don't have tables at all.

'The dealer would sit at one end and there would be a slot in the board with an old Oxo tin underneath for all the money to go into. It was dice, but not the way they play it in casinos, more the way that kids play it in the streets.

'The ways it works is that the shooter, that is the person who has the dice, establishes a point, then tries to make that point. The people placing the bets either bet with the shooter (on the point) or against the shooter (on the 7). Someone must "fade" the shooter (cover the bet) in order for the game to continue.

'Once the bet is covered, the shooter can throw the dice. The object of the game is to throw a 7 or an 11 on the first roll. If you do that you win. But if you throw a 2, 3 or 12 (two sixes) then you lose. If you don't hit a 2, 3, 7, 11 or 12 first time, then whatever number you hit becomes your point and that's what you then play against. You carry on throwing until you either hit your point or a 7. So it's easy: 7 you win, 11 you win, but 7 you're out if you're looking for your point.

'It might sound complicated, but it's a million times easier than playing dice in a casino. There all the players are playing against the house rather than the person throwing the dice and there are about a million more betting combinations that you can get into.

'When we played in my club, I would take a "tax" of a shilling in the pound. That meant that any money that was placed on the table, I'd take a percentage of. If someone won £40, then £2 of it would go into my Oxo tin.

'The place in Balham was always pretty busy and I was earning a nice little packet out of it, so before too long I decided to expand. There was a club called the Crown in Croydon – a beautiful big club – and the owner let me set up a dice game there in one of the upstairs rooms.

'The place was open all hours and by this time I had four guys working for me, all big strong men who could all look after themselves. Every now and then the club downstairs would get a bit rowdy and the owner would run up and ask one of my guys to go downstairs and help him sort it out. The original deal was that I was supposed to pay rent but I assumed that because we had been helping him out so much, that that was no longer the case. I was wrong.

'One day the owner came to see me.

'"Joey, you ain't paid me no rent. What's going on?"

'"Why should I pay you rent? You're using my people to help sort out trouble and that is worth more money than the rent could ever come to."

'"That's not true. Anyway, I don't need anyone. I've got a manager now."

'He called his fella over, this flat-nosed idiot, and introduced him as the manager. I looked him up and down. He didn't look like he could handle spicy food let alone a row.

'"I've been told you don't need any help looking after the place," I said.

'"That's right," the new manager replied. "I can look after my own club."

'"Are you sure? Are you sure you're never going to need any help?"

'"Never."

'"OK. If that's how you want it."

'The next night, five blokes came to the club and set on the manager. They were really laying into him and we could hear him screaming out for help. My lot were all there but did nothing. He came out of hospital a couple of days later all done up in bandages and plasters. Then the owner came to see me. "Joe, just to let you know, I got your message. Let's forget about the rent."

'My two gambling clubs were doing well and money was really starting to come in. Each table would pull in around £150 per night. I had to pay rent for the place in Balham, but it was never very much. The owners wanted me there because the games brought in a lot of extra people, more customers. There was never a bar up in the gaming room so people would have to go down to the bar to get drinks. And whenever anyone won big, the first thing they would do is go and splash out on drinks all round, so the club owners were always happy. It wasn't a fortune or anything like it, but I was making a good living.

'The thing is, I was still young then and at that age the only things you need money for are some flashy clothes and a flashy car. You don't want to buy a house; you certainly don't want any kids. You're just out to have a good time.

'I was still into clothes in a big way. Everything I wore in those days was tailor made; I made a point of never buying anything off the peg. There was a man called Barry Scott who lived up in Neasden Hill, and I'd go down there to get measured up and then come back and pick up the suit two weeks later. I took a real pride in my appearance because that was an important part of showing that you were someone who demanded respect.

'It was the same with the cars that I drove; it was all about having a status symbol. That's changed a bit these days. Today you could be a millionaire and still be happy to drive about in a Ford Poplar, but back then, if you had it, you had to flaunt it. A flash car was a sure sign of success, a sign that you were doing very well thank you very much. I went through a lot of cars in those days. I had Rolls Royces, Maseratis; I had a Lamborghini and a whole load of Mercs.

'Having the dice clubs made me realise just how much money there was in gambling and, not soon after that, Waggy approached me with a business proposition. He had a thing going where he was getting paid to look after clubs like the Bagatel and the Astor. With all the casinos opening up there was more and more demand for his services – more than he could cope with – so he asked if me and the Nash brothers wanted to go into business with him.

'Pretty soon we were getting a "pension" from four or five clubs and used to go round every Friday to collect our money from the owners. Then we were looking after the casinos as well, so that was even more money. There would be at least a couple of grand to share between us, so it meant a nice fat wage packet every week. It was good knowing where your next penny was coming from – it was almost like having a proper job but without the grind. And you knew there would never be any problem about getting paid.

'When people talk about protection money, they imagine people going in somewhere and smashing a place up, but it doesn't work like that at all. If you have a man and you are taking money from him but he doesn't want to pay you, then sooner or later that man will turn. There are all sorts of strokes he can pull and he will look for an out. It might be telling the police what you are doing or it might be calling in another firm to get rid of you. But if he doesn't want to be paying you, then sooner or later it will cause you trouble. On the other hand, if you have a man who wants to pay you, who doesn't want you to leave, and the minute he does want you to leave then you are happy to go, then that's a happy situation all round. That's the way Waggy worked it and that's the way me and the Nash brothers worked it too.

'I'd got the work as a direct result of the reputation I had gained after the Pen Club incident. But once you're in that position, as the Nash brothers had already found, you become a target. People want to challenge you because they knew if they can best you, they take your reputation with them. Like it or not, you have to fight just to stay where you are.

'People will try it on. If they owe money, they will go without paying just to see what happens. They want to know who is going to come after them and how aggressive they are going to be. If you try to be kind and understanding, sympathetic, sometimes you can come across as being weak and people will take advantage of that. But you can't ever let that happen.

'I was out one night with Johnny Nash and his brother, Ronnie, in an illegal drinking and gambling joint called the Panda Club, which was based above a restaurant on Streatham High Street.

'As we went inside, John recognised a bloke who had asked Ronnie Diamond, a well-known and well-respected villain, to cut someone for him – offered him some money to do it. Diamond had taken the bloke at his word and gone and done the deed, leaving the bloke needing something like 25 stitches. He had even got caught for it and was doing bird, but the man who had ordered it hadn't paid up.

'It was well out of order that the only reason Ronnie was in prison was because he'd accepted a bit of work. Ronnie was a decent man and there was no way he'd ever tell the police that he was offered money to do it or say anything to get the bloke who wanted it done into trouble. And that just made it even worse that the bloke was taking the piss.

'John went over to confront the bloke, who was standing by the entrance to the toilets, and pretty soon the two of them were having a bit of an argument. Me and Ronnie went over to join John and see what was going on, and other people in the club started taking an interest.

'There was two brothers in the club that night, Terry and George Samson, who came out of the Elephant and Castle. They had a big reputation and were there with about half a dozen of their mob. I guess one of them, I think it was Terry, must have known this bloke John was talking to because he came over and asked him if he needed any help.

'I looked across at this bloke. "Yeah, he's all right. What the fuck has it go to do with you?"

'The next thing I know it's off. John has hit the Samson brother and the bloke he was talking to has grabbed a fire extinguisher off the wall and cracked me over the back of the head with it. For a few seconds I'm seeing stars, and then when I look, I see the whole Samson mob, six or seven of them, steaming towards us.

'We're right by the entrance to the toilets and there's nowhere to go, so we force open the window and drop down into the kitchen of the restaurant below. In the meantime the Samson mob start running down the stairs to get us. They appear at the end of this narrow passageway that leads from the kitchen to the front door.

'They started running towards us, so we grab the first thing to hand – loads of cans of food – and we start chucking them. That keeps them back for a bit but then we run out of cans and we know that before too long they're gonna start coming forward again. I look on the kitchen counter and I see a couple of knives. I grab one and start running down the passageway. That's when George Samson appeared. He put his foot up on one side of the wall and his back against the other. "You ain't going nowhere mate," he said.

'I didn't even slow down, I just looked at him, growled "fuck off" and chopped the knife right into his leg. The blood went spurting up the wall and he went down, screaming. Behind me Terry had jumped out to try to stop Johnny, who had stuck a knife right up his Derby. He too went down screaming and we made it to the door. The three of us jumped on a bus that was passing by and that was it, we'd managed to get away.

'The next day we all met up at the Nashes' house in Hoxton. All the brothers were there and we started talking about what might happen next. As far as we're concerned, we're all suddenly at war with the Samson brothers and they were bound to try and retaliate.

'But then a message came over from a guy called Aggie, a friend of the Samsons who was also friendly with the Nash brothers. He told us that the Samsons had only just realised who it was they were dealing with. They simply hadn't recognised us before.

'Although they were the only ones who were injured, they said they didn't want to take it any further. Instead, they were going to lick their wounds and forget the whole thing. That suited us down to the ground and so that was the end of it.'

In those days, reputation was everything and the only possible way to respond to any kind of challenge was to meet it head on.

'Back then it seemed to happen on a regular basis. I remember being in a club in Notting Hill and having a little chat to this girl I met down there. She seemed nice and we got on pretty well but nothing happened and at the end of the evening I went home. The next day someone told me that I was in big trouble, that the girl was seeing a bloke by the name of Mad Ronnie Fryer, who was now planning to chop my head off for trying to chat up his bird.

'Mad Ronnie was a doorman and had a reputation as a bit of a hard nut. I knew if I didn't do anything that it would count against me, so I had no choice but to go down to the club again the next night. I got myself tooled up – a shooter and a knife – and went down there with a couple of mates. When we arrived Ronnie was outside. He turned out to be as nice as pie. Apparently he hadn't been threatening me at all, it was just someone trying to stir things up. We had a good laugh about it, and a few weeks later he had moved down south London way and ended up working for me.'

But challenges didn't always end so peacefully.

'Once I was in a basement club in a mews in the West End and a bloke called Dukie got into an argument with one of the crowd I was with. He went outside and pulled a shotgun out of his car and then started threatening the doormen. He was screaming at the top of his voice: "Get that fucking wanker up here, I'm gonna blow his fucking head off," and all that.

'I went outside to see what all the noise was about, pulled my gun out of my trousers and crouched down so Dukie couldn't see me. Then I started creeping up behind some parked cars and vans until I was level with where he was. It was funny because all the people he was threatening with the shotgun could see what I was doing and knew what was coming, but old Dukie never had a clue. He was too busy being the big man: "Who wants some, come on then. I'll take you all on."

'I knew I didn't want to kill him. As soon as I was close enough I jumped up, aimed nice and low and shot him in the leg. He screamed, dropped the shotgun and limped off as fast as he could, while everyone pissed themselves laughing. Then

I tucked the gun back into my trousers and went back into the club for another drink.'

'I valued my reputation, not just for its own sake but also because it was a key part of how I made my living. As the new gambling clubs opened, people with reputations were exactly what the casino bosses wanted. It was a whole different game to working the clubs and pubs. Casinos are not the sorts of places where people get mad drunk or start fights. And it's not even like being a bouncer because you don't stand outside the door or walk around in an evening suit.

'The reason the casinos wanted people there was to stop any kind of skulduggery, to stop folk from trying to pull scams. Let's say you have someone who goes into a casino and tries to buy chips with fake money. Well if we found out that they were doing that, we would ask them to stop. And out of respect for the sort of people that we were, they would do; they would go and try it on somewhere else. You would literally say to people: "Hey. We've got a pension here, so behave yourself."

'It was the same when you had punters who owed a lot of money on credit. It would be our job to tell them to pay the money or pay the consequences. Collecting the debts would also be a nice little earner because you'd get a commission on the money.

'One of the first people me and Johnny had to collect from was Cubby Broccoli, the man who produced all the early James Bond films. He had built up a debt of £40,000 and when we went round there he tried to get a bit tough with us. At first he refused to let us into his office and then, when he finally did, he had all his minders around him. The funny thing was, the minders knew us and once Broccoli realised that, he knew that he had no protection at all. He paid up in full the same day.

'When we weren't chasing debtors, we were looking out for scams. The signs are always there, but only if you know what to look for. The people with the fake money buy lots of chips but only play a few of them before changing them back; the card counters bet small most of the time, then go through a run of betting – and winning – big.

'It's a whole new world with a whole new language. There are "hand muckers" who mark the cards so they recognise them when they come up again, and "holdout men" who have extra cards and switch them during play. Then there are the "mechanics", either card mechanics or dice mechanics, who manipulate things for their own benefit. And then there are the "spookers" – the people who try to stand behind dealers or other players, peek at the cards and try to secretly convey information to a co-conspirator sitting at the table.

'Some of the time it wasn't the players but the dealers you had to watch out for. They could work hand-in-hand with the players and give them an unfair advantage, splitting the proceeds later.

'One of the biggest scams at the time was on the baccarat table, where people would try to use special cards which would slightly bevel up so you could see what the next card was. And on the blackjack table I've seen people using little mirrors to check a card and then take the second one if it works out better for their hand.

'It wasn't our job to look out for these people, but working the casino circuit, you soon got to learn about all the different tricks that people got up to. And if anyone got spotted pulling a stroke, then it was our job to sort them out and make sure they never did it again. No matter who they were.

'I had a good friend, Ray, who never used to gamble his whole life, but one day for some unknown reason he decided to start. The bug got hold of him something rotten. He'd be in and out of casinos all day and all night. It took a while before we realised just how bad things had got. He'd started out as a successful businessman with a few greengrocers' shops to his name. After a year of non-stop gambling, he'd almost lost the lot. Yet still he couldn't stop.

'There would be times when I saw him and he'd be crouched over a table, biting his nails down to the hilt. It was painful to watch because you always knew that something big was riding on the next spin of the wheel but there was nothing you could do. As far as Ray was concerned nothing else mattered and telling him to slow it down or give it up was just a waste of time.

'One time I was looking after the Olympic casino and Ray came in. I was standing by the roulette table, keeping an eye on the game, and Ray came up and stood right next to me.

' "How you doing today Ray?"

' "Losing. This is my last bet, I'm off home after this."

With that he pulled a sealed envelope out of his jacket pocket. In those days whenever you won £500, you could go to the desk and, instead of getting chips, they would give you a special envelope with a wax seal. Just as the wheel started spinning Ray slung the envelope down on red.

'All the dealers and staff in the place knew I was security, so when they saw Ray standing next to me, they assumed he must have been all right. The dealer looks at me, then looks at the envelope, assumed it had £500 inside and carried on with the game. The ball landed on red and right away, even before the dealer had paid him out, Ray snatched the envelope back. And that's when I twigged.

'I let him get his winnings then I took him into a quiet corner.

' "What's in the envelope Ray?"

He said nothing, just looked sheepishly at the floor. I put my hand down on his shoulder. "Ray, what's in the fucking envelope?"

' "Newspaper," he mumbled.

' "You bastard! You were standing right next to me, the dealer saw it, and you pull a stroke like that. How would it make me look if you had lost?"

Ray shrugged his shoulders.

' "I'd have had to give you a dig wouldn't I?"

' "Yeah, but I had to take the chance. It was worth it, I knew it meant a beating off you and getting thrown out but I just had to take the chance."

'One of the golden rules about looking after casinos was that you were not allowed to gamble there. But I've been a bit of a gambler all my life and sometimes the temptation is just too hard to resist.

'When things got a bit quiet at the Olympic one day, I decided to put a few quid down, try my luck. The owner was in his office and couldn't see me so I thought I'd be able to get away with it. I did, but as luck would have it, I was losing my shirt. I was putting down twenty pound or thirty pound and it was all vanishing right in front of my eyes. I was down a few hundred quid, quite a lot of money for me to lose, and had gone right down to betting two pound chips, waiting for my luck to change.

'I was sitting on the stool in front of the table when I sensed someone walk up right behind me. I glanced over my shoulder and saw that it was the actor Telly Savalas, later to be the star of *Kojak*, but at the time known for his roles in *Kelly's Heroes*, *The Dirty Dozen* and as the main villain in one of the Bond films. He was dressed up all smart and had a beautiful woman a good few years younger than him, hanging off his arm.

'I looked back and started concentrating on the cards. Then all of a sudden Telly's came in over my shoulder and put down a twenty quid chip in my box alongside my two pound one. Now that didn't bother me – there's nothing to stop other people betting in your box – but what happened next did.

'The first card had been a nine and second was a seven. The dealer looked at me to see what I wanted to do next.

' "No card," I said, firmly.

' "Card," said a voice behind me. I looked around and Telly Savalas was pointing at the dealer. "Card," he said again.

' "No card," I said once more, this time a little more loudly.

' "Card," repeated Savalas.

'I whipped round in my stool. "Who the fuck do you think you are? This is my box and it's down to me to say if I want a card or not."

'"It might be your box, but I've got the bigger bet. I've got twenty quid down there."

'"I don't give a fuck. You ain't in some fucking James Bond film now you know."

'By now the owner, who like Savalas also happened to be half Greek, was out of his office and running across the casino floor.

'"Jesus Christ Joey, what do you think you're playing at? You know you're not supposed to gamble in here."

'"It's OK, I'm losing."

'"I don't care. Don't gamble."

'"Well I'm waiting to see if I've won."

'"Don't gamble!"

'"I'm in the middle of a bet." Then Savalas piped up. "And so am I."

'The owner ran his hands through his hair, pulling out a few clumps on the way. All he could see was a valued celebrity customer leaving the place because of me and my two pound bet. Either that or the next day's newspaper headlines about a Hollywood villain getting a right hander from a real East End villain. He reached across to the dealer's end of the table, grabbed a fifty quid chip and pushed it into my hands.

'"Please Joey, take this and just leave the table. And from now on, no gambling."'

4. 'THE WORST THING I COULD DO IS START GIVING YOU A LOT OF MONEY NOW BECAUSE IF I DO THAT, YOU MIGHT START SHOWING OUT AND THEN IT WILL COME BACK TO ME. BUT WHEN THE TIME COMES FOR ME TO LEAVE, I'LL MAKE SURE I SORT YOU OUT'

The big man with the close-cropped hair and high collar had been hovering outside the newsagent's in Windmill Road for nearly ten minutes before he finally pushed his way inside. 'Watchya mate,' he said, in a thick Australian accent. 'I saw the sign in ya window there, 'bout the flat you're renting out. I'd like to take a gander.'

Rita Poole, the middle-aged woman behind the counter, eyed the man cautiously, fazed by both his formidable appearance – the swollen knuckles and flattened nose hinted at a life of violence – and the fact that for the first time in her life, someone had referred to her as 'mate'. Leaning back on her chair she asked the stranger to wait a minute and called out to her husband who was checking stock in the back room.

From the way he had sighed when asked to wait, it was clear that the Australian was already losing patience and, by the time Albert appeared, he was struggling to keep his temper under control.

'G'day. It's about the flat you've got in the window,' he said briskly. 'I want the keys so I can go take a look, see if it's the kind of thing I'm looking for.'

Albert shook his head. 'It doesn't work like that. We don't have the keys here.'

The big man's jaw fell open. 'What do you mean you don't have the keys here? What the fuck are you talking about. How can you advertise a flat for rent and not keep the keys? Is this some kind of joke?'

'But it's not my flat,' Albert interrupted.

'I know it ain't your flat, but in Australia, if you ask to see a flat, you get the keys straight away. None of this fucking about. No wonder this country is such a fucking mess. You people ain't got a clue. Nothing makes any fucking sense.'

As the insults flew thick and fast it soon became Albert's turn to lose patience. 'Look mate, I don't know what your problem is. You say things are different in Australia. Well you're not in Australia any more. If you don't like the way we do things over here, why don't you just piss off out of it and go back to your own country.'

At that moment the argument was balanced on a knife-edge and could have gone either way. The Australian stood in the centre of the shop, his nostrils flaring as he glared at the couple. Rita would later tell friends that she was glued to the spot with fear. Albert, on the other hand, stood firm, comforted by the fact he was well within arm's reach of the heavy monkey wrench he kept under the counter for protection. But as quickly as it had started, so it finished.

'It all right mate,' said the Australian. 'It's not you. I'm sorry I lost my rag. It's not you, it's just this whole fucking country. It just pisses me off sometimes.'

The flat in question sat above a dry-cleaners a few streets away, in Handcroft Road. The cleaners itself was managed by a man called Ernie Finn who ran the place in partnership with none other than Joey Pyle. Finn, at Pyle's suggestion, had spent a good deal of time and money doing the flat up, adding a new bathroom and small kitchenette. It had been two days since Finn had placed the card advertising the property in the newsagent's window and this was his first caller – he was eager to get a return.

Albert wasn't certain about putting forward the Aussie with the hair-trigger temper as a client but the flat was nowhere near his property, and he would have nothing more to do with him. Also, escorting the man to meet Finn seemed the best way to get him out of the shop before he flared up again.

Albert hung around as Finn gave the Australian a tour of the flat. Built on two storeys, the living room and kitchenette were on the ground floor, directly behind the shop, and the bedroom was on the top floor, set back from the road with the roof of the shop jutting out directly underneath the bedroom windows. To get in, you walked along a narrow alleyway to the left of the shop, covered by plastic sheeting, and through a wooden gate into a small yard area. It took only a matter of minutes for the Aussie to make up his mind. 'I reckon,' he said with a grin, 'that this is just the place I'm looking for.'

Later that same day, Finn called Pyle to tell him that the flat had been let.

'He told me some Australian had taken it and paid six months worth of rent in advance. In cash. It almost covered the cost of all the work he'd had done. He was well chuffed. Of course, I knew about it long before Finn called. The money was genuine but all the rest of it was a set up. I'd met up with the Australian a couple of days before and told him that there was only one thing he needed to do when he went into that shop – to make sure that the owners remembered him. And he did that rather brilliantly, deserved a fucking Academy Award.'

Two days later it wasn't the Australian who moved in but a woman called Franny Reynolds and her husband Bruce, who at the time just happened to be one of the most wanted men in the country.

'I'd met Bruce a couple of years earlier when he was doing time in the boob with my mate Ronnie Osborne. They were banged up in Brixton and Bruce, who was having terrible problems at home, was desperate to get out as early as he could. The girl he'd been seeing was having an affair and not being able to put a stop to it, or at least find out where he stood, was driving him mad. There was no point in trying to escape – he didn't want to be looking over his shoulder for the rest of his life – so he came up with a plan.

'A few years earlier Billy Hill had been released six months early after arranging for his friend to attack a screw so that he could heroically jump in and rescue the bloke. The friend who did the attack, Jack, had spent a month in the punishment block but had been well rewarded by Billy when he finished his own sentence. Using that as his guide, Bruce came up with a similar idea. He knew that prisons are always well pleased with any prisoner who helps to foil an escape. Of course, Bruce was no grass and there was no way he was going to risk his reputation by actually fucking up some other lag's plans to do a runner. Instead he got someone to smuggle a gun – an old Browning with a clip full of ammo – into the prison grounds, pretended that he'd heard some prisoners plotting to use it to escape, and then tipped off the screws about where they could find it.

'At first it all seemed to be working like a dream and Bruce was moved to the block to protect him from the prisoners whose "escape plot" he had uncovered. The Deputy Governor even told him to start packing up his gear as he was in line for a big reduction. But it's one thing going to all the trouble of making an elaborate plan and quite another being believed. The trouble was, no one believed Bruce, mainly because he refused to name the prisoners who had been talking about the gun. Instead of going home early, Bruce was put back in an ordinary cell and told to get on with the rest of his sentence.

'Bruce protested to the Governor. He told him he'd been receiving death threats and needed to be let out or he'd be dead in a matter of days. He gave a good performance as a man in real fear of his life, but got sent away with a flea in his ear. "That's your problem," the Governor told him. "If you were man enough to bring the gun to me in the first place, then you're man enough to deal with the threats you're getting as a result." That meant there was only one thing for it – Bruce had to arrange an attack on himself, and that was where Ronnie came in.

'Ronnie was working as a cleaner in the bathhouse, the place where the prisoners went a couple of times a week to pick up fresh clothes and bits and pieces like that. Bruce smuggled a knife out of the workshop and offered Ronnie £500 to stab him with it. That was a decent lump in those days and it didn't take Ronnie long to agree to do the business. Bruce sent £250 to Ronnie's old lady straight away and promised to pay the rest once the job was done.

'It's all set for one Saturday in July. Bruce walks in and Ronnie stabs him, but not very hard. It's only a flesh wound. Doesn't look that bad. So Ronnie does him again. Another flesh wound. So Ronnie does him again and really goes for it. This time it's the real thing, the knife goes into Bruce's chest and punctures one of his lungs. Claret everywhere, screaming, and poor old Ronnie thinks he's fucking killed him.

'The screws run in, storm the place, but by the time they get to Bruce, Ronnie is lost among the crowd of other lags and no one is saying anything. Bruce spends two weeks in intensive care and meanwhile the papers are going ape shit. They get hold of the story that he'd foiled an escape attempt and told the authorities that his life was in danger, but the Governor had told him to go fuck himself. The Home Office got a lot of stick but they refused to give in. Rather than let Bruce out, they transferred him to Durham and made him serve out nine months of the last year of his sentence. During that time he finally ended it with the girl he'd been seeing, and started going out with her younger sister, Franny, and eventually married her.

'So Bruce got a result of sorts and ended up happy, but Ronnie didn't come off so well. Bruce had never let on who had stabbed him, but when Ronnie finished his own sentence a couple of years later he still hadn't had a sniff of the £250 that Bruce owed him. The two of us had been out in the West End one night, drinking at the Pigalle, when someone mentioned they had seen Bruce over at the Bagatelle – so we shot straight over to confront him.

'He'd just finished a job where his gang had got a good result, though it ended up being less than a tenth of what they had been expecting, and he'd been on holiday in Casablanca living it up. When we got down to the club, he was sitting in a booth with a couple of hostesses, smoking on a fat cigar. We didn't get the £250, but Bruce and I got to know each other a little. He said he'd be able to give us the money pretty soon as he had a big job coming up. He said he might even try to put a bit of work our way. It was all pretty reasonable and by the time we left, I couldn't help liking the guy. He made it sound as though we'd be better off in the long run waiting for the bit of work rather than tapping him for the £250. So that's what we did. I saw him a couple of times after that and we became pals – not close or anything, but pals. But then he went off and did his next bit of work without us. And I have to say, I'm fucking glad I never got involved.'

The 'bit of work' turned out to be a job that, more than four decades later, remains the most famous heist ever to take place on British soil.

At exactly 3.03 a.m. on 8 August 1963, the London mail train, travelling south from Glasgow, was brought to a halt close to Bridego Bridge in Buckinghamshire by a fake red signal. Within seconds the train driver, Jack Mills, found his cab had been filled with men in balaclavas, one of whom coshed him over the head as he struggled. The rear coaches were uncoupled, and the engine and front two carriages were driven down the line while other members of the gang overpowered the five postal clerks working in the High Values Packages Coach.

The train was brought to a halt and the staff made to lie on the floor while the fifteen or so members of the gang formed a human chain, passing 120 sacks bulging with banknotes across to a waiting lorry and two Land Rovers. In just 24 minutes, two and a half tons of bags containing a total of £2.6 million had been stolen, the equivalent of around £30 million today. Telling the terrified workers 'not to move for half an hour' the robbers fled the scene.

The man chosen to lead the hunt for the Great Train Robbers was Flying Squad chief Tommy Butler. A hugely experienced detective who had been at the forefront of many a gangland murder inquiry, Butler was a man who lived for nothing apart from his work. At the age of fifty he was single, still lived with his mother and, when asked to describe his hobbies, would reply curtly: 'catching crooks'.

Intrigued by the 'half an hour' comment, Butler correctly guessed that the gang must have initially hidden out somewhere close to the scene of the crime, and focused his efforts within a tight radius. Five days later the police uncovered the gang's hideout at Leatherslade Farm, twenty miles away.

The gang had long gone, having split their mammoth haul seventeen ways – around £150,000 per man – and they believed they had wiped clean every surface. But Butler's forensic team found enough prints left behind to link the crime to several known London villains. Within five weeks, five of the gang had been arrested, and wanted posters were pasted up across the country in a bid to track down those who had escaped the initial sweep and gone on the run, including Bruce Reynolds.

Reynolds, who described himself as an antiques dealer, was quickly identified as the organiser of the entire raid. Seen as the 'intellectual' of the gang, Reynolds was well known in police circles for living extravagantly. He enjoyed dinners at the Ritz and the Savoy, drove an Aston Martin and took regular holidays in the south of France. Butler was determined to get him, even staying on past his retirement to continue the hunt.

Within hours the robbery had become headline news around the world and in the days that followed literally thousands of column inches had been devoted to covering each new development. The pressure on Butler's team to get a result was enormous and he responded by using every trick in the book. His ultimate plan was to cut off every possible escape route or sanctuary the fugitives might turn to and then turn every member of the public into an unpaid lookout.

There were hourly press briefings, constant radio and television appeals. House-to-house enquiries were taking place on a vast scale and as many as fifty addresses were being raided each and every day. Anyone who had ever had even the most fleeting contact with one of the robbers found themselves being turned over by the Flying Squad time and again. Within weeks most of the leading faces in the London underworld, who had spent years working alongside the robbers, had become so fed up with the harassment that they point-blank refused even to speak to them, let alone help to hide them. Butler's plan was working to a tee – more gang members were being rounded up – and Reynolds was quickly running out of options.

'Bruce called me up a couple of weeks after the robbery and asked if I could help him hide until the heat died down. I knew it wasn't going to be easy – his picture was plastered all over the papers and billboards. It seemed as though every single policeman in the country was looking for him, but I said I'd give it a go.

'My brother had a council flat in Cobham, a tatty council prefab that he'd kept on even though he no longer lived there. We set Bruce up in that and thought that was the end of it, but within two or three days he was back on the phone. "I can't stay here Joey, it's too fucking quiet. It's frightening the life out of me. Every time I see someone walk past the curtains I think they're coming for me." At the time I'd never been on the run myself, but I'd known enough people who had to know just how stressful it can be. It don't matter how much money you've got, it's miserable as fuck and once the paranoia gets into your blood, you can't get rid of it.

'I was living in a little flat in Clapham South and I realised that if I was going to carry on helping Bruce there was only one thing for it – I'd have to let him move in with me. I only had the one bedroom and I wasn't giving that up for anyone, so Bruce made up a bed for himself on the settee. It was a bit cramped but it gave us the chance to get to know each other better and we thought it was only going to be a temporary thing. But the weeks started to fly by and Bruce was still there. Then Franny came and joined him and I had the two of them living there. That was when things started to get really claustrophobic, especially since Bruce could never leave the flat.

'There was one time I fancied a bit of a night on the town and arranged to take this girl I was seeing – who knew all about me hiding Bruce – out to the pictures. On the way I was going through my pockets and my wallet and I suddenly realised that I didn't have enough cash to pay for the tickets. I asked the girl if she could lend me the money and she just looked at me. "You're fucking mad you are, you've got a man up there, a fucking train robber, with all that money and you haven't even got enough to go to the pictures." Bruce had been with me for a couple of months and during the whole time, we'd never discussed what I'd be getting for helping him out.

'It had come out in the papers, as other members of the gang had been caught, that they'd all been paying untold sums, thousands of pounds, for safe houses and the like, but I hadn't had a penny. Bruce didn't have all the money on him – most of it was stashed away – but he always kept a briefcase with about £12,000 of what he called "movers money" in case he needed to be on his toes in a hurry.

'What the girl had said really made me think, so right there and then I went back up to the flat. I said to Bruce, "Look, I've got to sort this out with you. I've just tried to go to the pictures and I didn't have enough money; I had to get it off my old lady. This can't go on." Bruce was smoking a cigarette and looked up at me, stubbing it out in an ashtray. "Don't worry Joey, you know I'm going to look after you and I will. But the worst thing I could do is start giving you a lot of money now because if I do that, you might start showing out and then it will come back to me. But rest assured, when the time comes for me to leave, I'll make sure I sort you out. That will be the first thing I'll do."

'Bruce had arrived at my flat around the back end of August and almost immediately I'd spoken to Ernie Finn about doing up the flat above the cleaners shop in Handcroft Road. But before they could move in, we knew we had to set things up so that no one would suspect anything. It had been Bruce's idea to put the advert in the newsagent's window and he himself had supplied the loud Australian who had gone in and made all the fuss. In the end, what with all the renovations the place needed, it had all taken much longer than expected. It wasn't until November that the place was finally ready and although Bruce and I had become very pally, I was more than happy to have my flat back.'

With the Reynolds' situation well under control, Joey turned his attention to a new money-making enterprise devised by his new friend Billy Falco, one half of yet another prominent London family. His elder brother, Tommy, was a bookmaker and driver for gangster Albert Dimes, and had once narrowly escaped being shot at a meeting with the Kray twins when they pressed home their claim to take a cut of illegal horseracing bets. Billy was the quieter of the pair and known more as a gambler than as a hardman.

'Billy was seeing this bird who would have done absolutely anything for him, so he persuaded her to take a job as a kennel maid down at Wembley dog track. The idea was that by having someone on the inside, me, him and Waggy Whitnall, who was also in on the deal, would be able to fix races and have ourselves a nice little earner.

'We had to wait until there was a race where one trainer had at least three out of the six dogs in the race. Ideally, we wanted four dogs but three was pretty good. What would happen then was that Billy's girlfriend would mix something in with the food or the water that the dogs got given before the race – I never knew exactly what 'cos Billy took care of that side of things – to totally fuck them up. Say there were three dogs from one stable – they'd all be knocked out and then we would bet on the best of the remaining three, picking a winner but also doing each way bets and combination forecasts to cover ourselves.

'We took it fairly slowly to start out, experimenting with different drugs and timings until we knew we could control things the way we wanted to. After a couple of weeks it was all going smoothly and we had a few nice touches – nothing major but enough to show that the system worked and pushed the odds right over in our favour.

'Then one day, the dream race came along. This one trainer had four dogs in the main race of the afternoon. We all got together and knew this was going to be big. Billy told his girl to knock all four of the dogs out and, because one of the two remaining runners was a real outsider, it meant we'd have practically a dead cert for the winner. At lunchtime Billy's girl came to meet us outside the track and told us that she'd doped three of the dogs but hadn't managed to get her hands on the fourth one. She still reckoned she'd be able to do it before the race though.

'She told us that if she managed to get the dog doped, she'd stand up when she came out to watch the races in the kennel maids' enclosure. If she didn't manage to do it, she'd sit down. After checking the signals to make sure we were clear about what was what, we sent the girl back to the kennels and headed off to see our bookmakers.

'I needed all the money I could get my hands on but some of my regular sources were a bit short of cash. The night before I stopped off down in Croydon, went to see Bruce Reynolds and told him what was happening. He opened his briefcase and handed over about three grand. I told him we were on such a golden opportunity that it hardly seemed like gambling at all.

'I got back to the track and found Waggy and Billy. We were all waiting for the girl to get to the enclosure so she could give us the signal and we'd know what to do with our bets. She finally came out with a few of the other kennel maids, moved to the corner by the railing and sat down. Oh fuck, I thought, she hasn't done the last dog. But then she stood up. And then she sat down again. I didn't know what was going on. Had she doped the fourth dog or not? Had she forgotten the signal? There was no way of knowing. We just had time to place our final bets before the race got underway.

'Out of the dogs that didn't belong to the one trainer, one was the 7-4 favourite, and the other was a 20-1 outsider which no one thought had a chance. We put all our money on the favourite to win and had a few combinations to cover ourselves in case the girl had only doped three of the other four.

'The race starts and by the time the second lap is on, me, Billy and Waggy are gripping onto the rail so tight our knuckles have turned white. We're all screaming at the tops of our voices because it's all gone exactly the way we planned. The 7-4 favourite is out in front, the 20-1 dog is behind it and the other four dogs are behind them in single file. It seems as though she had doped them all and we know we've got a big payday coming. Then it gets to the last bend and it's still the same order; and then, as it gets within a few feet of the finishing line, the dog in front does a somersault – a fucking somersault – and ends up lying on the ground. The race is still going but the fucking dog is just lying there, looking at the sky with these big stupid eyes. Then the 20-1 rag comes up, overtakes it and wins; then the doped dog comes in second. We can't believe it. We're standing there watching it all but none of us can fucking believe it. We can't say anything. I'm so choked up that no words come out of my mouth no matter how hard I try.

'We go outside and sit in Billy's motor in the car park, waiting for the girl to turn up. The second she climbs in we're onto her: "What the fuck happened? Why did you stand up? Why did you sit down? Did you dope the wrong fucking dog or what?" The poor girl was almost on the verge of tears.

'"I was trying to warn you," she says.

'"Warn us about what?"

'"I was trying to warn you not to put any money on the favourite because he suffers from rheumatism."

'There was a pause before the three of us spoke together. "He does what?"

'"He suffers from rheumatism. That's why he did that somersault. It's because of the rheumatism."

'Billy looked at me:

'"Fucking rheumatism."

'I looked at Waggy.

'"Fucking rheumatism," he said.

'Waggy looked at Billy.

'"Fucking rheumatism."

'After that we decided to give up the dog doping game and go back to other forms of crime instead. It was all just too much trouble.'

Out of pocket some three grand, Bruce Reynolds, happily ensconced in the Croydon flat, could not have agreed more. He would later refer to the requests for money as 'a subtle form of extortion', but knowing the huge sums being paid out by others who were on the run, he decided to accept it. Besides, he had far more important things to worry about.

At 6.30 p.m. on 3 December, Bruce and Franny were listening to the radio when a news flash came on to say that yet another of the Great Train Robbers had been arrested. Disillusioned by the news and the unmistakable knowledge that the net was getting ever tighter, the pair decided to get drunk enough to forget about it, at least for a few hours.

As the wine flowed, Bruce asked Franny to go up and check on the 'movers money'. Somewhat unsteady on her feet, she vanished up the stairs for a few seconds and then came down hurriedly with a worried look on her face. 'Bruce,' she gasped, 'the police are here.' The words had barely got out of her mouth before there was a knock at the door.

'Franny had reached the bedroom and been shocked to see this copper coming in through the window. He had place a ladder at the front of the dry cleaning shop and scrambled across the short roof. "What are you doing here?" she asked him.

'"Sorry love, we didn't know anybody was living here, we're just following up a report of a burglary."

'"Right, well you'd better come in, but not like that, go round the side and use the main door."

'"OK. Is it just you on your own then?"

'"Yes, it's just me."

'Bruce had to think fast because Franny was moving across the room towards the door – there was nothing else she could do, she had to let them in. Bruce had already guessed that the officers were nothing to do with the Flying Squad. They would have stormed the place commando-style rather than knocking on the door.

'As the team entered, Bruce ducked behind the sofa in the living room and took off all his clothes. Then stood up, shamefaced. It was a ploy he'd used once before when he had been caught with a girl in a stolen car on Mitcham Common. What had happened then happened again now. Confronted by the sight of a naked man the police officers suddenly got really self-conscious. They didn't know what to do with themselves. They were looking anywhere and everywhere expect at Bruce. Everywhere except his face.

'"I thought you said you were here on your own," one officer said to Franny.

'She was one step ahead of the game and put in an Academy Award-winning performance of her own, sobbing gently. "You see, my husband is a lorry driver and he's away at the moment . . . and this is my boyfriend . . ."

'So now all the coppers are grinning to themselves and winking at Franny, but still not looking at Bruce. "You'd better get your clothes on mate," they say, "and make yourself scarce before the old man gets home." They take a name and address, just to be on the safe side, but Bruce gives them false ones and before too long the coppers are on their way.

'The law were quite happy with the whole thing until they got back to the police station and saw the wanted posters stuck up outside. They recognised Franny first and then they realised who Bruce was. But that's where they messed it up. Instead of going straight back round there they called DCS Butler. I think Butler had given orders that, if any of the robbers were spotted, no one was to move until he had been informed. He immediately set up roadblocks all over the place and surrounded the whole area. He tried to tighten the net but the few minutes' delay meant Bruce had time to escape.

'Even though he'd bought some time, Bruce got himself into a real panic. One of the last things his solicitor has said to him was that if he got caught, it should be without the money, as that was the principal evidence against him. He called me to explain what had happened and I dropped everything to get over there.

'When I arrived Bruce was in the yard out the back, trying to stick his briefcase with all the money into a dustbin. I said to him what do you think you're doing? Just take that with you. We jumped in the car, he ducked down in the back, and I took him down to Tooting Bec tube station where he met his friend Terry, who looked after him from there. It was only when he'd gone that I realised he'd never given me anything for looking after him. From Tooting he stayed on the run for another year before he was eventually caught, and by that time virtually all the money had gone.'

Believing they still had the element of surprise, the police waited several hours before finally raiding the shop, smashing their way in through the doors and windows. But Bruce and Franny had long gone.

Butler was on the case straight away and within minutes had tracked down ownership of the flat to Ernie Finn. When they grilled him about who was staying there he had no hesitation in telling them everything he knew – he had advertised the flat in the window of a local newspaper shop and the flat had been leased to some bloke who had responded to the ad. Within minutes the police followed up the lead and dropped in on Albert and Rita Poole. Was there, the officers wondered, any chance that they remembered who had leased a flat advertised in their shop five months earlier?

'I remember exactly,' Rita told them, barely able to contain her excitement. The officers gathered around her, licking their pencils and eager to get all the details. 'It was this horrible big Australian man. Scared the life out of me. I'll never forget him. Made a terrible fuss because we didn't have the keys, didn't he Albert? What's he been up to? No good I bet. You can tell his sort a mile off.'

Of course the police suspected that Pyle might have had something to do with the fact that the Reynolds had ended up living there, but neither Finn nor the couple who owned the newsagents had any criminal connections, and the detectives knew that if they attempted to take the case to court, it would collapse at the first hurdle.

But deep in the vaults of Scotland Yard, the file on Joey Pyle got a little thicker. The man who once faced the death penalty for the Pen Club murder, and was known to be heavily involved in the world of illegal gambling, was now inextricably linked to the biggest robbery the country had ever known.

And from that moment on, Joey wasn't just a top London gangster – he was a target.

5. 'I HEARD HE WAS SITTING IN THE PUB AND I THOUGHT FUCK IT. I'LL JUST GO AND KILL HIM'

By the spring of 1966, Joey Pyle had known the Kray twins for more than a decade and, thanks to their habit of getting photographed standing alongside as many top celebrities as possible, he had seen their reputation grow rapidly.

The years had been kind to the Twins: Ronnie was taking medication which seemed to be going some way towards controlling his paranoia, and he was also coming to terms with his homosexuality, attending gay parties and stepping out with a variety of good looking boys. Reggie had found a different kind of love in the arms of Frances Shea. They had married the year before and although there had been difficulties – not least of which was the fact that Ronnie could not stand the sight of his brother's bride – which had led to a split, there seemed to be hope for a reconciliation.

Business had boomed following the legalising of gambling under the 1960 Gaming Act. This had unwittingly given the Twins a whole new source of income as their ruthless nature allowed them to sweep aside a softer generation of old-style mobsters and take over the running of gaming clubs through-out the capital.

In 1960 they had forcibly taken over Esmerelda's Barn in Knightsbridge and, by encouraging villains to consider the place a home from home, made it into a huge success. The Krays even persuaded Lord Effingham, a silly but entirely honest member of the House of Lords, to join them on the board of Esmeralda's Barn, a move that brought the rich and famous to the venue in droves.

It didn't take long for their friends in high places to prove useful. In 1965 the Twins had been arrested for demanding money with menaces from the owner of a club called the Hideaway. Remanded in custody to Brixton prison, questions were soon asked in the House of Lords by Lord Boothby as to how long it would be before they were granted bail.

Ronnie Kray had first met Lord Boothby through one of the many gay parties that they both attended. Boothby then began making plans to join the Krays in a business venture involving a seaside development in Nigeria but the scheme collapsed. Stories of the meetings began to leak out and the *Sunday Mirror* ran a story about 'The Peer and the Gangster'.

Boothby sued the paper, claiming that he was unaware of Ronnie Kray being involved in crime, that he was not gay and that he had never attended any parties of that nature. He was paid damages of £40,000 and while papers continued to feature pictures of the Krays, it would be some years before they dared write about their gangland associations once more.

The American Mafia also came to town in 1966. Attracted by the opportunity to set up new casinos in London, they had come over to seek what they called 'The Arm'.

In America, setting up a casino without the protection of the Mob was and is a ticket for disaster. Those who try find themselves the victims of weekly, sometimes daily, robberies where men with guns rush in and scoop up all the cash they can find. The only way to avoid this problem is to pay off the local Mafia family. The word then goes out that the casino is protected and the only problem then is ensuring you don't forget to make your payments.

When the Americans arrived in London, they fully expected the situation to be the same, and set about finding the top local gangsters so they could establish a business relationship with them. For Ronnie the prospect of being approached by the Mob was a dream come true. He had long modelled himself on American gangsters of the kind portrayed by film stars like James Cagney and George Raft. There was no concern, no thought of competition. It could only be seen as a good thing. The Americans had money and they would be bringing business. And the Krays wanted to make sure they got a piece of it.

'Around that time the Krays had a hell of a lot of influence,' Joey recalls. 'They were well respected by everyone and I had a lot of time and respect for them. They had a style about them that was and remains very hard to explain to people. They always dressed very smart and they were always together. And in those days they were still identical, you couldn't tell one from the other. No matter what you did, you couldn't get away from the powerful sense of togetherness that they generated. It was rare to see them alone. It almost never happened. You knew that if you pushed one, you had to push the two of them. And that was something extra; that made them special.

'There were other gangs that were just as powerful in their own part of London, but the Krays were better known because they were so much in the public eye. So far as ordinary people were concerned, the type of folk I like to call civilians, it must have seemed like the Krays were running everything but that was nothing like the truth.'

To the west of the Krays, covering most of Islington, the Nash brothers and Joey Pyle ran the show; just south of the river, covering the area around Lambeth and Bermondsey, was a mob run by notorious 'pavement artist' and general hard man Freddie Foreman. To the extreme south was a firm run by brothers Charlie and Eddie Richardson, supported by their friends 'Mad' Frankie Fraser, George Cornell and others.

'I'd met Eddie Richardson a few years earlier through the scrap metal game. There was a bloke I knew who worked on the railways and he used to nick silver ingots. He'd pass them on to me and I'd sell them to Eddie. That was my first real introduction to him and we became pretty pally after that.

'They'd hang out mainly in south London and every now and then I would go down and see them. Sometimes they would turn up at the Thomas à Becket pub and I would have a drink with them there. Sometimes they came up to the West

End and they could come into a club that I was looking after with the Nashes and we'd end up having a few drinks together there.

'Like the Twins, the Richardson brothers had both been boxers when they were younger. They were good, though Eddie was the better of the two in my opinion. And after that, like the Twins, they grew up into a pair of game fuckers – that was pretty obvious from the times I had been out drinking with them. You don't have to see someone have a row to know he can handle himself; you go by the way he talks, the way he holds himself.

'Everyone who knew the Richardsons knew that they were men of honour – they were never the sort of blokes who went around having rows in public, that wasn't their style. Not to say there was no trouble, it's just that in their firm, anything like that was always done in private.'

While the Krays seemingly concentrated on raising their profile to the highest possible levels, the Richardsons turned their attention to expanding their business interests. Charlie began making regular trips abroad and investing in African mines, while Eddie started up Atlantic Machines Ltd, with which he hoped to cash in on the lucrative gaming machine market: even in the smallest club, a single one-armed bandit could easily turn a profit of £100 per week, paying for itself in no time and thereafter producing a healthy, ongoing return.

Soon after launching his new company, Eddie Richardson was approached by a couple of club owners who hoped he might be able to help them out. Their establishment went by the unlikely name of Mr Smiths and the Witchdoctor but was usually referred to simply as Mr Smiths, and was based in Rushey Green, Catford. In a previous life the venue had been a cinema and then a bingo hall, but after being taken over by Paddy McGrath and Owen Ratcliffe, it had evolved into something far more profitable. Hoping to use Mr Smiths as a base from which to expand their business into London after scoring considerable success in their native Manchester, the pair had spared no expense. Mr Smiths boasted a nightclub with a small stage for bands, a dance floor and a casino.

The problems started almost straight away, as the new club found favour with a rough and ready clientele prone to brawling. Two local brothers, Billy and 'Flash' Harry Hayward, were installed at the club to deal with trouble in exchange for free drinks. Well known and well respected throughout south London, the Haywards were a good choice but, as the weeks went on, McGrath and Ratcliffe began to suspect that they were on the verge of being ousted and that their minders were beginning to use the club as their own headquarters.

In desperation, they turned to Eddie Richardson and a deal was quickly struck. In return for clearing out the Hayward brothers, Richardson would be given the chance to install gaming machines on the premises. It was a licence to print money.

To celebrate the start of this lucrative new venture, Eddie Richardson, Mad Frankie Fraser and a few of their friends stopped by Mr Smiths for a drink. Also in the club that night was Billy Hayward and his friend Dickie Hart, a loose ally of the Krays and vague member of the Firm. Hart had drifted in and out of jobs ever since leaving school and had picked up a conviction for hijacking a lorry. He had failed to impress either of the Richardson brothers, who had dubbed him the 'Catford Fart'.

The scene was set for a violent confrontation that would leave one man dead and forever change the face of London's gangland.

As the night wore on more and more of the Richardson mob began to appear at Mr Smiths and Billy Hayward began to suspect that something was about to go down. He had been having an affair with the wife of Eddie and Mad Frank's mechanic and feared he was about to be confronted over it. Convinced that the Richardson gang would be tooled up to the teeth, Hayward sent out for more weapons, including a

.410 shotgun, which he concealed under his coat. An excited Hart told Hayward not to bother on his account – he already had a pistol with him.

During the course of the next couple of hours the atmosphere in the club seemed to mellow out. The Richardson gang and the Hayward gang were drinking in two groups on separate tables, but occasionally a conversation would begin which involved both groups. The drinks and laughter flowed freely and it seemed like just another night in a south London club.

At around 3.30 in the morning Billy Hayward and his mob were still sitting there. The club only had a licence till 3 a.m., so the manager asked Eddie Richardson if he could have a word with them. 'Right then, drink up, that's your lot,' Richardson told them, only to receive a wave of protest in reply from Hayward's group. After all, the Richardson mob were still being served and were showing no signs of leaving. Peter Hennessey, one of a number of brothers, was drinking with Hayward. He called Richardson a ponce and challenged him to a fight. The pair walked into the centre of the dance floor and began pounding one another. Then all hell broke loose.

Dickie Hart pulled his gun out, a large revolver, moved to the edge of the room and began firing at random. The bullets were going all over the place, hitting the roof, legs of chairs and finally people. One, Harry Rawlings, was hit in the shoulder and arm – one of the shots severing an artery and producing a fountain of blood. Hart continued firing, hitting Richardson in the thigh and buttocks. Ronnie Jeffrey took one in the groin and Billy Hayward received serious head injuries.

Hart was still firing as friends of Rawlings applied a tourniquet to his arm and tried to drag him to safety. Frankie Fraser sneaked up on Hart and tried to grab the gun, but Hart fired again, sending a bullet through Fraser's thigh.

By the time police arrived Mr Smiths was swimming in blood and Hart had been shot in the face with a .45

automatic. He died in hospital later that day while lying in a bed right next to the injured Frankie Fraser.

With one or two notable exceptions, virtually every written account of the underworld of the 1960s talks about growing tensions between the Kray twins and the Richardson brothers, about how the two groups hated one another and teetered on the brink of all-out warfare.

In line with this is the theory that the real reason Eddie Richardson and his friends went to Mr Smiths that night was that they intended to wipe out the Kray gang because they were getting too powerful and were eating into the Richardsons' club interests. The fact that Hart, a close ally of the Krays, was responsible for many of the shootings and was ultimately killed is seen as proof that the battle of Mr Smiths was the culmination of a series of incidents during which members of the Firm had been warned to be on their guard.

At one point, so the story goes, every member of the Kray Firm was said to have been issued with an automatic pistol and told to keep it on their person at all times. Another claim was that guns and caches of ammunition were being hidden across London so they would be available at a moment's notice, regardless of where the fighting actually broke out.

Ronnie Kray, it is said, wanted something more in line with his status within the Firm, and equipped himself with two large Browning machine guns, bought for £75 each. The Twins were also said to have invested in a pair of bullet-proof jackets.

It didn't end there. There were plans for raids into enemy territory, which involved large vans, packed with dozens of heavily armed men. This, Ronnie said, would ensure the Firm had the element of surprise all to itself.

And it wasn't only the Krays who were after blood. One night, a few minutes after the Twins had left the Widow's pub in Tapp Street, a car drove past and gunshots blazed out, shattering windows and leaving bullets embedded in the floor and ceiling. A few days later, a man with the misfortune to bear a striking resemblance to Ronnie Kray, was run down by a car, which, according to eyewitnesses, deliberately mounted the pavement along Vallance Road where the Twins lived. Both incidents were soon attributed to growing tensions with the Richardson brothers.

The truth, however, was far less dramatic. There was no war with the Richardson brothers. The Twins knew Charlie well, and had done so ever since the three of them found themselves in the same army detention centre during their National Service days.

Joey explains: 'Though I was never part of the Firm, never getting a pension from the Twins, I was more than pally with them. I'd go round their mum's house for meetings and all sorts, or we'd go out drinking or in and out of clubs and casinos.

'It was the same with me and the Richardsons and no one on the Firm ever had a problem with that. Sometimes the Twins and the Richardsons would be in the same club at the same time but nothing ever sparked off while I was around.

'Sure there was tension some of the time, but that was just a typical north and south London thing, nothing more. There would be a bit of looking, sizing up, and that would be it. All this stuff you read about them being at each other's throats – it wasn't like that at all.

'If anyone had wanted to go to war with the Richardsons, there were plenty of opportunities. One night – one of the rare nights that John Nash and I were not looking after the place – there had been a fight at the Astor Club involving the Richardson gang and some Scots. As Eddie and Frankie Fraser were leaving they bumped into a bloke called Eric Mason, a good friend of the Krays and the Nashes. According to Fraser, Mason insulted him, so he kidnapped him and hit him over the head with an axe, dumping him, badly injured, in a hospital car park.

'A few days later, Mason came to see me and Johnny Nash and we asked if he wanted us to retaliate against the

Richardsons. He said no. The Krays asked him the same thing and he said no. It was just one of those things, people falling out with one another, nothing more.

'In fact, a little bit of tension occasionally cropped up between all the gangs – even the Nashes and the Krays – purely because we were all in the same business; although London was a big place, there was only so much any one gang could do.'

Even if there had been a war in the offing, the notion became redundant after the battle at Mr Smiths. Frankie Fraser would later be charged (and ultimately acquitted) with the murder of Dickie Hart. He and Eddie Richardson were also charged with Affray and each received a sentence of five years.

A short while later, police moved in to arrest what remained of the Richardson gang, including Charlie himself. The trial, which centred around allegations of fraud with intimidation and extreme violence, saw Charlie sentenced to 25 years, with additional 10-year sentences handed out to Fraser and Richardson.

Although stories of tensions between the two gangs have been greatly exaggerated, the jailing of the Richardsons meant the Kray Twins, along with the Nash gang and the Foreman mob, had all of London to themselves.

It was around this time that Ronnie first came up with an idea for what he described as a 'federation' of gangs. He wanted to set up a treaty that said if one gang were attacked, the others would come to their aid. If someone got killed on the territory of one gang, it would be up to the people in charge of that territory to avenge it.

'The whole thing came up soon after gambling got legalised and the Yanks started coming in and opening up their casinos. We knew they would be coming to us to look after the places, but no one knew who was going to be working where. It made sense to set things up so it worked like one big strong firm rather that a few little ones, otherwise people would have been running around all over the place.

'We had a few meetings over the amalgamation plan between the Twins, me and the Nash brothers and Freddie Foreman who represented south London. The Richardson brothers couldn't come because they were being detained at Her Majesty's pleasure, otherwise it is more than likely that they would have been there too.

'The first couple of meets went well and then the Twins called me and John in for another at the Pigalle to discuss splitting the money. As far as we were concerned, the arrangement only applied to the new work that was going to be coming into London, not the arrangements we already had established in the West End. Smaller firms would sometimes pay the Twins a "sub" to be allowed to operate on their patch, but me and the Nashes were too well established for that.

'We got to the club and there were about fifteen of the Firm there, with Reggie and Ronnie sitting at a table on their own. They called us over and Ronnie started talking about sharing stuff up. "Whatever we get we all put into the kitty," he said. "Anything we do in the clubs and the casinos, we all put in there and share it. So for starters, there's that book shop in the West End the two of you look after."

'As Ronnie spoke, I could see the veins in John's neck start to swell up. "Book shop? So fucking what. We don't ask you what you've got. That book shop is nothing to do with this."

'"Isn't it?" said Ronnie.

John was getting really angry. "I hope you're not giving us a fucking pull here."

Ronnie shook his head. "No John, nothing like that."

'I was thinking Fuck, it's all gonna go off here. Me and John against fifteen of the Firm plus the Twins. I looked across at the rest of them and saw they were starting to shuffle about in their seats. My hands went underneath the table, ready to flip it over and give us a bit of an advantage.

'John was getting more and more heated and I could see that he meant it because his face was going bright red. "I hope you're not giving us a fucking pull are you?" Then Reg jumped in. "No, we wouldn't do that with you and Joe, you're wrong, we're not trying to do anything like that."

'And right away it calmed down. That was that. We agreed to amalgamate but didn't have to give up our share of the clubs that we already had on our books. After that the meetings took place on a regular basis, and then things started getting quite strange.

'Ronnie would produce a list of names and tell us that these were the people he wanted killed. He'd run his finger down the names and say, "We'll do him, you do him, er . . . you do him, I'll do that one", and so on. That was how he used to talk about it, all very businesslike. You wouldn't believe some of the names that were down on that list. Even poor old Albert Dimes was down there. There didn't seem to be any rhyme or reason to it but Ronnie was obsessed. I guess he was just itching to kill someone.'

Just before 8.30 p.m. on Wednesday 9 March 1966, two days after the gun battle at Mr Smiths, George Cornell spoke the six short words that would ultimately cost him his life.

He was drinking in the Blind Beggar pub with his friend, bookmaker Albert Woods, who, concerned that they were going to be late for a nine o'clock meeting in Walworth, south London, had suggested they leave. Cornell had shaken his head and pointed to the bar. 'Let's have one for the road,' he said.

Cornell had originally been part of the Firm, having got to know the Twins well when they were imprisoned together, along with Charlie Richardson, in an army detention centre during their National Service days. A year or so earlier, Cornell had moved to south London and joined forces with the Richardson gang after marrying a girl from the other side of the river – a move which did little to endear him to the Krays.

He and Woods had been visiting a friend of theirs who was in hospital and had decided to have a few drinks afterwards.

Despite the events that had taken place two nights earlier, Cornell seemed unconcerned about sinking a few pints in the heart of Kray territory.

They were sitting at the far end of the empty L-shaped bar, Cornell on a stool with his back to the public bar partition and Woods opposite. With a juke box playing quietly in the background Cornell ordered another beer for himself and another gin for his friend, lining them up on the bar.

At that same moment two men walked in. 'Well, look who's here,' said Cornell. Ronnie Kray had walked in, along with Firm member Ian Barrie. They were both carrying guns and Barrie fired two shots into the ceiling, sending the barmaid and other customers diving for cover. Kray then walked over to where Cornell was sitting, held the gun up inches from his head and pulled the trigger.

The area around the bar filled with a dense pall of blue smoke, blood from the wound spattered across the room and the barmaid began screaming hysterically. Woods dropped to the ground, eyes shut and quivering with fear as he waited for a bullet of his own. It never came. Ronnie Kray strolled calmly out of the pub and into a waiting car.

Woods knew he could do little to help Cornell and had no desire to be there when the police arrived, so he left the pub and ran to the nearest phone box where he called Cornell's wife: 'I have some bad news, George has been shot in the Blind Beggar,' he told her. 'Get over there as quick as you can.'

Woods then climbed into his car and drove to the home of Charlie Richardson. 'I told Charlie what happened and he said "You'd better have a wash and brush up." My blue suit was covered in Cornell's blood. Then we watched TV and a series of news flashes came on. The first said a man had been shot, the next, an hour later, that he had been taken to a hospital in Maida Vale; the third that he had died.'

Exactly why Cornell was executed remains something of a mystery. It is certainly true that he was on the 'wrong' side of the river and that he had angered Ronnie Kray by calling him a 'fat poof' in public, but many believe there must have been more. One theory is that Cornell had been at Mr Smiths during the battle and that it was he who had shot Dickie Hart, running off into the night long before the police arrived. Another is that, as a member of the Richardson mob, he was simply attacked to avenge Hart's death.

Years later, even Ronnie Kray was hard pressed to explain exactly why Cornell had to die: 'I didn't know then but I think now it was my mental illness, my paranoia,' he wrote in his autobiography. 'I just couldn't stop myself from hurting people, especially if I thought that they were slighting me or plotting against me. Also I like the feeling of guns, although I was usually happier with my fists or a knife.'

'Everyone in London, come to think of it everyone in the country knew Ronnie had done Cornell because he went straight into hiding, in this little flat above a barbers shop,' says Joey. 'Me and Johnny went to see him while he was holed up there and he made no bones about it. "Yeah. I done him," he told us. "I heard he was sitting in the pub and I thought fuck it. I'll just go and kill him. All right, so it might have been hasty, it might have been rash but it's done now, it's over with. So what." That was the way that Ron looked at it, he was happy with it all.

'I didn't know George Cornell and, to be perfectly honest, I didn't like him. It was never really based on anything. I'd seen him once or twice but never really spoken to him. I didn't like his appearance or the way he held himself, but I guess he might have been a nice guy for all I know.

'The fact that Ron had killed him didn't bother me in the slightest, but doing it the way he had hadn't made much sense. Reggie was the only one who said what we were all thinking. "It was fucking stupid, doing it right out in the open like that. You could have done it sensibly. You're a fucking idiot, you've put us all at risk," Reggie told him.

'Ron hit back. "Fuck you. You don't know what you're talking about. It might have been mad and impulsive but fuck it. I've done him and that's that. What is there to moan about? It's done. There's no sense in going on about it."'

Although he had gone into hiding, Ronnie refused to believe there was any danger. He had not only killed for the first time but he had done it in classic gangster style – in public with loads of witnesses. It had been like something out of a Mafia film, and Ronnie was convinced that the fearful reputation he had strived so long to establish would keep him safe.

And so it proved to be. When Detective Chief Superintendent Tommy Butler, the man appointed to lead the murder inquiry, asked Woods for the name of the man who had shot his friend, Woods insisted he had seen only feet, not faces.

Butler knew the truth, of course, but the only person who even hinted that they had actually seen Ronnie Kray pull the trigger was the barmaid of the Blind Beggar, a woman who to this day continues to be known as Mrs X in order to protect her identity.

She was, however, terrified and refused to make a written statement. She also told Butler that if pressed, she would deny having seen anything or mentioning any names. With a firm offer of police protection in place, she seemed on the verge of changing her mind, but the Twins had been out spreading the word and making it clear what would happen to anyone who betrayed them. When Mrs X was called in as the star witness in an ID parade attended by both Twins, she nervously told Butler that she simply didn't recognise any of the men before her.

With no forensic evidence and no willing witnesses willing to identify the gunman, there was no way Butler would be able to pin it on Ronnie Kray. Within weeks the murder team had exhausted all possible leads and members of the squad were reassigned to other duties.

The only person willing to put their head above the parapet was Olive Cornell, George's widow. She mounted a vicious campaign against the Krays, denouncing them as murderers at every opportunity and even going so far as to smash windows at their Vallance Road home. She was arrested and brought before a magistrate but was let off with a small fine. The Twins briefly discussed sending her on her way to join her husband but soon abandoned the idea – though everyone in London knew that Ronnie had killed Cornell, no one was talking about it and Olive had no evidence. For the time being, one murder would be enough.

At the end of 1966, the Twins hatched a plot to free their friend Frank Mitchell from prison. In the course of his fantastically unsuccessful criminal career, Mitchell had been birched and flogged, and had passed through almost every prison in England – and both its secure mental hospitals.

A good-looking man in prime physical condition, Mitchell stood 6ft 2in tall and tipped the scales at 16 stone, all of it muscle. His strength was almost super-human: one time, at Marylebone Court, it had taken thirteen policemen to hold him down. Mitchell exercised at every opportunity, getting through a couple of hundred press-ups and sit-ups every day. If weights were not available, he would select a couple of inmates, pick one up in each hand and use them like dumbbells.

The Twins had met him at Wandsworth where he was serving time for breaking into the home of an elderly couple in 1958 and holding them hostage with an axe that he had found. It was the latest in a long line of offences (he was on the run from Broadmoor at the time), and Mitchell was sentenced to life imprisonment with no date for eventual release.

The Twins had tried to establish a reputation for looking after friends of theirs who found themselves behind bars. Such people were referred to as being 'away', and a special fund was set up to provide them with whatever luxuries were available. In the case of Mitchell, these soon became plentiful.

After four years, his behaviour had improved to the point that he was transferred to Dartmoor prison and put onto an incredibly liberal regime. From May 1965 he was given the privilege of working on the Honour Party. This consisted of six of the most trustworthy prisoners who had given their word of honour not to escape, and who worked under the supervision of just one officer on the moors surrounding the prison.

With money provided by the Krays, Mitchell became a regular in a local pub and would while away the hours with women of easy virtue, also provided by the Twins. He would often return to the prison after a day's 'work' with a crate of beer under one arm.

Despite these abuses, the turnaround in Mitchell's behaviour had been noted by the Dartmoor governor, Denis Malone, who supported Mitchell's demand to be given a fixed date of release in order to have something to work towards. At the time this was something that every prisoner serving life could expect to be given at some point during their sentence.

Malone wrote in his report:

> Mitchell has continued to progress and improve. He has made every effort to demonstrate his reliability and the absence of risk to the public. I sincerely believe that Frank Mitchell will make a great effort to justify the trust placed in him.

But repeated applications to the Home Office were dismissed without explanation, leaving Mitchell bitter and frustrated. When Malone retired, it seemed all hope was gone. During a regular visit with the Kray Twins, Mitchell bemoaned his plight: 'They're messing me about, Ron. They offered me this deal, if I behaved myself I would get a date. Now the governor's gone.'

'Don't worry,' said Ronnie. 'We'll get you home, we'll get you home.'

It wasn't a wholly altruistic gesture. The original plan had been to use Mitchell as additional muscle, but with Frankie

Fraser and most of the Richardson gang behind bars, this became rather irrelevant. Instead the status-conscious Kray twins were drawn to Mitchell's prestige more than his character. It was as important to them to be seen with the right villains as it was to be seen with celebrities from the entertainment world. With their reputation on the slide in the East End the Twins hoped that springing Mitchell would put them back in favour with those who accused them of caring only about themselves.

Thanks to the relaxed prison regime, the escape was not particularly complex. All the Twins had to do was provide a car to pick Mitchell up at the edge of the moor and somewhere for him to hide out. Knowing they could not afford to keep him at large for ever, the long-term plan was to start a campaign to get his case re-investigated so he would get a release date. Once this goal had been achieved, Mitchell would give himself up and return to prison.

The plan was executed on 12 December 1966, when two members of the Kray Firm, Albert Donaghue and Billy Williams, whisked him away. Within hours Mitchell was holed up in a tiny flat in Whitechapel.

For the first few days Mitchell was more than a little unhappy. He had been led to believe that he would be hidden in more salubrious surroundings than those eventually provided. The flat belonged to Lennie 'Books' Dunn, a porn merchant and bookshop owner who was one of the Firm's brighter recruits.

Mitchell cheered up considerably when hostess Lisa Prescott, a striking blonde who had been picked up from Winston's nightclub and paid to provide the escapee with sex, showed up. Mitchell promptly fell in love and started planning a new life. Lisa soon became fond of Mitchell but her feelings were nowhere near as strong.

Mitchell was a simple soul and had been classified subnormal as a child. Writing letters to newspapers to campaign for better treatment was far beyond his capabilities, so this was left to Dunn. Mitchell added a thumbprint in lieu of a signature to prove the letters were authentic.

Sir, the reason for my absence from Dartmoor was to bring to the notice of my unhappy plight, to be truthful, I am asking for a possible date of release. From the age of nine I have not been completely free, always under some act or other. Sir, I ask you, where is the fairness in this. I am not a murderer or a sex maniac, nor do I think I am a danger to the public. I think that I have been more than punished for the wrongs I have done.

The story and letter were carried by the papers and at first the Home Secretary agreed to meet with Mitchell and discuss his case. He quickly amended this proposal, saying this would only happen if Mitchell gave himself up first.

As the weeks went by and the press interest waned, the Twins realised that Mitchell was becoming more of a liability. Confined to the Whitechapel flat he felt he had simply exchanged one prison cell for another and began to make demands to be taken places and visit his family. The Twins suggested he take up the offer of the Home Secretary and return to prison but he vehemently refused: to have done so would have almost certainly meant more time on his sentence, and Mitchell decided that he, and Lisa, should take their chances on the outside. 'They'll never take me alive,' he told Dunn. 'And I'll kill a dozen policeman rather than go back inside.'

The stress was soon getting to the Twins. Ronnie in particular became ever more addicted to the tranquilliser pills he had started taking.

A few days before Christmas, Albert Donaghue turned up at the Whitechapel flat and told Mitchell he was being moved to a new safe house, one where it would be possible for others to visit him more easily. Lisa, he was told, would be following on.

'I never knew Mitchell personally because he was in the nick virtually all his life but I'd heard about him because he had become good mates with Roy Shaw and the Twins. We heard he had escaped on the grapevine and pretty soon we knew that it was the Twins that had broken him out – everyone knew that – and we wanted to do our best to support him.

'A few months earlier a thief called Harry Roberts and two members of his gang had shot three policemen dead just outside Wormwood Scrubs. The other two had been caught but Roberts had gone on the run and was hiding out. There wasn't a villain in London that didn't feel sorry for him. We were convinced the police were going to find him and shoot him dead. I'd met Harry a couple of times and thought he was a decent fella. I felt sorry for the poor fucker.

'Some of his mates organised little benefits and collections and I remember putting a bit of money in the pot for him. It was a tradition; it was just what people in that world did. So when Mitchell was broken out, we didn't think anything of doing the same. Me and Johnny Nash were in a pub one night over Christmas and started drinking with the Twins. At one point John pulled out a wad of notes and pushed them across the table towards Reggie. "There you go mate, there's a few quid from me and Joe for Frank."

'Reggie slowly pushed the notes back. "You're all right. He doesn't need any money." It was only later that we found out why he didn't need any money: he was brown bread. They had fucking killed him.'

Once Mitchell had made it clear that there was no way he was going back to prison, the Krays found they had boxed themselves into a corner. Their pride and reputation was at stake and the only way out was to eliminate Mitchell.

Ronnie had met up with his friend Freddie Foreman and asked him to get rid of Mitchell as a personal favour. Thanks to the co-operative amalgamation of London gangs, Foreman now operated a mutual assistance pact with the Krays, which put serious money in the pockets of both sides. When Foreman received a call from Ronnie asking him to get rid of Mitchell, he was duty bound to oblige.

Foreman, along with Albert Donaghue and a man called Alfie Gerrad, escorted Mitchell into a waiting van. Mitchell had swallowed the story about being taken to join Ronnie at a farm in Kent and climbed into the van without fuss.

As soon as the passenger door shut the first shots rang out. Mitchell fell back, groaning, another bullet was fired into his heart and he went quiet, only to start groaning again a few minutes later. The final shot was fired from a gun placed behind his ear and Mitchell was dead.

There was no police investigation: so far as the law was concerned, Mitchell was still alive and still on the run. The underworld knew far better and for months after he disappeared, ugly rumours about Mitchell's fate circulated all around the East End. One story was that he had ended up in the foundations of the Bow Road flyover, another that his dismembered body had been fed to pigs, yet another that his body had been 'doubled up' in a coffin and cremated.

The truth was far simpler. Mitchell's body was trussed in chicken wire, weighted down and dumped in the middle of the English Channel.

For the second time in less than a year, the Twins seemingly had got away with murder.

6. 'THE WAY IT WORKS IS THIS: IN AMERICA, YOU'RE THE GOVERNORS BUT OVER HERE, WE'RE THE FUCKING GOVERNORS AND WE'RE RUNNING THE SHOW. RIGHT?'

'Jackie Buggy, the man who had shot Charlie Reeder outside the Pigalle, and I had become good friends during our time in the nick. Good enough for me to promise to try and break him out as soon as I was able. Me and Peter Marshall had spent a good amount of time planning the thing. We nicked a car, an old Ford Zodiac, dressed up in overalls and had hats pulled down low over our heads so that no one would be able to recognise us.

'We drove to the prison, backed the car up against the wall and took out a rope with a big lump of iron tied to one end to weigh it down. The rope had a big knot tied into every eighteen inches to make it easy to climb up. We tied the free end to a tree and then got ready to throw the anchor end over the wall and into the prison yard.

'Timing was everything. Jackie had told us to do it dead on 2 p.m. because that was the time he would be out in the yard moving from one wing to another, on his way to collect his week's wages.

'As soon as the second hand of my watch reached the 12, I threw the rope over. Inside the prison yard Jackie saw it come over and broke into a run. But the screw who does all the PT saw Jackie sprinting, realised what was about to go down and gave chase. Jackie jumps up, grabs the rope and tries to pull himself up. At the same time, the screw jumps up and grabs hold of Jackie's legs, holding on for dear life and pulling him down to the ground.

'I can feel the weight on the other end of the rope and I'm trying to pull it over, doing my best to help Jackie. But then when the screw grabs him he starts shouting and screaming, and the screw is doing the same, and as soon as we hear all the schmozzle we decide to fuck off out of there. We left the car and just legged it.

'The police knew it was me. My brother-in-law was in the nick at the same time, and they went to see him. "Oi! Derek," they told him, "Joey's at it again, throwing ropes over the wall." They shipped Jackie out to a new prison – a high security one. I laid low for a couple of weeks, but nothing more happened so I decided it was safe to go back to living my normal life.

'They moved Jackie to Leicester nick and I used to go up and visit him regularly. We had a good laugh about the time I tried to break him out and we stayed pally all through the time that he was doing his bird. When he got out, I went along for a drink with him, his Auntie Mag and all his family.

'Mag was wonderful, a real rough-and-ready woman who owned a greengrocers and lived just five minutes down the road from me. Jackie had told me all about her when we were inside and when I got out, I went around and introduced myself. We soon became pretty friendly and she became the main way that Jackie and I used to get messages to each other. She knew I was a villain before I'd even opened my mouth. She reckoned she had some sort of psychic powers and that she was always seeing the future, but I never paid too much mind to all of that.

'When Jackie finally got out I knew he'd be looking for work and I ended up going into partnership with him and Waggy Whitnall. It all went well for a while but then I fell out with Waggy.

'Billy Hill had got involved with a little gang that were planning to run a few scams at casinos throughout London including one with me, Waggy and Johnny Nash were looking after. The deal among all those involved in the underworld at the time was that, if you were going to pull a stroke like that, you had to give a cut of the profits. In this case, Hill figured our end would be £20,000 and he duly handed over the money to Waggy. The idea was that the money would be shared between the three of us but Waggy decided to keep it all to himself. I don't know what made him think I wouldn't find out. I did, of course, and after that I started to get very cold with Waggy.

'One Sunday morning Waggy came round to my house. "You've got the needle with me Joe ain't ya?"

'I didn't say anything; I just looked at him.

'"What's it over then Joe? What have I done?"

'"I don't want to say. I haven't got absolute proof yet, but as soon as I do, I'll tell you what it's over. But you're right. I have got the needle with you."

'"Is it over twenty grand?"

'"Yes, that's right," I told him.

'"Well that's nothing to worry about. I put it in the club we've got."

'Between the three of us we had invested in a club, the Chez Nous, in Inverness Terrace in Bayswater. I was taken aback. "You put it in the club? What? Without telling anyone? Well it would have been nice to know that it was my own money that was going into it and not you treating me. And what about Johnny Nash? He was supposed to get a share of that twenty grand, but you took other money off of him to put in the club. I've got to tell John about this now because he's my partner and I'll be a slag if I don't do it."

'I told John what had happened the next day, and before long we had realised that there was only one option. We arranged a meet with Waggy and told him the good news: he was sacked. We no longer wanted him as a partner.'

News of what Whitnall had done spread through the club scene like wildfire. He spent almost every afternoon playing cards at the Mount Street Bridge Club, a once-fashionable and upmarket venue that had descended into little more than an illegal gambling den, along with a bunch of regulars including Jackie Buggy, an old fellow called Pinky who worked as a bookmaker, and the club's owner, Franny Daniels, who also happened to be Waggy Whitnall's uncle. One day, not long after he'd been sacked from Joey's club someone put a small bomb behind one of the radiators, which caused a fair amount of damage to Franny's club.

'It wasn't enough to close the place down but it certainly caused a bit of concern. The next day all the card players were back and Franny Daniels was wondering what was going on. He told Waggy that the only reason someone would be having a go at him was if they were trying to get to Waggy. And with that Jackie Buggy shouted out: "Yeah, if you played the game and didn't fuck people for money, then these things wouldn't happen."

'Waggy was pretty pissed off and called Jackie into his office. After that . . . well, no one knows what happened. But poor old Jackie wasn't seen again.

'A couple of days later his aunt rang me and asked if I'd seen Jack. I'd heard stories circulating around the West End that Waggy had done something, but they were only stories and I didn't want to worry the old girl.

'"I haven't seen him Mag. He might be out with a bird or something . . ."

'"Listen Joe, he went out in a T-shirt and he hasn't come back or phoned for three days. And that's not my Jackie. I think something's wrong."

'Then one morning I got a phone call from Waggy. I hadn't spoken to him for a while and wasn't that happy to hear from him, especially once he started talking. It was common knowledge that various members of the Firm, and people who were connected to the Krays were having their phone lines bugged. Waggy seemed eager to get me into as much trouble as possible.

'"Hello Joe, have you seen Jack?"

'"What do you mean have I seen Jack?"

' "Well I heard that you have seen him recently."

' "No. I heard you were the fucking last to see him. Why are you saying this to me?"

' "Well look Joe, people are coming over to my house trying to shoot me."

' "What are you talking about? Are you trying to say it's me?"

' "Nah mate, not you, not you."

' "You're right it's not me. If I had the hump with you I'd fucking tell you."

' "I know you would Joe, I know you from old. But it's the others, the Nashes and the Krays. Someone was over the tennis courts last night because the dogs went mad and when I went out into the garden, I swear I saw someone jumping over the fence."

' "Waggy, I don't know what you're talking about."

' "All right. It's like that is it? Well in that case let's just meet in a field and we each have a gun and whoever comes off best comes off best. Let's sort it that way."

' "You're talking like a fucking idiot. I don't know what you're talking about and as far as Jackie Buggy is concerned, I understand that you were the last one to see him." And with that I put the phone down.

'After that I decided to arrange a meeting with Pinky, the old boy who used to go to the Mount Street club every day. I asked him to come down to Mag's house with me so he could tell her what had happened – put her mind at rest. If Waggy was starting to spread rumours about what had happened to Jackie and dragging my name through the mud, I wanted to make sure that she knew it was a load of all rubbish.

'The three of us sat down and I asked Pinky if he knew where Jackie was. He looked a bit sheepish, and then he asked Mag to go out of the room because he didn't feel comfortable telling me with her there. As soon as she was out of sight Pinky told me that he was almost certain that Waggy had shot Buggy. After the two of them had gone into the office, three shots had rung out. Waggy had come back out and told everyone to go home for the rest of the day. No one knew what had happened to the body but Pinky didn't think it would ever be found. But I knew that until it was, Mag wouldn't be able to even begin to stop worrying.

'A few nights after that, Mag called me up. Her voice was filled with tears and sadness.

'"Joey, Jack's dead."

'"How do you know that?"

'"Because I had a dream last night. And in this dream all I could see was an arm sticking out of the ocean."

'"Well that could be anything. How do you know it's Jack?"

'"I saw the tattoos on his arm. I recognised the tattoos and that's when I knew he was dead."

'"Aw come on Mag, you can't put any weight on dreams. I'm sure he'll turn up. Don't you worry about it any more."

'A couple of days after that, two fishermen were out in Peacehaven near Brighton when they saw a body floating in the water. The body had been weighed down with chains and lying on the bottom for weeks, but then a Navy submarine had passed by doing underwater manoeuvres and had broken the bonds, letting the body float to the surface.

'The body was so badly decomposed that you could no longer recognise the face. In fact the whole thing was such a mess that almost everyone who looked at it ended up losing their lunch. They suspected it might be the body of Jackie Buggy and arranged for Auntie Mag to go down and identify it. Only they didn't risk showing her his face. Instead, as the body lay on the mortuary slab, the policeman pulled back the sheet to reveal a single tattooed arm, and asked her if she recognised it.

'It had all happened just the way she had seen it in her dream. I guess she was a psychic after all.'

One of the most remarkable things about the way things operate at the highest levels of organised crime is how closely the pattern of activity mirrors what goes on in the corporate world.

By the early 1960s, the American Mafia was coming to the end of a thirty-year run of almost constant expansion. During this time the Mafia had remained largely hidden from public view and, as a result, had received little if any attention from law enforcement officers. Now the winds of change were blowing and the Mafia found itself confronted with the same problem that eventually hits every big company: how to expand its markets to ensure future economic survival.

In America, and in New York in particular, the future was beginning to look decidedly shaky. JFK had been elected president and his brother Bobby appointed Attorney General; both had campaigned hard on the issue of the strong anti-crime stance they would adopt if they were to get into power; one of the Mob's key markets for illegal gambling and racketeering – Cuba – had been lost following the leftist revolution led by Fidel Castro; and, as if all that wasn't enough, the infamous Mafia code of silence, Omerta, was now being broken on a regular basis. Compared to America, Great Britain seemed naïve and ripe for the picking.

The man who masterminded the move to the new territory was a certain Meyer 'The Brain' Lansky, the infamous financial wizard who effectively controlled the Mafia's money.

Lansky was born in Grodno, Russia, as Maier Suchowljansky, in 1902. He and his family migrated to New York in 1911, abbreviating and simplifying their names in the process. Like most young Jewish children, Meyer found himself being picked on by older boys who would demand protection money or beat and rob their victims. Unlike the other children, Meyer refused to play ball.

Soon after arriving in New York he was accosted by a strapping Sicilian boy, about five years older than Lansky. The boy demanded money and little Meyer told him to fuck off. The Sicilian started to laugh, admiring the boy's guts. 'OK kid,' he told him. 'You got protection for free.'

It was the beginning of one of the most notorious partnerships in American organised crime – the Sicilian boy was none other than Charles 'Lucky' Luciano. Before he was out of his teens, Meyer had secured the friendship of another youngster who would become an equally legendary figure: Bugsy Seigel.

As with many others, it was the introduction of Prohibition that really started Meyer's criminal career rolling. By the late 1920s, working alongside Bugsy and Lucky, Meyer had put together a bootlegging syndicate, which evolved into the dominant force in organised crime for the next two decades. After Prohibition Lansky moved into gambling, establishing the so-called 'Gold Coast' in Florida with its hotels and casinos and all but founding Las Vegas. From there he spread out into Cuba, Haiti and the Bahamas, investing Mafia money into a network of enterprises.

In Cuba he had set up a croupier school in Havana to train staff to work in the casinos. He had appointed his most trusted deputy, a Sicilian by the name of Dino Cellini, to run the place. The students were put through a gruelling regime of lecture and practice and only knew they had graduated when Dino called them up out of class and sent them off to have their dinner jackets fitted.

When the Cuban empire collapsed, Cellini was sent to London to set up a Mayfair version of the Havana school to work in a new London venture, which was to be known as the Colony Club.

The fashion of the time was for upmarket London clubs to employ celebrity 'greeters' to shake hands with customers and then mingle around the gaming tables, ensuring everyone was having a good time. The Krays had managed to convince Lord Effingham to fulfil the role at Esmerelda's Barn, and the shareholders of the Colony, who included Meyer Lansky and dozens of major names in American organised crime, realised they would have to do the same.

It didn't take long for one name to stand out from the rest as a possible candidate. During the 1930s the actor George

Raft, a smooth-looking American, had made a name for himself (and a small fortune) playing sinister gangsters in much the same way as his contemporary James Cagney had done, in films like *The Glass Key*, *Souls at Sea* and *Each Dawn I Die*.

Raft had continued working through the 1940s and 50s, picking up minor roles in classics including *Some Like It Hot*, *Around the World in Eighty Days* and the original version of *Ocean's Eleven*. The 50s were rounded off by the release of a film biopic, *The George Raft Story*. However, by the mid-1960s his star was beginning to fade and Raft was the perfect front-man for the Colony.

He eagerly accepted the position. He had long-standing Mob connections and in his memoirs, published in the 1950s, boasted about the fact the he knew all the leading New York gangsters of the bootleg era.

'Big groups of Americans had been coming to London on gambling junkets ever since gambling had been legalised and the first few casinos had opened up,' explains Joey Pyle. 'It was clear that eventually, they would be opening up places of their own, but at first all they wanted to do was gamble.

'There was no animosity: we welcomed them with open arms because they brought clout, money and a kind of glamour. The Krays in particular had long idolised American gangsters. They had been dressing like them for years and preferred American cars.

'Most of the Yanks were straight up but a few of them were trying things on. There was a lot of cheating going on in those days. I got to know quite a few of them while I was working at the Astor and eventually started working a few scams.

'I met up with an American called Ben and we played with crooked dice. We would pretend not to be together. I would be at one end of the craps table and throw the dice. He would pick them up and throw them back. Only, when he picked them up, he would switch them for a pair of crooked dice that would not be able to come up to certain numbers. I'd play with those for a while and then we'd switch back and I'd keep playing, just to prevent anyone getting suspicious. It would look as if I'd just had an incredible lucky streak.

'We hit one club called the Apron Strings out in Fulham. There was no one looking after the place otherwise we would not have been able to do it without permission. In the end I won so much money and had so many chips in front of me that the casino ran out. They had to buy the chips back off of me so that they could continue with the game.

'It was through Ben that I first got introduced to an American called Joe Nesline, a well-connected man who was travelling to London regularly in order to gamble. We got pretty friendly, and after a while he told me that he had put some money into a place setting up in Mayfair, the Colony Club, which was going to be the first American-owned casino to set up shop in London. By then he was only too well aware of the kind of business I was involved in and told me and Johnny Nash that he'd been looking to us to protect the place.

'I didn't see him for a little while after that but then I got a phone call out of the blue. Joe was back over in London and staying at the Hilton. He wanted me and Johnny to go over and see him. When we arrived he explained that the Colony was going to be opening up in less than a week's time and that he wanted us to meet the host, George Raft. The club was only around the corner from the hotel so we all strolled round there.

'The place was still being fixed up: there were builders running around doing bits and pieces and some of the carpet was still being laid. As we walked in, we could see George Raft walking around, making suggestions and giving orders. Then Joe called him over.

'"Hey George, I want you to meet some friends of mine. This is John and this is Joey. I want you to look after them: they're the arm."

'To be honest, I was a bit in awe and so was John. I'd seen loads of his films and the guy was a real hero to my mum and dad. And here I was, shaking him by the hand. I tried to be cool – I didn't want to come across like a fucking groupie – and we settled down and started talking.

'George was a really nice guy, very down-to-earth. He was telling us how much he loved England because the climate suited him much more than it did back in the States. Then he shook our hands again and told us to come in when the club opened and talk business.

'Three days later, John and I went down to the Colony to iron out the details. As we walked into the restaurant, I saw Ronnie and Reggie sitting down with Albert Dimes and another man I didn't recognise.

'Ronnie saw us and came running over; he was rubbing his hands together with excitement. "I've got some good business here," he said, nodding across to the table where he'd been sitting. "Me and Reg are right in here and you're gonna come in with us." I couldn't help but let out a laugh. "Fuck me John, looks like we've got a couple of partners and we didn't even know about it."

'I was a bit taken aback at first but it didn't take long to sort it all out. The man sitting with Ron turned out to be Dino Cellini. Not knowing that Joe Nesline had approached John and I about being the arm, he had decided to play the race card and approach another Italian: Albert Dimes. Dimes, in turn, had gone to the Twins and so it was that they all came to be at the Colony the night John and I thought we were due to start working there.

'After the Colony, a few other places opened up and we set up similar agreements. The Yanks would come over and there would be meetings between them and the Twins, the Nashes and me, usually at a suite in some flashy hotel like the Dorchester or in one of the clubs. Occasionally the Americans would be invited over to Vallance Road, and God knows that they made of that – the idea of these two blokes still living with their mum. They'd be having a meeting in one of the upstairs rooms and their mum would be in the kitchen, cooking bacon and eggs for about twenty people. And they had this mynah bird, which Ronnie had taught to say, "Gotta get some money", and it would be going on and on, every time someone walked past. It was a complete madhouse.

'But wherever they were held, the meetings were always a bit strange, because the Americans had no problem about paying – they expected the arm to come on them as soon as they opened up, so it was them who came looking for us rather than the other way round. But even so, Ronnie was always really aggressive about it.

'I remember one meeting where he started slamming his hands down on the table to emphasise the point. "The way it works is this," he said. "In America, you're the governors but over here, we're the fucking governors and we're running the show. Right?" The Yanks took it well enough, but it seemed a bit over the top. But then the Twins were starting to act more and more strangely all the time.

'When my son Joey was born, I went over to the Blade pub in Bethnal Green. The place was packed out with faces, including the Twins, and right away Ronnie came running up to me. "Joe, great to see you and congratulations. We got you something for the boy, hang on a minute and I'll get it for you."

'Ronnie came back with this fucking great big toy panda. It was absolutely massive; I mean it was almost the size of me. I thought to myself, what the fuck is my little baby supposed to do with it? "We didn't know what to get for the boy, so we got this, brilliant ain't it?" he told me.

'I felt a right twat standing at the bar holding this fucking panda, so I gave it to the barman and asked him to look after it for me. Of all the presents that I got that day, this had to be the worst by far. A few drinks and a lot of celebrating later, it was time to go. I was halfway out the door when Ron started screaming at me, loud enough so that everyone in the place stopped and stared. "Joey, Joey, don't forget the panda." He ran over to the bar, picked it up and handed it to me.

'By now everyone was looking and every face in the place was creased into a smile. I just knew they were going to piss their pants the second I stepped out of the door. Gangster Joe? Not that night. I felt like a right prat.

'Another night me and Johnny Nash were in the Colony with the Twins, sitting at a table in the restaurant with George Raft. He was keeping us all entertained with stories about the old days and what it was like working with James Cagney, Humphrey Bogart and people like that. Then one of the junior managers came up to him and said, "Excuse me Mr Raft, Mr Frank Sinatra has just come into the casino."

'George slowly got to his feet. "Sorry lads, I'm going to have to leave you now because Frank has just come in and I want to go and make sure he's being looked after properly." It was no problem, we all understood, it was his job after all. So we wished him well.

'He left the table and started walking away. Then he suddenly stopped after about three paces and came back. "Tell you what I'll do," he said. "I'll bring him in here. I'm sure he'd like to meet you." I felt this rush of excitement running through me. I was going to meet the legendary Frank Sinatra. "Cheers George, that'll be great," I said. But then Ronnie reached across the table and squeezed my arm to shut me up.

'"It's all right George," said Ronnie. "You're all right. You don't need to bring him in here. Don't worry about it." George asked if Ronnie was sure and Ronnie assured him that he was. George looked a little puzzled but knew better than to argue, so he went on his way. Once he was out of earshot I turned to Ronnie, trying to hide my disappointment.

'"What's wrong Ron, don't you want to meet him?"

'Ronnie shook his head slowly. "Nah, that Sinatra's a flash bastard. If he came in here, I'd end up hitting him on the chin."'

Sinatra was just one of a host of major celebrities who passed through the doors of the Colony Club during the mid-1960s, soon making it one of the most famous venues in the city.

In the meantime, senior figures in the British government were getting concerned about the possibilities of American organised crime getting a foothold in London. The authorities suspected that Meyer Lansky was the secret owner of the Colony Club – a notion that not only fitted with the picture of Lansky as the worldwide master of organised crime, but which was also supported by lots of circumstantial evidence.

There was the fact that Dino Cellini and several other known Lansky associates were regular faces in the club. Many gamblers and some of the staff who worked there were also known to have worked with Meyer at different times, particularly in Cuba.

A few weeks before the club had opened, Scotland Yard had tracked Lansky right into London, a stop-off on a pan-European trip that culminated in a visit to Switzerland to supervise some of the Mob's many, anonymous, numbered bank accounts. In London, Lansky had headed straight for the Colony Club and cast his eye over the layout of the gaming floor, making a number of suggestions.

Scotland Yard had also received information direct from the United States that links were being forged between the East Coast criminal syndicates and those in London. There had been increasing travel by certain people within Lansky's circle. During a raid on the offices of a leading Manhattan bookmaker who was suspected of having Mob ties, the man jumped out of a window and died from a heart attack before his body hit the ground. A search of his office revealed papers that indicated that Lansky and several other well-known figures were shareholders in the Colony.

The papers also showed plans to host a conference to discuss how the introduction of yet more gaming legislation in Britain would affect the West End. This information was passed over to Scotland Yard. Meanwhile, closer to home, pictures of George Raft and the Kray twins were appearing in the papers on a regular basis.

Soon afterwards, the then Home Secretary, Roy Jenkins, was presented with a list of eight men whom, it was said, had strong links to the Mafia. The list included the names of George Raft and Dino Cellini.

And so it was that in 1967, Raft and Cellini were deported. It was said their presence in the country was 'not conducive to the public good' and that was the end of it. 'We were sorry to see him go,' says Joey. 'He had been good to us and paying over two grand per month which ended up being split three ways between me, the Twins and the Nash brothers.'

George Raft never quite got over being kicked out. Years later he would claim that, at the time the pictures were taken, he had no idea who the Twins were or that they had any connection to organised crime. He made two requests to be allowed to re-enter Britain. Both were turned down. 'The ban ruined everything for me,' Raft would say later. 'I was just getting back on my feet after the American government had taken everything from me for tax evasion. I loved London, and the English. My only crime was knowing people.'

He would eventually die alone and almost forgotten in Los Angeles in 1980, his vast wealth – accumulated during a career spanning 105 films – frittered away, gambled on horses and unwise investments.

'The Americans brought loads of work with them and not all of it was based in London. I got asked to go on a job by some Americans who were, in turn, helping out some friends of theirs from Germany. The German team had been taken for a ride at a casino in Stockholm. They were sure the place was moody and that they'd been ripped off. They wanted all their money back so I got asked to go over and do the business.

'I took Johnny Nash and two others, Ray Kennet and Johnny Davis. We got to Stockholm and went straight to the casino and confronted the manager in his office. I told him straight what I thought he was doing – being a fucking cheat. He denied it, of course, and it was only after a few heated arguments that he agreed to close the place down and send all the customers out so we could have a look round.

'It didn't take long to uncover the scam. The German gamblers only ever played roulette and whenever they did, they always bet on the same two or three numbers. When we looked at the roulette wheels, we saw that the manager had put a double thickness of felt on the numbers that the Germans were betting on. That meant that the ball would be far more likely to bounce out of those numbers and go elsewhere.

'Once he knew he was caught, the geezer put his hands up to it right away. He admitted cheating the Germans out of a small fortune and agreed to give all the money back. No argument. The only problem, he explained, was that he didn't have the money with him in Stockholm and that he'd have to go and get it from Denmark the following day.

'We decided to stick around and wait – just to make sure he paid up – and after that the atmosphere became much nicer. We met up with him the next day and had a cup of tea. Everything was kosher and we were enjoying the chance to relax and see a bit of the city. But then in the afternoon he called us into his office and said there was a bit of a delay, and that it would be at least another three or four days before he could pick up the money.

'I'd seen more than enough of Stockholm, and so had Nashy, so we both decided to come back to London, leaving the other two out there to make sure the bloke didn't forget to pay what he owed.

'Before I left I told the fellas to be careful. I wasn't worried about the casino boss getting up to any villainy, I was more concerned about him going to the law and getting them nicked. "Make sure you get him to come to the hotel and pay you, don't go back to the casino, it will be safer that way."

'John and I went home and a couple of days later the manager phones the hotel and says he has the money but wants the lads to go to the casino and pick it up. Ray and Johnny decide to go.

'They should have sussed it right away. The first time we went the door was all locked up. You had to ring a bell and a man would come up and slide a little panel over to see who it was. This time, they get there and find the door has been left open, just slightly ajar. And as they push it, a pack of cards falls down to the floor. Someone had balanced them on top of the door to give them a bit of warning when anyone came in.

'But even that didn't give them the message. They go straight into the casino and, of course, the manager had heard the cards and now he's waiting for them. Not only that but he's got three or four other guys with him. So Ray shouts out "Where's the money?" and the manager pulls out a gun. "I ain't got no money, but I've got this." Then Ray picks up a chair and throws it at him, telling him to go and fuck himself. And that's when he starts firing the gun.

'Ray got hit at least ten times and Johnny took almost as many himself. The miracle was that they both lived. I think they'd been using a .22 or something. As soon as we heard we flew back over and picked them up at the airport. Ray still had at least one bullet inside him, one that was too close to his vital organs to be removed. We brought them back to London and decided that Sweden was somewhere we didn't have any plans to return to in the near future.

'It wasn't the end for the casino boss though. A little while later someone shot him dead on the doorstep of his home. I guess he must have made a few enemies somewhere along the way.'

In the 1990 film *The Krays*, there is a key scene that takes place at a fair in Victoria Park. The twins happen across a boxing booth and, after Ron wins against one of the booth's boxers, Reggie jumps into the ring to take him on. It's a titanic battle, awesome in its brutality and bravery. The audience is shocked and their older brother, Charlie, rushes home in a panic to fetch their mother.

Violet Kray rushes to the park and jumps into the ring to break up the fight. 'Listen to me,' she tells them, fighting back her tears. 'We don't fight each other. We stick together. That's how we're strong. If you want something . . . yes . . . you fight to get it. Like I fight, like mum fights. Fight them out there . . . But we don't fight each other . . . Not for fun . . . Not for no money . . . Not for no reason . . . You hear me? We never fight each other.'

The Twins then each take one of their mother's hands and kiss it. 'We're sorry, Mum,' they say in unison.

Although the scene is based on actual events, the truth is that the Twins fought all the time. During their careers as amateur boxers they met on a number of occasions and even when that was all behind them, they would often resort to using their fists to settle personal disputes.

'By mid 1967, around the time that George Raft was being expelled, everyone started to notice that the Twins were arguing more than ever. There would be times when I'd turn up at Vallance Road and the two of them would be out in the back garden, rolling around in the dirt and beating the shit out of each other.

'No one would ever dare to interfere but every now and then Charlie would jump in there, put himself in the middle and shout "turn it in lads", and then they would both turn on him, tell him to mind his own fucking business.

'Whenever they fought, it was always Reggie who used to come out on top. The weird thing was, although Ron was the mad one, Reggie was the more dangerous of the two. Ron was so crazy that he couldn't hold anything in. If he wanted to do something, he'd have to just go out there and do it, no hesitation, no thinking. Just like when he killed Cornell.

'If you'd pissed Ron off and you walked up to him in a bar, he'd tell you to piss off there and then. He might even throw you a right-hander. Now Reggie would be different. He'd say hello mate, how you doing and put his arm around you. When you go to the toilet he'd go along with you. And then, when you least expect it, he'd cut you.

'With Ronnie you knew where you stood. With Reggie you didn't.

'When they weren't fighting each other, they were winding each other up. I remember one time when Ronnie had this little Alsatian puppy and was carrying it around with him. Now Reggie didn't like dogs at all and Ronnie knew it. He kept pushing the dog into Reggie's face, telling him to give it a stroke and all that. And Reggie was getting really pissed off, telling Ron to take the fucking thing out of it. Then Ronnie started saying in this sing-song voice: "Look at the big gangster, scared of a little doggy."

'None of us realised it right away but it soon became clear what was behind it all. The Twins were the best known and among the most feared gangsters in London. Although they had both beaten, cut and maimed people over the years, only Ronnie had actually killed someone. And he wouldn't let Reggie forget it.

'One night we were in the Astor club and the two of them were having a real go at each other in a corner. We could see them arguing – it looked like it was going to get violent at any second – but none of us could hear what they were saying. Then Ronnie came over in a real rage and grabbed hold of me. I could tell he was really upset. "That fucking bastard," he said, nodding towards Reg who was scowling in the corner. "That bastard my brother. Look at him Joey. He's talking about Bobby, saying I fucked Bobby's wife and you know I'd never do that, you know I'd never because I fucking love that boy."

'Bobby was a well-known singer and one of Ronnie's boyfriends. Ronnie had fallen head over heels in love with the man and was seeing him on a regular basis. "I love that boy and that bastard is accusing me of fucking his wife, that bastard." I could see Reggie looking at us, getting more and more wound up because he knew what Ron was saying. Then he calls me and Johnny Nash over.

'"Have you got a piece on you?" said Reg.

'I shook my head. "What do you want a piece for Reg?"

'"I'm gonna go and do someone ain't I."

'"Who you gonna do?"

'"I'm gonna fucking go and do Dimes."

'"Dimes? What, Albert? What the fuck you gonna do him for?"

'"To show Ron that he ain't the only one who can fucking go and shoot someone. He thinks he's the only one who can go and kill someone. I can fucking do it too."

'Then Ronnie started shouting out loud so that everyone in the club could hear it. "What, are you going to go and shoot someone tonight? Is that what you're going to do? Oh good. Well, when you do it, just make sure you do it right. Don't fuck it up. Make sure you kill them with the first shot, just like I did with Cornell."

'If I'd had a gun on me that night, I'm pretty sure that Albert Dimes would have been killed. As it was, Reggie's first kill was going to have to wait for another day.'

7. 'AFTER THE FIRST ONE I DON'T KNOW WHAT HAPPENED, I JUST WENT MAD. I JUST KEPT ON WHACKING HIM ON THE BACK WITH THE AXE, AGAIN AND AGAIN, EACH ONE HARDER THAN THE LAST'

Joey Pyle and Mickey Inglefield met for the first time on the day they tried to kill each other.

Pyle was enjoying a drink at the Springfield Club in Garratt Lane with his old friend Oliver Reed who, despite growing notoriety as an actor, had never lost touch with the south London boys with whom he had grown up. And regardless of the amount of time he spent in the company of starlets, the real Oliver Reed was never far away.

Reed's first job had been working as a doorman in a Soho nightclub, and in 1963 he had needed 36 stitches in his face following a fight in a bar. The scars to his cheek that he received as a result boosted his career by adding a touch of menace to an already distinctive look.

During the early 60s Reed had risen to prominence through performances in films including *The Dammed*, *The System* and Ken Russell's *The Jokers*, but was yet to feature in the trio of back-to-back films – *Oliver!*, *Hannibal Brooks* and *Women in Love* – that would catapult him to superstardom. As Joey recalls,

'Olly was with his wife, Katie, and the three of us were sitting in a corner, drinking and chatting. The club was pretty quiet – there were a few people milling about and an old boy drinking on his own at the bar, but apart from that it was pretty much empty.

'All that changed at around 1 a.m. when a little crowd came in. There was Bernie Bingham, Jumbo Parsons and Mickey Inglefield. I knew the first two quite well – they were a pair of blaggers and well known among the chaps – but Inglefield was a stranger to me. I knew him through reputation and the fact that he was a feared man in the area, but we'd never actually been introduced.'

The three men were in the company of their wives and girlfriends and by the time they stumbled through the door of the Springfield, they were already the worse for wear. The trio had successfully pulled off a robbery earlier in the evening, netting more than £50,000, and the celebrations were far from finished.

Inglefield stomped over to the bar and hammered down his fist, demanding beer and champagne. As he looked around, the old man mumbled something about the fact that Inglefield was clearly celebrating and offered to buy him a drink. Inglefield's eyes suddenly focused sharply.

'You want to buy me a drink? Why do you want to buy me a fucking drink? Are you a poof or something?'

Realising his kindly gesture had been completely miscon-strued, and not wishing to antagonise the large, aggressive Inglefield any further, the old man reached for his pint and shuffled further along the bar. But in his nervousness, he took the wrong drink with him.

'Oi! Put that down! It's my fucking drink,' yelled Inglefield.

The old man mumbled an apology but it was too late. Inglefield lashed out and, as Joey Pyle looked up, the old man fell to the floor.

Pyle rushed over, picked the fellow up, sat him down on a chair and got him some scotch. He was half unconscious, still a bit dazed but starting to come round. Then Joey went over to the bar, his face puffing up with anger. Bernie and Jumbo tried to calm him down.

'It's all right Joey, it's all right,' said Jumbo, but Joey wasn't having any of it.

'Nah, nah, nah. It's not all right. You don't do that. This is some old man, you don't go around knocking them out for nothing.'

Then Inglefield moved closer. 'What's all this? Why are you making yourself busy?'

Jumbo turned to him. 'It's all right Mick, leave it. It's all right.'

Pyle and Inglefield locked eyes for the first time. 'So what if I am making myself busy?' asked Pyle.

'Well you shouldn't,' Inglefield replied. 'It's none of your fucking business.'

'OK. If that's your attitude.'

Pyle returned to his seat.

'I wanted Inglefield. I wasn't going to do anything there and then because I thought the others might turn on me too and I wasn't going to make myself a mug over it. Before I went back to the table I got on the phone, called up a couple of pals and told them to get over to the club sharpish. Then I went back to see Olly.

' "Do yourself a favour mate. My pals are coming down and it's going to be going off in here. You'd better make yourself scarce."

'Katie looked scared and started tugging at his arm to get him to go, but Olly just shook her off. Then he said in that wonderful voice of his, "No Joey, I am with you one million per cent. That bastard over there deserves it. You know me. I love a fight. I'm with you. I'm just in the mood for a good punch up."

'About half an hour later, two of my mates turned up and I went back to the bar with them and Olly standing beside me. Inglefield was facing away and I pulled him around. "You had something to say for yourself earlier when you had people with you. Well now I've got people with me so what have you got to say for yourself now?"

'Inglefield turned to face me and put his glass down on the bar. "You think I'm fucking scared of you?" He started ranting but I wasn't listening. As soon as his drink hit the bar – bosh – I hit him with a right-hander. He went down hard, hitting his head on the brass rail.

'The next thing I knew, his wife was hitting me over the head with her handbag. I don't know what she had in it but it weighed a ton. It was crash, bang, wallop and I didn't know what to do so I back off. Then Inglefield picks himself up, grabs the bag off his wife and pulls something out. Then I see it's a tiny axe, all chrome, and that he is raising it high above his head and charging towards me.

'I managed to get my hand up in front of my face just in time and the axe went into the back of my hand. The cut was really deep, right down to the bone, and there was blood everywhere. You couldn't tell where my fingers joined my hand. There was so much blood that it looked like they were all falling off.

'Inglefield pulls back for another strike so I rush towards him and throw my arms around him like a boxer in a clinch. Then we start wrestling, I'm trying to get the axe out of his hand. We're falling this way and that, all over the place. In the meantime the whole place has gone off. My mates have pulled knives and coshes out of their jackets and Parsons and Bingham have done the same. I saw Parsons get hit over the head with something and Bingham get hit in the face with something else. It was a complete madhouse.'

It was a big bar and the whole place was in uproar. There had been about 25 people in the club and most of them were fighting. The others were pressed up against the walls trying to keep out of it.

'Then out of the corner of my eye I saw Olly running out the back door, dragging Kate behind him. He had legged it at the first sign of the knives.

'Inglefield and I were still wrestling and fighting when I managed to get the axe away from him. As I pull it out of his hand he spins and starts falling to the ground because of the way we were fighting. So I hit him with the axe. The first blow catches him on the shoulder and there's a fountain of blood and I hear him scream.

'After the first one I don't know what happened, I just went mad. I just kept on whacking him on the back with the axe, again and again, each one harder than the last. I just kept doing it and I only stopped when my mates grabbed me and pulled me off of him. They said something about my thumb hanging off my hand and stuck me in the car and took me around St Thomas's.

'It turned out that I wasn't too badly injured. I had a few stitches and had my arm in a sling but none of my fingers had to be sewn back on. I'd come away relatively unscathed.'

The same wasn't true for Inglefield, who had ended up in intensive care.

The next night Pyle was in a pub in Tooting and a policeman called Palmer came in to see him. Pyle denied all knowledge of the fight, but with his arm in a sling it was pretty clear that he had been involved in trouble.

'All right Joey. Here's the thing. He's on the danger list and if he dies, we're going to do you for murder.'

The police had gone to visit Inglefield earlier that evening as he lay in intensive care. 'We've got witnesses,' Palmer had told him. 'We know that Joey Pyle did this to you. You might not have long left. Tell us what we need to hear.'

Inglefield looked at Palmer and then spoke, struggling to breathe. 'I ain't gonna help you. If I die, then you're gonna have to nick him under your own steam so fuck off and do that now. You'll get nothing from me.'

'While some of the people at the club had told the police that they had seen me hitting Inglefield with the axe, none of them were willing to make statements. Without Inglefield's testimony there was no way they could be able to pin anything on me.

'At first I was worried but once I found out what Inglefield had said, I knew it was going to be all right. A few days later I heard that he'd pulled through. Then six weeks after the fight I was out with Johnny Nash and the two of us were walking into the Astor club when I saw Bernie Bingham across the road. I shouted out to him and he turned around just as he got to the corner of Berkley Square. He came back and said hello and then I noticed who he was with. It was Inglefield.

'"So, what have you got to say for yourself?" I asked. "What's your attitude?"

'"What do you mean?"

'"Well, what's your attitude, how's it going to be?"

'"Well, I got done in the back but I did your hand didn't I?"

'"Yeah."

'"Well, I will take that as my innings."

'"Well that's fair play."

'"But I don't want to have to go out with a suit of armour every time every time I step out of my front door."

'"Well that works both ways. Shall we call it quits?"

'"Yeah, that will be it. It's over."

'And it was. If we hadn't agreed to end it there, we could have been going at each other for God knows how long. The whole thing could have escalated into a little war. Instead we called a halt to it. I never liked Inglefield, but I couldn't help respect and admire him for sticking to the code like that. Inglefield was no friend of mine – I wouldn't have come close to killing him if he had been – but I won't hear a bad word against him.'

'Dino Cellini and I had remained good friends even after he'd got kicked out of the country along with George Raft in the spring of 1967.

'The first thing Dino did was decamp to Holland and set up shop over there. He set up a casino called The Cabaret in the middle of the red light district and I went over there to see him a few times. It was while I was there that I met his brother, Bobby, for the first time. We really hit it off and in time we became good pals.

'Then Joe Nesline set up a new casino in Yugoslavia in the

town of Split and asked me to arrange for groups of big time gamblers to go out there on junkets.

'The way it used to work was this. There would be about thirty people in the party overall and the attraction for them was that the whole thing was dirt cheap and they would be able to spend all their time gambling. But out of that thirty at least eight or nine of them would be my pals. They were not gamblers; they were just working for me and got little more out of it than a free holiday. I just had them there to make the tables look busy.

'The shields could go up to the cashier and get as many chips as they wanted without having to pay anything for them. Whether they won or lost didn't matter because at the end of the day, any chips they had would go right back to the casino.

'People used to fight over themselves to get places on the trip because I told them I had an in with one of the croupiers. "Tell you what I'm going to do for you," I'd tell them. "I'm going to arrange for you to get fed chips from the dealer. I don't know how much it will be, but it will be a nice amount, a nice little earner. The only thing you have to do is play big, you have to play big otherwise he can't do it."

'The thing about people who love to gamble is that, more than anything, they love to win. The fact that it was dirt cheap to get out over there and the hotel would also cost nothing was attractive. But what really pulled them in was the idea that the game was going to be crooked, that they were going to get a chance to beat the system.

'I'd even tell them that they'd get a chance to meet the dealer before the game began so they would know for sure that the whole thing was bent. He would come along into their room and explain to them that, as long as they played big – several hundred pounds at a time – he would be able to slide some money over to them. "I'll do it cleverly and cunningly," he would explain. "Stand right on the left of me. I'll make sure there's a space for you and you'll be right near the stick man so he won't be able to see what I'm doing. And as soon as I get a chance and the pit boss is not looking, I'll slide the chips over. You need to look away for a second too, but next time you look down, you'll have an extra couple of grand there."

'All that made the punters more eager than ever. They would start to play and they would have changed up about five grand-worth of chips. They would play and play and almost always they'd find they were losing all their money fast until they only had a couple of grand left. When that happened they would start looking to me and looking to the dealer, waiting to get sent over what they are supposed to be getting.

'What would happen next was almost comical. The floor manager would suddenly be distracted and have to look away at something and at that same moment, the dealer would take the opportunity to slide over a big stack of high value chips, as much as two or three grand at a time. The punters would be delighted and they would go back to their playing with a new sense of excitement.'

It was, of course, a classic double bluff. The crooked dealer, who was giving away free chips, was working for the casino and he was also using crooked dice to make sure all the gamblers at the table lost.

The players would get down to £2,000 and then the dealer would slide over another £2,000 so then they'd be back up to £4,000. They would keep playing and keep losing and eventually they'd get down to nothing. When that happened, then they would have to write out another cheque. And then the same thing would happen all over again.

'The junkets would last for a week and during that time we would keep robbing them and robbing them until the very last night, when we would take absolutely everything they had. I used to get a percentage of it and I would use that to pay all my mates who had been running around helping. Of course, none of them knew it was a scam and even if they suspected, they could never have proved it. Plenty of people were winning and walking away with the money – it's just that they were all my mates and that at the end of the day, they'd have to give the cash back.

'The real punters didn't stand a chance. Any bet they made, they would never fucking win. So they would be losing their own money and then losing the money that they'd be given as well. At the end of the night I'd say to them how are you doing and they'd say fuck me Joe, I'm down seven grand. And I'd say how can you be down that much, the man's given you more than ten grand-worth of chips.'

It was the perfect crime.

It had been more than twenty months since the murder of George Cornell and the taunts that flowed back and forth between the Kray twins were as vicious as ever. And at the same time, their behaviour, particularly that of Ronnie, was becoming increasingly bizarre.

Joey recalls: 'The heat was on the whole time. The Twins and I decided to travel up to Manchester to collect on a few bits of business from bookmakers and nightclubs up there. We had planned to stay for a few days and make a bit of a holiday out of it. We arrived late in the afternoon, booked into our hotel and then went out on the town.

'The next morning we came down for breakfast and the whole place was full of police. They were everywhere, in every nook and cranny, just standing around, not staying a word to us or anyone else. Their governor was this bloke with a big pipe. He took a couple of steps forward and just stared at me and the Twins. He didn't have to say anything. We knew that he was telling us to get out of his town. We also knew that if we didn't, we were almost certainly going to get fitted up with something.

'We jumped in a cab and went right down to the train station and the police followed us there. The whole platform was just one big line of uniforms. Ronnie Kray looked up and down the ranks of coppers and scowled. Then he said to me. "Hey Joey, remember when Angelo Bruno came over? He said that if he has a problem with the law, he gets them shifted. I'd like to see him shift this fucking lot."

'As we pulled in towards London, about twenty minutes from Euston, Ronnie took off his jacket and rolled up his sleeves. He explained that the police were bound to be waiting at the station but he had a cunning plan to fool them. He was going to disguise himself as a porter and carry some cases through the ticket gate.

' "You soppy bastard," said Reggie. "Don't you think they know you? And I'm your fucking twin. As soon as they see me the game will be up." But Ronnie wouldn't listen. There were times when he was as mad as a March hare.

'The train pulled in at Euston and Ronnie picked up a couple of cases, loaded them onto a trolley and walked along whistling to himself. Me and Reggie walked behind, shaking our heads and not quite believing what he was up to. When we got to the ticket barrier there were three Old Bill waiting there, including Tommy Butler. They recognised Ronnie right away of course. They never said a word; they just stared at him as he walked past.

'The funny thing was, when we met up outside the station, Ronnie was convinced that he had fooled them all.'

Ever since Cornell's murder, the police had been receiving a steady stream of information about who had been responsible, though none of it had moved them any closer towards being able to pin the crime on Ronnie Kray.

Most of the information had been received in the form of anonymous notes. One letter, typed and dated 9 August 1966, says:

Keep plugging at it. Ronnie Kray did the shooting.

And a handwritten note reads:

You had the right ones for the murder of George Cornell. The Kray twins done it. People in the Blind Beggar know. We can expect another murder in the East End soon. They are the guilty ones [Krays]. Watch them.

A memo from Detective Superintendent Tommy Butler of the Flying Squad reveals how officers knew as early as 1960 what a formidable force the Krays were, and the police's frustration at being unable to stop them. Mr Butler wrote:

During the past three years, the Kray twins have welded themselves into a formidable criminal association. At present this is directed towards club owners, cafe proprietors, billiard hall owners, publicans and motor car dealers operating in the East End of London.

They have organised the protection technique, and the keystones of their confederacy are violence and intimidation. That they will spread their operations to other districts in due course may be taken for granted. Their reputation is already such that persons threatened almost frantically deny visitations by anyone connected with the Kray twins.

Not one victim can be persuaded to give evidence against anyone connected with their organization. [The police knew the Krays were careful not to link themselves directly with any crime.] [The Krays] are content to remain in the background, emerging only to convince any particularly difficult client of the force of their demands.

For this reason their arrest will only be achieved by unorthodox police methods, or by very good fortune.

The fact that Ronald Kray is certainly mentally unstable (to put it at its very least) is of immense importance to the others, and adds considerably to the victim's urge to comply with demands made upon him, and to his atrocious memory when questioned by police.

The ruthlessness with which the Krays used to silence witnesses was revealed in documents from a police file relating to a court case in 1965.

A police inspector, known only as G, said: 'Coercion of the main witness was an astute move on the part of the Kray advisers. From the outset I concluded this witness was the stronger of the two main ones for the prosecution. The main witness became a complete turncoat, and this in my mind was directly influenced by the pressure of the Krays in particular.'

The Old Bailey court case collapsed, and the Krays and another man were acquitted of conspiring to extort money.

Other letters accused the police of being in league with the Krays. One said:

> It is pretty evident that these men [the Krays] are not doing these things without some assistance from the police why is this being allowed to continue they are getting money from all sorts of operations they have been known to have machine guns and shot guns in hordes what exactly is going on when it is common knowledge and the police are powerless to do anything about it.
>
> There are two families here in the east end namely the Nashes and the Krays brothers that have been having a glorious time on the proceeds of violence and crime so I think that it is about time that you stepped in and has this thing stopped. It will not stop at this one murder.

Despite the continuing police interest, by the summer of 1967, things started looking up for both the Kray twins, and for Reggie in particular. Two years earlier he had married Frances Shea, a simple and uncomplicated woman who had first caught his eye as a strikingly pretty fourteen-year-old living around the corner from Vallance Road.

Like Ronnie, Reggie was actually far more attracted to men but lacked the same level of confidence that would have

Left Dad.

Below My mother, Cath. She loved boxing almost as much as my dad did.

Above The young boxer, 'the most stylish boxer in Surrey'.

Left In the army, with Joe Vaughan.

THE FANTAST
A 'RESORT

iddle that remains: Who?
id shoot Selwyn Cooney

A witness is to be smuggled out by air

At last — the amazing truth about 6 men who fight the law with fear

THE
WICKEDEST BR

FRIGHTENED
WITNESSES

A father writes . . .

Above The Pen Club murder marked me out in the eyes of the police.

A night out with Tony Baldessare. Along with Jack 'the hat' McVitie, we made a good tea

Meeting with the Kray twins: Johnny Nash, Ronnie, Peter Marshall and Reggie standing behind, Alex Steen, me.

Johnny Nash, me, Eusebio the footballer and Sulky, manager of the Astor Club.

Brian Hill, Terry Downes, Mick O'Neill the boxer, me, John Nash, Oliver Reed. Olly liked a fight but did a runner the night I was attacked with an axe.

Above With Alex in New York City.

Right With Alex and Roy Shaw. Roy was too old for legitimate matches when he came out of prison, so we started up unlicensed fights with the famous match against Donny 'The Bull' Adams.

With Joe Louis, my hero.

I was best man at Ronnie Kray's wedding. Charlie Kray and Alex Steen came along as well.

With Charlie Richardson and Alex Steen.

Zagreb airport, where we used to fly out gamblers for one of our casino scams: me, Terry Plumber, 'Mad' Ronnie Fryer, Ronnie Warner, Terry Marsh. Ronnie killed Terry a few years later.

Sparring with my son, Joe Jr.

With Joe Jr and Freddie Foreman.

Above Dino Cellini's brothers, Bobby and Eddie, at their casino in Africa.

Left With my beautiful bride, Julie at our wedding in Las Vegas in 2002.

enabled him to be as frank and forthright about his sexuality in the way that Ronnie was. Instead, Reggie began courting Frances in the most chivalrous fashion possible, taking her out to all the best places, showering her with gifts and always behaving like a true gentleman: on trips to Barcelona and Italy, he always insisted on separate hotel rooms.

The East End 'wedding of the year' took place in April 1965 at St James the Less Church in Bethnal Green, with celebrities including the film star Diana Dors, pianist Lenny Peters (of Peters and Lee fame) and one time world boxing champion Ted 'Kid' Lewis. The event was photographed by none other than David Bailey, then a rising star in the London fashion world, whom the Twins had got to know a few weeks earlier.

The marriage had gone wrong right from the start. Reggie moved them in to a flat near Marble Arch – an attempt to move upmarket. But away from the East End and her family and friends, Frances was lonely and miserable. And so was Reggie.

A month later they had moved back to the East End, but their problems continued. For one thing the marriage was never consummated – Reggie preferring drink and long chats with Ron and friends to nights with his bride. Then there was the fact that Ron hated Frances for coming between him and his brother and made no secret of it. Dismayed by the constant presence of thugs and criminals, as well as the menacing atmosphere, Frances left the marital home after just eight weeks.

Reggie continued to pursue her, standing in the street outside her mother's house – she refused to let him enter – and talking to Frances as she leaned out of a window. Both Frances and Reggie seemed irresistibly drawn to one another, even though they were clearly unsuited and the relationship brought both more misery than joy. For Frances in particular, ten years younger than her husband, the strain was beginning to show. Always nervous and highly strung, she suffered a nervous breakdown three months after the marriage and was hospitalised after trying to kill herself.

By the June of 1967, Frances seemed to be on the mend and it looked as though she and Reggie might be making another go of things. Reggie arranged for the two of them to go on holiday, a second honeymoon, but it was not to be. The day they were due to leave for Ibiza, Frances took another overdose and died.

Reggie was heartbroken. He went into a deep depression for months, starting drinking all the time and was crazy with grief. Ronnie continued to boast about having killed Cornell and to goad Reggie into doing a murder himself. Although Reggie had lost his temper on dozens of occasions and had made idle threats, he always had sufficient self-control to prevent things from going too far. The death of his wife finally pushed him over the edge.

Joey Pyle's childhood friend, Jack McVitie, had grown up to become a tough brawler and big drinker who was deeply embarrassed to find he was losing his hair in his early thirties. He took to covering the bald patch, even when he was indoors, thus earning the nickname Jack 'The Hat'.

Jack had never really been part of the Firm, more of a hanger-on. He dabbled in the Purple Heart business, in which the Twins had some interest, and did a few little jobs for them. His chance to become a fully-fledged Firm member came when he was offered £100 to kill Leslie Payne, a former business manager of the Twins. However, Jack had been getting high on his own drug supply and kept the money without ever fulfilling the contract.

In the weeks that followed, Jack's drink and drug habits raged out of control. Fearless and dangerous even when sober, Jack's bravado increased to the point that he was openly criticising and threatening the Krays wherever he went. It was only a matter of time before his words got back to Vallance Road.

Joey recalls, 'I never knew him as Jack The Hat, I knew him as Mac from back when he was younger and I used to run around with him and Tony Baldessare in south London. I remember Ronnie phoning me up several times and asking me to tell Mac to shut up.

' "What has he done now?"

' "Listen Joey, he's going around saying that he's going to kill us and whenever he sees one of our firm, he goes right up to them and says: 'Ah, you work for the Slay – the Slay Twins. Ha ha. Have they been taking it up the bum lately? Ha ha.' And then he's going up to people and saying: 'Ah, I just missed the Twins last night. I was gonna shoot them. I was waiting outside the boozer but they went out the other door.' Have a word with him Joey, get him to straighten himself out will you?"

'Ronnie was well pissed off. Mac had been winding them up big time and he was playing a dangerous game. I called him up.

' "Mac, why don't you turn it in? You're going around slagging the Firm and saying this and saying that. If you carry on like this, one day, you're gonna get it."

I could hear Mac grinning down the other end of the phone line. "Don't worry Joey," he told me. "The Twins will be dead tomorrow. I'm gonna go round and shoot them."

'This didn't just happen once, it must have happened at least half a dozen times. I would call Mac up and warn him to be more careful; he would reassure me that any day now, he would personally take the Twins out of the game. You didn't have to be a clairvoyant to work out what was going to happen next.'

On the night of 28 October 1967 Jack McVitie was having a drink at the Carpenters Arms in Bethnal Green when two members of the Firm, Tony and Chris Lambrianou, invited him to a party in nearby Evering Road.

And drunken Jack arrived at the basement flat a few minutes later expecting birds and booze, instead he found himself face to face with the Kray twins and half a dozen others. The plan had been that as soon as Jack walked in, Reggie would shoot him in the head with his .32 automatic, but the gun jammed.

'What have I done?' asked Jack, suddenly sober.

'You know what you've done,' Reggie told him.

Jack sat on the sofa. 'I'm sorry. It won't happen again.' If Reggie had been on his own, Jack might have had a chance of talking his way out of it, but Ronnie was in a fury, his eyes were bulging and Jack knew it was only a matter of time.

He ran to the window in the corner of the room that looked out on the garden, punching out the pane with his fist. He tried to jump through but members of the Firm grabbed his legs, dragged him back into the room and hauled him to his feet.

'Be a man Jack,' screamed Ronnie.

'Yes, I'll be a man, but I don't want to die like one.'

Ronnie moved forward and grabbed Jack from behind, locking his elbows together and forcing his chest forward. Ronnie spun him round to face Reggie who was now holding a 12-inch butcher's knife.

'Kill him Reg,' hissed Ronnie. 'Do him, don't stop now.'

The first blow hit McVitie in the face, just below the eye. McVitie sank to his knees and gasped 'Why are you doing this to me Reg?' The only reply was more thrusts of the knife, first in the stomach, then the chest and finally through the throat with a blow so hard it penetrated the floorboards underneath. Another member of the Firm placed his hand on McVitie's chest and pronounced him dead. It was over.

As Joey Pyle says, 'Jack got silly. He knew he was going to get it – maybe it was a death wish he had – because everyone knows that you can't go around saying things like that without it coming back to bite you.

'At the end of the day I can't blame the Twins for what they did. If someone goes around saying they are gonna kill you, then you don't have a lot of choice – you have to do them first. But Jack should never have died the way he did. He died like a fucking rat, everyone in the room jumping on him and all that. The Twins killed him as if he was a grass and he was entitled to a lot more respect than that. He wasn't scum and if he had to go, he should have been allowed to go with dignity.'

While Ronnie spent the best part of two years bragging that he'd killed Cornell, both the brothers were tight lipped when it came to the death of Jack the Hat.

'A few days after he had gone missing there were rumours flying round London about what had happened to him, most of them pointing at the Krays. Me and Johnny Nash went to see them. I remember saying to Reggie that there was a lot of talk that he had done it. His expression never changed. "Yeah, I heard that too. But it ain't nothing to do with us."

'The Twins put some stories about that Jack had been killed in a car crash on the Westway near Hammersmith – some bollocks like that. But pretty soon we all knew it was them. I like to think the reason they didn't brag this time was because of the way that they had done it. Maybe they knew it was wrong. There was nothing honourable about the way Jack died, and anyone who took credit for killing him would have to live with that.'

'I first met Roy Shaw when I was out in the 58 Club in Westbourne Grove with my mate Peter Tilley. I was still a teenager at the time and making my living as a professional boxer. Roy was thinking of turning pro himself and came over to ask my advice. I knew of him and him of me, not through villainy but through the boxing. We were both aware of each other's reputations as game fighters.

'We got on really well – we had lots in common – and it was clear that we were going to become good friends. After that the next time I saw Roy was when I was banged up for the Pen Club murder and he was in the Scrubs doing time for armed robbery. That was when our friendship really grew, and once I got out I would continue to visit him on a regular basis.

'Roy had a hard time in prison. On one occasion a bloke called Brown started threatening Roy's friend, Bert Coster, because of an argument over a football match. Roy stepped in and they started fighting at the top of a flight of steps. Brown fell backwards and ended up slumped at the bottom with blood trickling from his mouth. Two days later, Brown died and Roy and Coster were charged with murder, even though his death was nothing more than a tragic accident.'

Much to the annoyance of the authorities, who were looking for an excuse to keep him behind bars, Shaw narrowly escaped being convicted when the two prosecution witnesses – other prisoners who had been at the top of the stairs when the fight started – changed their minds and gave evidence that put both him and Coster in the clear.

It was soon after that Shaw developed a reputation as the most violent man inside any jail. He attacked warders and even governors, sometimes with startling brutality. As a result he was eventually transferred to Broadmoor, the hospital for the criminally insane. One doctor wrote: 'Shaw is the most powerful and dangerous man I have ever attempted to treat', but they eventually decided that his crimes were not triggered by madness – it was simply that violence was his way of life.

'It was on one of my regular visits to Broadmoor that Roy asked if I could do him a favour. There was a bloke who had been having it away with Roy's wife while he had been on the inside, some trader who worked on Romford market. I was happy to help him and started making plans, but then something came up.

'Although I had moved away from doing jobs across the pavement after coming out of prison for the Pen Club case, I was still involved in little things every now and then, mostly in south London rather than anywhere else. I worked on a firm with Peter Tilley, Peter Marshall and another friend, Bertie Cox. There was also another local lad that I knew less well – Vic Scallion.

'We did stuff together, but we also did little things on our own as well like debt collection. One time Bertie got unlucky and ended up getting three years for demanding money with menaces. He was banged up and we all did what we could for him to make the time go by quicker. We used to try and visit as much as we could and Vic used to drive Bertie's girlfriend up once a week so that she could get to see him too.

'After a while the rest of us started to get a bit suspicious. Vic seemed to be getting closer and closer to Bertie's girl and, what with him being away that just didn't seem right. And then Vic went in to see Bertie and told him that he was going to marry his girlfriend. Now Bertie was really in love with this girl. It was bad enough losing her but losing her to someone he had trusted and considered a friend – that was just too much.

'The rest of us felt the same way: it was right out of order. So we had a chat about it and decided there was only one thing we could do. Vic Scallion was going to have to die.

'Doing the deed wasn't going to be a problem; disposing of the body was. After a bit more discussion we decided to use acid. Peter Tilley had a big scrap metal yard where it would be easy to hide big vats of acid. The idea was we were going to mullah him and put him in the acid until the body had completely vanished.

'None of us had used acid for that before and we needed to be sure that it worked. We decided to try it out on some dead rats. We got three of them and threw them in my bath then poured some of the acid we were going to use over them. Within seconds they had turned into a red sludge. The stage was set. All we had to do was kill Scallion.

'But then one afternoon me and the two Peters were in a club and in walked Vic Scallion and Bertie Cox's girlfriend. As soon as I saw them, I just went into one. I rushed over to Vic and started screaming at him: "You fucking bastard, you no good dirty cunt, how could you do that to Bertie", and all that. I couldn't help myself. I just lost it. But that blew the plan. The club had been packed to the rafters and there was no way we could do anything after that because the police would have been on us right away.

'A couple of months later Bert got to the end of his sentence and I picked him up from Wandsworth prison. He was still furious over the whole thing and I told him that whatever he did, he had to stay away from Vic. He told me he would, that he wasn't going to do anything silly. But a week later he went round to his old flat to see his girlfriend and found Vic there, painting and decorating the place.

'Bert went into one, ran in there and the two of them started fighting. I don't know which one of them pulled the knife but it was Vic that ended up getting stabbed in the heart. There's blood pumping out of his chest and he's gasping. Bert realises that he's done the business and starts to carry Vic down the stairs, and that's when he runs into one of the neighbours.

'The neighbour is in a right panic because they can see all the blood – there's a dirty great trail of it running down the stairs. So Bertie tells them that Vic has had an accident and to stick their finger in the wound to stop the bleeding while he goes off to call an ambulance.

'After that Bert runs off, dumps the knife in a river and then calls Peter Marshall, telling him that he has stabbed Vic and thinks that he might have killed him. Peter picks Bert up and hides him out in a room in Putney; then he comes to see me.

'We both race round to Putney. It's just one room, bare apart from a mattress on the floor. We get inside and Bert is just sitting there on the mattress, looking a bit stunned. We know by now that Vic is dead and Bert says he has nothing left to live for. The way he's talking makes me feel a bit uneasy so I go into the kitchen and see that the door of the gas stove is open and that he's stuck wet bread all around the windows and door frames, making an airtight seal. And then I find a suicide note.

'I didn't say a word. I just walked back into the room and told Bert that it was a bad idea for him to stay in that house because the police would probably be able to track him down.

' "Nah, just let me stay here," said Bert.

' "You can't, you've got to come with us." '

'Bert shook his head slowly.

'Now Bert was a big man, at least six foot six, and I knew that if I tried to make him move by force, I was going to have a fight on my hands. I was pacing back and forth looking at him and decided that if it came to that, I was going to have to knock him out with the first blow. The angle he was at and the size of him meant it had to be a kick, a hard one, right on the chin. I got myself into position but then at the last minute, something inside me made me change my mind. Instead of a kick I rushed forward and grabbed Bertie by the arm and pulled him to his feet.

'Bertie was so distraught over everything that was happening, he didn't even have the strength to fight back. Peter and I jostled him out of the room and down the stairs, got him into the car and took him to my uncle's house in Stoke Newington. Once we had him settled in we headed back to south London and ended up stopping off for a drink in the Prince of Wales in Tooting.

'That night the local police commander, a bloke called Palmer, came in the pub and when he saw me and Peter, he came straight towards us.

' "We know you know where Bertie Cox is," he said. "And I advise you to tell him to give himself up."

' "You're wrong, I ain't got a clue where he is."

' "You're lying," he replied. "Tell him to come in."

' "Why, so you can verbal him up?"

'In those days police interviews were never taped and half the time they never even made proper notes of what was being said. It meant that "verballing", where the police made up confessions and all sorts, was commonplace. It was why so many crooks were meant to have said things like "You've got me bang to rights" and "You'll never take me alive copper". No one ever really said those things, it was all just made up by the police and everyone knew it.

'Palmer shook his head. "No, there won't be any verbal. It

will just be a straight forward nicking. We will listen to whatever he has to say. But he needs to come in."

' "Tell you what, if I happen to bump into him somewhere, I'll pass the message on."

'We went to see Bert a little later on in the evening. By then he had been listening to a little radio and had heard that Vic was dead.

' "What do you want to do Bert?"

' "I want to go in. I want to give myself up. I can't go on with my life like this."

'Bertie was a good friend of ours. He had only just come out of prison and neither of us wanted to see him go back. It wasn't like we could argue with what he had done, because only a couple of months earlier we had been planning to do the same thing ourselves. They had got rid of the death penalty for murder by then but we didn't want Bertie spending the rest of his life behind bars. I guess I felt a bit guilty in that if I had managed to control my temper in that club, the problem would never have come up because Scallion would have been poured down a drain somewhere.

'That's when I had an idea. I explained it to Bertie and he jumped at the chance. We found a bottle of whisky and gave him a couple of glasses to help dull the pain, and then we started. Bertie stood in the middle of the room and Peter and I laid into him. There were kicks and punches to the head and body. I hit him over the back of the head with a bottle; Peter jammed his elbow into the socket of one of Bertie's eyes.

'The whole thing had been almost funny and completely surreal. Bertie had wanted us to do it and just stood there taking the punishment, but he couldn't help yelping with pain and calling us every name under the sun each and every time we hit him. But then he'd tell us not to stop and to hit him harder.

'By the time we'd finished his lips and nose were busted to pieces, there was blood dripping from a split in the back of his skull and a couple of his teeth were coming loose. Peter and I were both out of breath.

'"OK Bertie," I said, glancing at my watch and sucking up a big lungful of air. "It's 2 a.m. Have a little sleep but whatever you do, don't have a wash and we'll come back and fetch you tomorrow and take you down the station."

'The next morning Peter and I picked Bertie up. He looked absolutely terrible. His face was covered in bruises including two nasty shiners, and all the blood had congealed around his cuts. We took him to a photography shop on Tooting High Street and got a few pictures done and then took him down to meet our solicitor, who escorted him into Tooting Police station.

'He made no comment through the interview and after half an hour of questioning, the police charged him with murder and locked him up in a cell. The police didn't bother taking any pictures of Bertie that day and they didn't know that any existed until halfway through the trial, when Bertie's solicitor produced them to support a claim that he had only killed Vic in self defence.

'It worked: the jury took one look at the snaps and decided that Bertie must have been fighting for his life to end up like that. Instead of ending up doing life for murder, Bertie got three years for manslaughter.

'Having seen the problems that Bertie ended up with, I knew I had to sort out the problem with Roy's wife as soon as. I was just about to move on it when I got another message from Roy. He told me to leave it because Ronnie Kray owed him a favour and had agreed to get it sorted.

'Kray had put two of the Firm, Ronnie Hart and Albert Donaghue on the job and they had agreed to get it done. A few days later they came back to Ronnie and said it was all done. After that Ronnie went up to see Roy and told him he had a nice present for him – that the bloke who had been fucking about with his wife had been dealt with. Roy was over the moon; it really made his day, his month, his year.

'It was only later that we all found out that Hart and Donaghue had done no such thing, that they had just been telling bald-faced lies when they said they had done the bloke. I'd never gotten to know Donaghue that well but I never had a lot of time for him. As it turned out my instincts were right: when the going got tough, he would be the first one of the Firm to crack. He would end up becoming the thing we all hated most: a grass.'

8. 'I TOOK THE CHAMPAGNE BOTTLE, SLIPPED IT UNDER THE TABLE AND PISSED IN IT, THEN PETER PISSED IN IT AS WELL. WHEN IT WAS FULL WE PUT IT BACK IN THE ICE BUCKET TO LET IT GET NICE AND COLD ...'

The summer of 1966 may have been a great one for English football but it was a bad one for law and order. In June thirteen convicted prisoners, nine of them prone to violence and constantly on the look out for chances to escape, were travelling in a coach to Parkhurst Prison on the Isle of Wight. The inmates had been called to court to give evidence in the trial of one prisoner who had been charged with stabbing another at the prison. But the whole case was a sham, set up and planned by the inmates purely to provide an opportunity to break out.

As the coach left Winchester, three of the convicts were handcuffed directly to prison officers and the other ten were handcuffed to one another in pairs. Despite being thoroughly searched they somehow managed to smuggle makeshift keys onto the coach. Hidden by the high seat backs in front of them, the ten men who were cuffed in pairs had managed to free themselves just minutes into the journey.

As they passed through Bishops Waltham on the way to Portsmouth Ferry terminal, they made their move, jumping off seats, leaping onto the prison officers and reaching for the steering wheel until the coach skidded to a halt across the middle of the road. Nine prisoners made it out, running in different directions, chased by two officers who had been following behind in a police car.

Within an hour, 120 police officers, 14 tracker dogs and an RAF helicopter were scouring the countryside around the South Downs. Swamping the area proved an effective solution: seven of the escapees were picked up after just a few hours, and one more the following day. After that only one man remained at large: John McVicar. Massive searches of the area around the coach continued but to no avail: it was as if he had vanished off the face of the earth.

McVicar had drifted into crime as a young boy and soon acquired a criminal record that included convictions for assault, robbery with violence and possession of offensive weapons. By the time of his escape he was a Category AA criminal of the first order and a well-respected man throughout the underworld.

'I'd known McVicar – Mac I call him – since he was young, as he used to be in a firm with Tony Baldessare and Georgie Nash,' says Joey. 'Nice bloke. There was a lot of respect and I knew that he trusted me. The escape was a couple of days old but still very much in the news the night that Peter Tilley and I went out on the town and ended up at the Celebrity Club. It was race night at the club. They had a giant screen up on one wall showing footage of horse races in America. Everyone who came in got a few tickets, each with a horse on it, and if you held the winning horse, you got a bottle of champagne.

'Well Peter and I won and they brought over this bottle of bubbly in a big ice bucket. It seemed like a nice touch until we poured it out and tasted it. It was absolute fucking rubbish, real cheap shit. After that one glass we just put it back in the ice bucket and sat there drinking scotch and chatting.

'A little while later, a few old lags that I vaguely knew came wandering in. There was Bert Mattie out of Hatton Garden, the old thief Dennis Stafford with the singer Selina Jones, a couple of others and a copper called Chris Pepper. Now Pepper was as bent as a nine bob note. He was well known for it. If you got into a bit of trouble, he was the sort of bloke you could bung a few quid to get you out of it. He was useful but he was no friend of mine, and neither were any of the others, but Pepper thought everyone loved him. There were a lot of bent coppers around at the time and a lot of them thought nothing of wandering in and out of boozers that were mostly frequented by the chaps, but it always pissed me off. I couldn't see why they had to come into our places when they had plenty of pubs of their own.

'We saw them all come in and a wicked idea suddenly popped into my head. I nodded towards the champagne. "Let's fill the bottle back up and then send it over to that bunch of cunts," I said. I took the bottle, slipped it under the table and then unzipped the fly of my trousers. I pissed in it, then passed it over to Peter and he pissed in it as well. When it was full we put it back in the ice bucket to let it get nice and cold.

'Soon after that Chris was up dancing around with Selina and came dancing over to our table, a big grin on his face.

'"Hello Pete, hello Joe, how you doing?"

'"All right Chris," I replied. "How's it going?"

He spotted the ice bucket in the middle of our table. "Is that champagne? You two must be doing well."

'"That? Oh we won that. We don't drink champagne. We're on the scotch. We haven't touched it. Tell you what Chris, you can have it if you like"

'"Really? Ah thanks mate, that'll be great."

'Chris lifted the bucket and took it over to his table. We watched as he filled five glasses and passed them out to the others in his group. Then they all turned towards us and held their glasses high.

'"Cheers"

'We held up our glasses in return. "All the best."

'And then they drank the lot.

'After that me and Peter went down the road and into one of our regular hangouts, the Olympic Casino, laughing ourselves silly all the way. We'd been there about half an hour or so and had met up with another friend, Ronnie Osborne, when the manager came over and told me I had a phone call. I went into the booth and picked up the receiver.

'"Hello mate, how are you?"

I recognised the voice immediately. It was John McVicar.

'"Hello, what's happening?"

'"I'm out. I'm down in Portsmouth and I can't fucking move. Everyone is looking for me. I need you to come down and get me out. I'll tell you what, come down on the A3 and when you come off the main road you'll see a street and a phone box. Drive down to the bottom and there's a railway bridge and another phone box. Go into that and I'll come out and meet you."

'I piled into the car with Ronnie and Peter and we started heading down towards the coast. All the way there, anytime we passed a bit of scrubland or a little wood, all you could see were police cars parked up with lines of coppers walked through, seeing if they could find anything. They knew McVicar was going to try to make it back to London and were looking for him every step of the way – no wonder he was starting to feel the pressure.

'A couple of miles from Portsmouth we stopped the car and tipped Osborne out. Loads of police had clocked us from a distance on the way down there and had been immediately suspicious because there were three of us in the car. There's something about three or more blokes in a car that instantly looks a bit dodgy and I didn't want to take any chances. I told Ronnie to get the train back to London and then we carried on driving down to pick up Mac.

'We found the road that he had been talking about and parked alongside the phone box. I got out and went over, pretending to make a call. It was a quiet street with a few houses, none of which had their lights on. The only noise was the sound of the car engine humming away. Tilley was in the driver's seat. He looked over at me and shrugged his shoulders. I started to think that maybe we'd got the wrong place but then, as I put the phone down, Mac came running across the road and jumped into the car.

'I pushed my seat back as far as it would go and told Mac to get down in the well, right under my feet, and slung a blanket over him. I was all dressed up for a night at the casino. I had a suit and tie and a nice pair of Italian-made leather shoes, but I noticed that Mac was barefoot – he had lost his shoes during his escape – and I told him to take mine in case he had to use his toes. You can run a lot faster in shoes that you can barefoot, especially where the ground is a bit rough.

'We got as far as Dorking. Up until then it had been pretty clear and there had been nothing to get spooked over. But then we came down a hill to see what looked like a new set of traffic lights next to a big bus depot. As we got closer we realised it wasn't traffic lights at all but a police roadblock. A team of officers had brought all the traffic to a halt and were checking each and every car before letting them drive on.

'Peter was driving and started slowing down. Mac was still under my feet and they were going to spot him right away. It's pretty clear there is nothing we can do. Even if we turned back, they would come after us because it would be obvious we were making a run for it.

' "Oh fuck," said Peter.

' "What's happening?" asked McVicar's voice from the floor.

' "It's on us mate," I told him, "it's fucking on us."

' "What are we gonna do?"

'I looked through the windscreen and saw a police officer standing in the middle of the road up ahead, directing the car in front of us to pull over to one side so he could peer inside with his torch. "Well we can't stop. I tell you what Pete, pull up right slow as if you're gonna stop and then when he says 'over here mate' put you foot down and go round him."

'And that's exactly what we did. Within seconds we were gunning it up the A3, tyres screeching as we skidded out into the middle of the street to get around the roadblock and back again in a bid to avoid the oncoming traffic.

'From that moment the chase was on. The cops all ran to their cars and starting coming after us like bats out of hell. We got to the next roundabout and chucked a right. There was no point in staying on the A3 – it was a main road and they'd just block off the next junction. Instead we headed into Dorking Town centre.

'We're turning left and right and left and we're just far enough ahead to give us the edge, but none of us know the town and we don't know where we're going, so they're gaining on us all the time. We pull another left and we realise we're in a cul-de-sac. But there's a big building site right at the end. I tell Peter to stop, push open the door and tell Mac to get out. Straight away, woosh, he runs out, scrambles over the fence and vanishes into the darkness. I see his shadow scoot under a bit of tarpaulin that someone has thrown over some breezeblocks and I know that no one's ever gonna find him there.

'I've only just managed to get the door shut when two panda cars come tearing round the corner. They're all fucking mob handed, come steaming out and grab me and Peter. There's four of them, all pulling at my arms and dragging me out of the car. As they get me up I start shouting and looking down at the ground, making sure my words are loud enough for everyone to hear.

'"Oi, where's me shoes? I want me fucking shoes, let me go back and get me shoes."

'"Fuck your shoes, you're coming with us," is the reply.

'I'm in one car and Peter's in the other and they carry us off down to the local nick and sling us into a couple of cells. They don't find Mac so as far as we're concerned, we ain't done nothing wrong, especially as the car isn't stolen or anything. They can suspect all they want but they can't prove anything. They tell us we're going to have to wait until the morning when the CID get there.

'We only get a few hours sleep before they wake us up and start with the questions:

'"Mr Pyle, where are your shoes?"

'"In the car."

'"We've searched the car, they're not there."

'"Well someone must have fucking nicked them then. I told your man about it as he was dragging me out, I wanted to go back and get them but he told me to get in the car."

'"Where have you been?"

'"We were going to drive down to the Isle of Wight. We thought we might go away for a few days, you know, a bit of a junket. But then when we got to Portsmouth we changed our minds and were just about to head back, go and see our wives."

'"You expect me to believe that story?"

'"I'm telling you the truth."

'"Really. Well suppose I tell you that there was a jeweller's shop in Portsmouth smashed open this morning and about one hundred thousand pounds-worth of jewellery nicked out of the windows. What would you say about that?"

'"Well what time did it happen?"

'"About 12.30 a.m."

'I couldn't help but allow myself a little smile. "Well if you're gonna try and stick that one on me, you're gonna come right undone."

'"And why's that then?"

'"Because at that time, I was in the Celebrity Club and I sent a Scotland Yard detective a bottle of champagne."

'"Oh really. Well we're gonna check that out."

'The sergeant returned about half an hour later, reached down and started unlocking the door to my cell. "OK then, we've phoned up the Yard and we've spoken to Detective Chris Pepper who backs up your story."

'"See, just like I said."

'"Pepper had a message for you though. He says that champagne you gave him was the worst he'd ever had. He'll never forget it. Said it tasted like a right load of piss."

'In the days and weeks that followed, I couldn't help chuckling to myself about the fact that something that had started out as a joke actually went on to get us off something far more serious. Normally these things come back and blow up right in your face.

'After that, I never saw McVicar again. He never phoned up to say thank you or passed me a message of any kind. And I never got my shoes back either.'

McVicar was eventually recaptured at the end of the summer during a botched raid on a security van and sent back to prison. A year later he would escape again, this time from the far more difficult Durham prison, helped by 'Angel Face' Wally Probyn, chairman of the prison's escape society. The move bought McVicar to prominence, partly because Durham was such a notoriously difficult prison to break out from, and also because he was immediately dubbed 'public enemy number one'. On his second shot at freedom, he remained on the run for two years until an informant, anxious to get his hands on the £10,000 reward, tipped off the police.

'About six weeks after that, Chris Pepper came down to a car site that I had down in Colliers Wood and held out his hand. He wanted paying off.

'"What for?"

'"What for? I got you out of it with them cozzers down in Dorking didn't I? You owe me at least a drink for that."

'"Got me out of it? All you did was tell the fucking truth for once. Why do I owe you a drink? Anyway, you've had a bottle of champagne off me. That's yer lot."

'Pepper was well known for being crooked and there were a lot like him around. If you wanted a favour, if someone was nicked, then he was the sort of bloke who, if they bunged a few quid his way, would be able to get them off. Pepper wasn't alone. At the time the West End was full of it, especially as far as the dirty book shops and the strip joints were concerned. Police were getting bungs off the lot of them.

'I knew one bloke, Jimmy Humphreys, pretty well and he was paying a fortune, literally tens of thousands of pounds each year, to people off the vice squad to keep them off his back. He also had contacts in the Flying Squad and all sorts of other divisions.

'It's just the way things were back then. I don't have anything against bent coppers. I wish we had more of them. The more there are, the better for us. But they have to be bent in the right way. The ones that fit you up, I think they want hanging. But the ones who take a bung and get you out of trouble, well how can you ever complain about them? The reason the prisons are so full up nowadays is nothing to do with there being any more crime – it's because before there were so many bent coppers around that you could get out of almost anything.'

It was after Jack McVitie's death that Leonard 'Nipper' Read was appointed by Scotland Yard and given responsibility for bringing the Krays to justice. He tried to turn some of the members of the Firm against them but it was no use. 'The Krays were both idolised and feared,' he said. 'People either loved them or were terrified of them. Either way, no one was going to talk about them. So I decided to go back to basics.'

None of this bothered the Kray twins. At Fort Vallance they bought two boa constrictors from Harrods and named them Read and Gerrard after 'Nipper' and Chief Superintendent Fred Gerrard, the other man who had been placed on the case.

'Sometime in the early part of 1968 me and Johnny Nash were in the Astor club when we got talking to Reggie Kray. He said he'd been talking to some crime reporter who was friendly with Nipper, and that the word was we were all going to get nicked. Me and John were going to get nicked first because the police figured that if we were behind bars, we wouldn't be able to help the Twins to get away. They didn't have anything to charge us with – they were going to fit us up with some moody bollocks just to get us out of the way.

'The very next day, John and I went to Spain. It wasn't anywhere near as built up as it is these days. As far as going places was concerned, there was Torremolinos and nothing else. I hired a villa right on the main coast road and John and I stayed there for a couple of months and it all blew up while we were away.

'It wasn't like we were trying to avoid getting arrested, just keeping out of the way. This was long before the Costa del Crime and they could have brought us right back if they wanted to. We were just trying to make ourselves scarce. There was no one on the run there and we weren't even on the run.'

Read sensed that the gang was staring to fall apart. He interviewed Billy Exley, who had been involved in the botched attempt on the life of Leslie Payne with Jack McVitie, but got nowhere. He then turned his attention to Payne himself whom, he correctly guessed would be feeling vulnerable and in need of police protection.

Payne spilt the beans almost immediately, providing evidence of the dozens of lucrative long firm frauds the Twins had run over the preceding years, to guarantee they would be held in custody. Though Read fully expected the charges to fail, it would give him weeks to work on his investigation.

In the early hours of the morning of 9 May 1968, the police struck as the Krays lay in bed after a heavy night at the Astor Club.

'As soon as we heard they had been arrested we knew it was safe to come back. The general consensus was that if they didn't do us straight away, then they weren't going to nick us at all because we didn't have anything to do with Cornell or McVitie. In that sense, it's just as well the Twins never told us anything about them.

'By the time I came back from Spain the Twins were on remand. I remember going to a club I had in Garratt Lane one night and being stopped by a copper on the front door. It was a bloke called Adams who was working on the Twins' case.

'"Hello Joey, I want to talk to you."

'"What do you want?"

'"Get in the car." He grabbed me and took me over to a waiting car. I knew it was going to be about the Twins.

'"I suppose you've heard about McVitie," he said.

'"What about him?"

'"Well, the Twins have done him and we've got them in the nick for it."

'"I thought you had them for fraud, I don't know anything about a murder charge."

'"Well we now know that they did him and we wondered if . . . well, we wondered how you feel about it. They've done McVitie. He was a pal of yours . . . so we were wondering if you can give us any help."

'I looked across at Adams and felt disgusted by what he was suggesting to me. I managed to control my temper, but only just. "Listen. Whatever I think about whatever has been done, and however I feel about it, that's my affair. I'm not going to tell you anything."

'"So, you're not going to help us then?"

'"No fucking way."

'"OK. Well I suppose we'll just have to do them for fraud."

'"You do whatever you have to." And with that I got out of the car and went back into the club.'

With the senior members of the Firm behind bars, Read found several others willing to come forward and give evidence or turn grass. They tried to turn every member of the Firm.

Albert Donaghue had been told by Ronnie Kray that he alone would have to take responsibility for the Firm's earlier murder of Frank Mitchell. Donaghue had initially refused to talk to the police but then changed his mind and named Freddie Foreman as the killer.

Faced with the prospect of years in jail, many others decided to co-operate. Billy Exley, who had helped the Twins run some of their long firm frauds, was one of the first to agree. Scotch Jack Dickson, and even the Krays' own cousin Ronnie Hart, both of whom had benefited considerably from their association with the Krays, also agreed to help the police. The move resulted in their being hated throughout the East End. Hart later attempted suicide.

The trial of the Kray twins opened at the Old Bailey on 7 January 1969. There were eleven men in the dock and court officials tried to hang placards with numbers around the necks of the defendants so that the jury would be able to tell who everyone was. Everyone in the dock objected strongly but none more so than Ronnie Kray, who tore his up shouting 'This is not a cattle market'. The court eventually relented, giving jurors a plan of the dock with all the names marked instead.

The trial was split into two sections: the first dealing with the murders of George Cornell and Jack McVitie, the second with the murder of Frank Mitchell. Further charges relating to fraud and assault were left on file to be heard at a later date.

The Kray twins received life sentences for the first two murders, while their brother, Charles and their top henchman, Freddie Foreman received ten years each for their parts in helping cover up the McVitie murder. Their fortunes changed in time for the trial over the murder of Frank Mitchell: both the twins and Foreman were acquitted. Ironically Donaghue, who had turned grass in order to avoid taking the rap for Mitchell's death, was sentenced to two years for being an accessory.

'I kept right away during the trial, I didn't go near the Old Bailey the whole time. That would have been asking for trouble. They had been confident but I think we all knew they were going to go down and get the sentences that they did. It didn't come as a surprise.

'With hindsight, it might seem like it wasn't that clever of them to stick around in London when they knew the net was closing in, but I don't think they ever saw it that way. I always knew they were going to stick around and face the music.

'The Twins never talked about going on the run or anything like that because they didn't think they had anything to hide. If they had tried to go somewhere, they would have found it impossible. They could not go somewhere and try to live as Bill Jones and Tommy Jones and get jobs as window cleaners or something stupid like that. They had to be themselves. They would always have to be Reggie and Ronnie Kray. They couldn't have been anyone else. The only way it might have worked is if they could have gone to different places, but there was no way they could live separate from each other, at least not by their own choice. Ronnie would have been useless at hiding out anyway. He would have spent his whole time phoning up all his mates in London and asking them to go out and see him. It would never have lasted.

'The question that people always ask is who replaced the Krays – who took over? But you can't answer that because there was nothing to take over. Nothing changed in London when the Twins went away, not one thing. The simple fact is that there has never been anybody running London. There have been stronger and stronger people doing this and getting involved in that, but no one actually running it. So there was no gap that the Twins left for anyone to move in and fill. They were just doing their own thing.

'Every now and then I read a book or see something in a newspaper where people are talking about the Kray empire. What fucking empire? They went into prison without a pot to piss in and died pot-less. The only money they ever had came from the books and the films and the documentaries. They never made any real money out of crime, only out of everything that happened afterwards. They ran lots of things and used lots of things but they never actually owned anything in their lives – not a car, not a club, not even a fucking house. At the end of the day, they were two blokes who lived in a council flat in Hoxton with their mum. If you're looking for an empire, that's all you're gonna find.'

9. 'I HATE YOUR FUCKING GUTS. I HATE EVERY FUCKING BONE IN YOUR BODY. I HOPE YOU DIE OF FUCKING CANCER. YOU'RE A SLAG AND I FUCKING HATE YOU'

It should have been a simple job. Five south London gangsters had travelled up to Blackpool with the intention of robbing a jeweller's shop on The Strand of at least £100,000 of gems.

The plan was to wait for a quiet moment, run in, brandish a few guns to show they meant business, grab the loot and then head back to London a.s.a.p. Not being from the area, there was no chance the gang would be recognised and the local police would have little to go on. That was the plan, but it all went horribly wrong.

During the raid on 23 August 1971 the shop manager managed to set off an alarm and the gang was forced to run for it with only a few handfuls of jewels. Police arrived on the scene in time to see the gang making their escape and followed. As the five men split up, other officers joined in the chase.

Superintendent Gerald Richardson, the head of Blackpool Borough Police and a man not afraid to get his hands dirty despite his rank, caught up with a man called Freddie Sewell and wrestled him to the ground. As they rolled about on the pavement, Sewell pulled his gun from the waistband of his trousers and shot Richardson twice at point blank range. 'He was too brave,' Sewell would say of the officer later.

Sewell made his escape and hid out in London, and for a while it seemed that every police officer in the capital was looking for him and that every major gangster south of the river was suspected of hiding him. Joey Pyle was top of the list.

'I'd been expecting them to come and search the house. The Flying Squad were looking for Freddie everywhere and anyone who knew him was getting a visit. It finally happened early one morning, eight or nine of them were outside the house and came steaming in. One of them, he had this fat gold ring with HH marked out in diamonds on his finger, showed me a warrant. "My name is Sergeant Harry Hannigan and we're looking for Freddie Sewell and we've got a warrant here to search for jewellery that was stolen in the raid in Blackpool." I knew it was a load of old bollocks but I had no choice but to let them in.

'They started going through the house, pulling everything apart and all the time saying, "Where's Fred? Where's Fred?" and after about half an hour of this I've had it up to here so I say listen you lot, I've fucking had enough of this shit. I don't know where he is, and even if I did know where he is I wouldn't fucking tell you. And I guess that was when they decided they were going to fit me up.

'They went out and looked in my car, but didn't find fuck all because there was fuck all there. Hannigan came back over to me and said he was taking me down the station. The missus was in the house the whole time and they said to her that I wouldn't be long. I knew it was true – I hadn't done fuck all and they hadn't found fuck all so obviously I was going to be coming home.

'They were supposed to be taking me over to Tintagel House, where his squad was based, to see Commander Bill Mooney, but they stopped off at Wimbledon station on the way. They stuck me in a cell while they all got washed up and had a bit of breakfast, because it was still ridiculously early in the morning at this time. And while I was in the cell they were still going on and on. "Where's Fred? Where's Fred?" and I just kept telling them to fuck off. Then I got taken upstairs into one of the interview rooms, where Hannigan was waiting for me.

' "OK Pyle, this is your last chance. Where's Sewell?"

' "I've told you before and I'll tell you again. I don't know, and even if I did, you'd be the last person I'd tell."

' "And that's your last word on it?"

' "Yeah, that's all I'm saying."

' "Well I've got news for you Pyle, you're nicked as from now."

' "How can you do that?"

' "Conspiracy."

' "What fucking conspiracy?"

' "Conspiracy with unknown persons to commit robbery on an unknown date at an unknown place."

' "How the fuck are you gonna make that one stand up."

' "Easy, we found a gun, pickaxe handles and ammunition in the boot of your car during the search."

'I couldn't believe what I was hearing. I was furious. "You did what? Well where are they then?" Hannigan flicked a glance at his watch. "I'll have them there in an hour. Until then, you're going back in the lock up."

'They put me back in the cell and slammed the door shut. I was pacing back and forth, trying to calm down. I honestly thought they were just winding me up, trying to put the frighteners on me, but it was a joke. It's the kind of thing they did with kids, not grown men. After an hour or so, Hannigan came down to the cells to see me.

'He started saying something or other but I just cut him off. "Don't fuck me about, I'm not a little boy. Why don't you stop with all these fucking silly games? I don't know where Freddie is, I ain't got a fucking clue."

'But all Hannigan said was that they were going to charge me. They put me in a holding cell and in the corridor I could hear the typewriter starting to go. And people were saying things like "how do you spell his surname?" and "what's his date of birth?" They were filling out the charge sheet and I was thinking, fuck me, they're serious about this.'

Joey was held overnight and the next morning he was released on bail, thanks to the magistrate who happened to be a close neighbour and knew him well enough to be satisfied that there was little risk in giving him his liberty.

After six weeks on the run, Sewell was caught. He had been betrayed by underworld colleagues who had been unable to resist the vast reward on offer for information leading to his whereabouts. But despite this development and it being clear that Joey had no link to Sewell's flight from justice, the charges against Joey remained and he knew he would eventually have to go to trial.

Then a few weeks later, Pyle was visited by a young reporter working for the *Sunday People* newspaper. The paper had run a story the previous year naming the main pornographers operating in Soho. That in itself wasn't news, but the *Sunday People* alleged that the reason they were able to operate so freely was because they were all involved in corrupt dealings with members of the local vice squad.

The allegations were true. At the time pornographers, including the likes of Frank Mifsud and Bernie Silver, would vie each other to see who could provide local detectives with the best tables at posh boxing and charity events. Wally Virgo, the senior CID commander, and Detective Chief Superintendent Bill Moody were alleged to have received regular payments for turning a blind eye to what was going on. Virgo took payments of £2,000 per month, with an extra two grand thrown in at Christmas.

Another player was a man called Jimmy Humphreys. He had come to the porn business late, having seen the profits that were there to be made in it, and successfully penetrating into the normally closed world. Along with his wife, Rusty, he was soon taking massive profits out of three clubs. To ensure few raids took place on his premises, Humphreys, according to his own diaries, had paid out around £53,000 to Virgo and Moody in the space of just six months.

In addition they and their junior officers had been treated

to cars, holidays, clothes and jewellery for their wives and girlfriends. Humphreys and the others never complained – their profits were high enough to pay the bribes and it was more than worth their while when it came to safeguarding their business. So that the vice squad could be seen to be doing its job, the pornographers even put forward the occasional mug, who would be arrested and portrayed as a Mr Big and take the rap for dozens of crimes, leaving the rest of Soho in peace for a few more weeks.

The *Sunday People* had run a story suggesting that many of the vice squad detectives were corrupt and that there were equal problems elsewhere, including on the Flying Squad run by Commander Ken Drury. An internal inquiry had been launched after the allegations and each of Soho's main pornographers had been interviewed; all but one denied that they had ever paid any money over to the police. The only one who refused to say anything was Jimmy Humphreys, who had refused to be interviewed altogether. He told the officers in the inquiry that his solicitor had recommended he say nothing, though in truth it was actually the corrupt officers on the force who had advised him to exercise his right to remain silent.

As 1971 began to draw to a close, the *Sunday People* decided it was time for a second bite of the police corruption cherry. The word on the street was that Pyle had been fitted up by the police good and proper and had the bang needle. A young reporter called Bill Thompson figured it might be worth approaching Pyle to see if he could help out with another case where someone had been framed.

'This bloke came over to the house and told me he was digging around and trying to find bits and pieces that would help me in my cause. He said he knew it was a fit up and that it was diabolical what they had done to me. Then he told me about another case. Ken Drury had fitted up a kid called Patsy Murphy with a murder charge over a killing that happened during a robbery on a post office in Luton. Patsy was the son of Stevie Murphy, who was a good pal of mine and also a pal of Johnny Nash. We all knew that the boy had nothing to do with the murder – it had been one of the other people in the gang, who had got off scot-free after turning grass. The reporter wanted to know if I knew anything about Drury because his paper was keen to try and get the lad off. "If there's anything you can think of, anything at all, then let me know because we can get this bastard," he said.

'At first I couldn't think of anything that might help and we were just chatting away about this and that, but then something popped into my head.

'"Well, he was in Cyprus the other week on holiday, I know that."

'"Oh yeah, who did he go with?"

'"Jimmy Humphreys."

'It just came out of the blue, and bang, that was that.'

On 27 February 1972 the *Sunday People* splashed the story that Commander Drury and his wife had recently returned from a holiday in Cyprus where they had been guests of a certain Mr Jimmy Humphreys. Drury immediately tried to wriggle his way out of trouble: he admitted going to Cyprus but denied that he had been a guest of Humphreys. He had paid his own way. Furthermore, despite the fact that he had taken his wife with him, it was far from a holiday. He had actually gone there in search of escaped train robber Ronnie Biggs, following up a tip that he had been seen on the island.

At first Humphreys supported him, but then Drury was suspended from duty and served with disciplinary papers. Drury then sold his story to the *News of the World* and, as part of his confessions, claimed that Humphreys had been a top police informer. Humphreys, keen to avoid certain death, or at the very least a good hiding as a result of the ultimate gangland betrayal, hit back. And, unlike Drury, he had the paperwork to back up his claims.

Humphreys made his own diaries public and showed that he had met Drury on no less than 58 occasions, and had paid in full for the entire Cyprus holiday. In fact, Drury and Humphreys had enjoyed so many good lunches and diners together that Humphreys had felt obliged to buy the Commander an exercise machine to help him lose the excess bulk.

In the meantime the newly established Serious Crimes Squad had started looking into the world of West End porn. Just as they began their probe, Peter Garfath, the lover of Rusty Humphreys, was given a severe beating at the Dauphin Club in Marylebone. Rusty had been in Holloway prison for a brief sentence over a firearms offence and the attack was said to have been a warning to Garfath not to resume his relationship with the woman.

The attack spurred the police team into action. Silver and Mifsud left the country, only too well aware that their entire businesses were likely to come crashing down and that, without the support of the police, they had been left horribly exposed. Humphreys himself fled to Amsterdam on a false passport but was arrested in December 1973.

Jailed for the attack on Garfath, despite protesting his innocence, Humphreys realised he had little left to lose. He made a series of statements implicating 38 detectives and quoting from his damming diaries, in which he had kept virtually every last detail of his dealings with the corrupt officers.

In February 1976 Drury, Virgo and Moody were arrested, along with nine other officers. Drury was taken from his home with a blanket over his head.

It was the biggest scandal to hit the police in decades. 'A good police force,' commented a sardonically dry police commissioner, Sir Robert Mark, 'is one which catches more criminals than it employs.' Of the 74 officers investigated, 12 resigned, 28 retired, 8 were dismissed and 13 were jailed.

But it didn't end there. A few years later, during an appeal against a conviction for the shotgun murder of the sub-postmaster, disturbing evidence emerged. A man who was originally charged with the murder had the charge withdrawn when he agreed to turn Queen's Evidence. The man had then received £2,000 in reward money from the post office. The money had been paid following a recommendation by the officer leading the investigation – Ken Drury of the Flying Squad. It was an allegation that would eventually uncover a massive abuse of the police informants' fund but, most importantly, Patsy Murphy, who had been convicted of the killing in the Luton post office, won his appeal and was released.

'That was the reason I did it, just to help Patsy out on the murder charge. I had nothing against Jimmy Humphreys, but he wouldn't help out so I felt something had to be done. I knew Humphreys well and I certainly wasn't out to do him any harm. I'd been over to his house many times, and quite often Drury had been there. It was no secret among the chaps. But I didn't want to do him any harm and it didn't. The thing he went to prison for was nothing to do with anything that I had said.

'Years later the story would go around that I was so pissed off about being fitted up with the guns over the Sewell stuff that I spilled the beans on Drury out of revenge, but it was never like that. It was just to help a friend get off a murder charge. But once that was done, I still had to face court over the guns and pickaxe handles they said they had found in my car.

'I hadn't been entirely sure what Hannigan's motives were, but it was only a matter of time before I found out. I was working on my car site in Peckham one day, about a week after I'd been arrested, when one of his minions came into the office.

'"I've got a message for you from Hannigan. He said he'll take a few quid and get you out of this. Six grand should do it."

'"You fucking what? Why should I give him any fucking money? The bastard fitted me up. Now he wants paying to get me out of it? It's a fucking liberty."

' "Hey, don't shoot the messenger. I'm just telling you what he told me to tell you."

' "So how do I get hold of him then?"

' "Well they're still holding your passport right? Phone up Tintagel House and speak to him, telling him you need your passport back. That way he's got a reason to come down and see you. Otherwise, because it's his case, he can't talk to you or be seen meeting you. Then you'll have a chance to sort it out."

'Now the only problem with the set up was that my passport was out of date, so there was no reason for me to ask for it back. I'd already applied for a new one. But I was so angry, I decided to use the situation to my advantage. I wanted the chance to tell Hannigan exactly what I thought of him and what he was doing. And I wanted everyone to know.

'I was too angry to speak to him there and then so I got my brother to call him and set up a meeting for the following day. I got my mate Terry Marsh to drive me over and all the way there I was rehearsing what to say to him in my mind. I knew I was taking a risk – they could have locked me up for it – but something inside me said I just had to do it.

'We got to his office and Terry waited outside while I went in and asked for Hannigan. A few minutes later he came down in the lift with another copper and a bunch of papers under his arm, including my passport. The reception area was full of people milling about – prying eyes were everywhere – and Hannigan was doing his best to make it look like a legitimate meeting.

' "Hello Joey, here's your passport," he said, loud enough for all those around us to hear. "That's what you came for isn't it?"

He held it out in his hand but I refused to take it.

' "I don't want it. I've just got one thing to say to you before you say anything."

' "What's that Joey?"

' "I hate your fucking guts. I hate every fucking bone in your body. I hope you die of fucking cancer. You're a slag and

I fucking hate you. And as for money, you're not going to have a fucking penny off me you fucking slag."

'Hannigan's face fell. He looked absolutely furious. He threw my passport at me, got me to sign for it and then ushered me out.

'As I walked back to the car, my chest was puffed out with pride. I felt so good about myself for having had the courage to say all that to him. It was better than having hit him on the chin. Fucking lovely.'

'Everyone knew I'd been fitted up over the weapons charges, but a lot of people said I should just take it as my innings. "Well Joe," they'd say, "what about all the things you've done in the past that you've got away with and got out of. This just makes things even."

'But I don't look at it that way. Imagine if you're a decent bloke and you go down the pub every night, have a few beers then get in your car and drive at a hundred miles an hour down the motorway, and you do this night after night. Then one night you don't have a drink and you drive at seventy but a copper nicks you, says you were doing a ton and that you were pissed. Would you accept it because the night before you were drinking and speeding? Would you fuck, you'd fight like anything. And that's just what I did.

'I knew that if I was going to accuse the police of corruption, the first thing I had to do was make an official complaint. If I didn't, the jury would think I had something to hide or was just saying anything to get out of it. I had to prove I was serious and willing to see it through.

'When they had charged me, Hannigan still hadn't managed to get his hands on any moody weapons, but he decided to go ahead anyway. In the statement I made to the complaints officer, I made sure that was one of the points I got across: "At no time when I was at the station was I ever shown a gun or pickaxe handle." In my mind, that proved beyond all doubt that the whole thing was a set-up. Surely if they had really found them in my car, they would have had them there and then.

'As I was out on bail I decided to make myself busy. I went to the offices of the Church of Scientology and took a lie detector test which the reporter Bill Thompson had arranged. I passed, of course, but my barrister, Ivan Lawrence, told me that such tests were not recognised by the British judicial system, so I'd never be able to use it in court. I told him not to worry and that somehow or other, I'd find a way to work it in.

'The first time I saw the gun they were fitting me up with was when we got to court. There it was in the middle of the exhibits table, the biggest gun I'd ever seen in my life, some enormous Japanese-made thing. Once I clapped eyes on it, I knew we were in for a bit of fun. According to Hannigan's statement, he had seen the weapons in the boot of my car, placed the gun in his pocket and then put a pickaxe handle under each arm. I knew Lawrence was going to have fun with this one.

'"Mr Hannigan, is that the same suit you were wearing on the day you raided Mr Pyle's house?"

'"Yes it is."

'"The exact same suit?"

'"Yes, it was this exact same one."

'"In that case, will you put the gun in your jacket pocket the way you did when you took it from the boot of the car?"

'"Yes, certainly."

'So Hannigan took the gun and put it in his pocket, but it was so big and heavy that right away it tipped over and fell out, landing on the floor with a huge crash. So Hannigan tried again and it fell out again. After that he was trying all sorts of things to keep it in place – putting it in sideways and slantways and backways and frontways, but no matter what he did, the gun kept falling out of his pocket. In the end, everyone in the jury was in fits of giggles. We'd won the first round: we'd proved that he was the one lying.

'It didn't take long for Lawrence to score another point. When I had been given bail the morning after my arrest, one of the conditions was that I had to surrender my passport. They took me from court to a police station across the road and said I'd have to wait there until my ex went home and picked up my passport.

'She was just about to leave when Hannigan stopped her, called over one of his sergeants and told him to go with her, whispering something in the man's ear before he left. I didn't think anything of it at the time – I just thought Hannigan was making sure she didn't get up to any funny business – but by the time the case came to trial, his actions suddenly became far more significant.

'Once Hannigan had finished giving his evidence, Lawrence called the sergeant into the box.

' "On the day Mr Pyle was given bail, his wife went home to fetch his passport and you went with her. Is that correct sergeant?"

' "Yes."

' "Why was that then? Was she under arrest?"

' "No."

' "Then what was the reason?"

'There was a long pause; a painfully long pause. The sergeant pulled out a handkerchief and mopped beads of sweat from his brow. Lawrence finally filled the void. "Did you just go along for the ride? Did you maybe think she wasn't coming back to the police station? After all, she wanted Mr Pyle to be released so it was more than likely that she would have got back as quickly as possible. Don't you think that would be the case?"

' "Yes, that would be the case."

' "Then why did you go?"

'The sergeant kept sweating but couldn't speak. He was choking on his own silence. Lawrence continued.

' "There must have been a reason. When you got to the house, where were you?"

' "Sitting in the back of the car."

' "And what happened then?"

' "She went into the house, got the passport and came back out."

' "Did she give the passport to you?"

' "No, she kept it. She took it to the station and handed it in there."

' "So you just sat there and watched all this?"

' "Er . . . yes."

' "Why?"

'Once more, the sergeant fell silent. Now was the time for Lawrence to play the winning hand.

' "I'll tell you why. When you and your colleagues framed Mr Pyle, you didn't decide on the details until you got back to the police station. That was when you decided to say that the weapons had been found in the back of his Mercedes car. You and your colleagues wrote your notes but then realised that none of you had made a record of the car's registration. You all wrote your notes anyway and left a gap. The reason, sergeant, that you went back to Mr Pyle's house that day was to see the car wasn't it?"

'The sergeant said nothing. He didn't have to. The second lie had been proved.

'The night of my arrest, my brother had gone over to the house and borrowed my car. When the sergeant arrived it was nowhere to be seen, which was why every single set of notes submitted by the police in the case had a gap left where they were going to fill in the car details. It was crystal clear that everything in the case was going my way, so that's when the police decided to start playing dirty.

'The following day they called a surprise witness: a uniformed inspector by the name of Smithson, who happened to be the custody officer of the police station where I had been charged.

'Now this was more than eighteen months after the event and there is no way on earth that the inspector could have possibly remembered anything about that night. It was one thing saying that a bunch of detectives were corrupt, because in those days it was widespread and everyone knew they were at it. But uniform coppers were a different kettle of fish. They were still thought of as *Dixon of Dock Green* characters and if you put one before a jury, you just knew they were going to believe every single word he said.

'I felt almost sorry for the inspector. He'd only been served with the papers the night before and was just going along with whatever he was told. The prosecutor, a man called Taylor, started his questioning by establishing what would soon become undisputable facts.

'"Mr Smithson. When you charged Mr Pyle, where were the weapons?"

'"They were right by the side of me," said the Inspector, indicating with his fingers. "The pickaxe handles were there and the gun was right there. And then I charged Mr Pyle."

'Now I knew I was fucked. They were going to use the statement I had made to the complaints division, even though it was supposed to be confidential, to show that I was a liar. If I told the truth – and Smithson was the one who was lying – then I'd turn the jury against me for sure. I had to think on my feet.

'Half an hour later I was back in the witness box facing Taylor, who was holding my statement in front of him with a look of glee in his eyes. I could tell he really thought he had me by the bollocks.

'"Mr Pyle, you heard the evidence of Mr Smithson so now let me ask you, did you see a gun or a pickaxe handle when you were at the station?"

'"Yes I did."

Taylor paused, taken aback for a moment, then continued.

'"I see. And where were they?"

'"They were right on the side of the table when the inspector charged me."

'"Very well. Then let me take you back to the statement you made soon after your arrest in support of allegations of police corruption."

'He started reading through and got to the bit where I had said that I had not been shown anything in the station.

'"Is that correct Mr Pyle?"

'"Yes it is."

'"But a few minutes ago you just said . . ."

I interrupted. "Don't get me wrong. Obviously I saw the gun and the pickaxe handles. I mean, they were right there on the table. But no one actually showed them to me. You see, I've left two words out of my statement. What I should have said was that I wasn't shown them 'for explanation', you know, no one said 'do these belong to you?' or anything like that."

'Taylor's face bulged and flushed red. If he hadn't been in court I'm sure he would have been swearing like a trooper. Instead he said nothing, threw my statement down on the floor in disgust and sat back in his chair, fuming.

'The following day I finally got a chance to mention the lie detector test. Taylor was back on the attack, going over some of the other bogus evidence and I was denying everything he was saying. Then he turned round and called me a liar.

'"I'm a liar am I?" I said. "Well let me tell you something – I took a lie detector test and I passed and I challenge every police officer on this case to take the same test . . ."

'The judge cut me off: "Mr Pyle. We'll hear no more of this. Members of the jury, discharge that remark from your minds, ignore it."

'"I'm sorry your honour," I said humbly. "I didn't realise I couldn't mention it."

'"Well you do now . . ."

'"It's just that how else can I let the jury know that I'm telling the truth . . ."

'"Mr Pyle! I said no more."

'After that I didn't have to mention it again. Despite what the judge had said, I knew the jury had it in their minds. I'd got the point across.

'The only other ace up my sleeve was the explanation about why all this had happened in the first place. Taylor was on his last legs when he finally asked me why on earth Hannigan would want to fit me up.

'"For money," I explained. "Mr Hannigan asked me to go down to Tintagel House on a pretext so that he could get six thousand pounds of out me. I met him there and I told him in front of a number of witnesses: 'Money, I would not give you one penny, you are nothing but a crooked copper', or words to that effect."

'"But surely, Mr Pyle," said Taylor, "the real reason you went to meet Mr Hannigan that day was because you needed to get your passport back."

'"But that's just my point," I replied. "I didn't need to get my passport back. It had expired. It was out of date. It was of no use to me whatsoever. Why would I want it back? He just wanted me there to get money from me."

'It was the final nail in the coffin as far as the police were concerned. Out of the corner of my eye I could see the jury nodding to themselves, agreeing with me, and I knew we'd won it.

'During his summing up, the judge said that if the jury acquitted me, not only were they saying that every one of the police officers who had given evidence had committed perjury, not only were they saying they were liars but they would be saying the officers on the squad had gone stark raving mad.

'Half an hour later the jury came back with a unanimous verdict: not guilty.'

A few months later Harold Hannigan was found guilty of trying to bribe a Sussex detective. He was given a conditional discharge and advised by the judge, Mr Justice Melford Stevenson, to see a psychiatrist.

'There is never a dull moment in the underworld. When you're not fighting the police, you are fighting among yourselves.

'A few months after the case had finished I was heading off to Monte Carlo to see a fight between Carlos Monzon and

Rodriguez Valdez, so I had had my friend Terry Marsh drive me to the airport. He took me out in the morning and a couple of hours later I was sunning myself on the beach and having a well-earned rest.

'When I got back to the hotel there was a message waiting for me, asking me to call my brother urgently: "Joey," he said when I got through. "Mad Ronnie has killed Terry Marsh."

'I couldn't sleep or anything after that. I came straight back the next morning and went round to see Terry's wife. I felt so sick, so sorry for her. She had three sons and the fact that they had lost their dad almost broke my heart. But at the same time it was hard to take sides because they were both my pals. I was more on Terry's side because he was the one who got killed, and I thought Mad Ronnie had taken a fucking liberty doing that, but I liked Ronnie and it was hard to think too badly of him.

'Later that day the law came to see me, looking for Mad Ronnie. They knew he had done it. Apparently what had happened is that after dropping me off at the airport, Terry had driven down to a car front in Tooting and seen Mad Ronnie. They started having an argument – a stupid argument. It was jealousy. Ronnie couldn't understand why I'd asked Terry to take me to the airport instead of him. They were like two kids in a playground fighting over which one teacher liked best. Then they started fighting, Ronnie pulled out a knife and did for Terry.

'The Old Bill asked if I knew where Ronnie was. "I'll tell you what," I said. "I hope you get to him before I do because when I see him, I'll fucking kill him. What he has done to that poor woman, Terry's wife, I'll fucking do him for it. When I see him it will be him or me. Either I'll be dead and he'll be doing life for it or it will be the other way round."

'Two days later Ronnie gave himself up and I found myself going round to see his wife, Maureen, as she was in a right state. I felt sorry for her and she felt sorry for Terry's wife. Although Ronnie was still alive, Maureen knew she'd lost him for good.

'A week or so later, Maureen rang me up.

' "Joey, you'd better come round quick."

' "Why? What's happened?"

' "It's Ronnie. He's dead. He's topped himself in his cell in Brixton. And the police are gonna do you for it."

' "Me! What the fuck has it got to do with me? How am I supposed to have done it? He's been in prison for fuck's sake."

'Maureen explained that Ronnie had taken an overdose of pills but they were not ones that were available in the prison hospital, meaning they must have been smuggled in from outside. The police had been looking around for someone with a motive and then they remembered what I had said when I'd seen them about killing Mad Ronnie if I ever got my hands on him.

'I was incredulous, and really worried. And Maureen must have been worried too. That night she went down to the police station and gave herself up. It turned out that she had smuggled the pills in to Ronnie, sewing them into the lining of a jacket that she had handed over when he asked for a change of clothes.

'Ronnie had decided that he couldn't go on living, knowing what he'd done to Terry and Terry's wife and family. He had pleaded with Maureen to help him and she had finally agreed. Even the police felt sorry for her – they didn't even charge her in the end.

'I was in the clear, but in the space of a fortnight, I'd lost two close friends.'

10. 'SO WHAT IF I'M SITTING HERE DRESSED LIKE THIS. THERE AIN'T NO LAW AGAINST IT. WHAT ARE THEY GONNA DO? ARREST ME?'

In the 1970s, long before anyone had heard of a crack house, and when the idea of pitched battles in the streets between teenagers armed with machine guns seemed ridiculous – even in America – cocaine meant only one thing: glamour.

Unlike today, when cocaine can be found in every club bathroom and its crack derivative in every ghetto, cocaine was the exclusive domain of the rich. Film stars, rock musicians and the aristocracy were the only ones who could afford it, and taking the drug meant buying into the lifestyle. Celebrated in songs like 'Cocaine' by Eric Clapton and by the comments of men like Robin Williams, who famously once said: 'Cocaine is God's way of telling you that you're making too much money.'

In those days prices were sky high. Just a few grams of high quality cocaine were worth several thousand pounds. You could make a fortune simply by bringing back no more than you could fit into a cigarette packet. For those who were prepared to take the risks, and knew enough wealthy people who wanted to buy the goods, it was a licence to print money.

Joey Pyle had little interest in drugs. He had shunned the fashion for pill popping during the 1960s and the snorting and injecting that followed sickened him still further. But despite this, Pyle, along with an American friend of his called Bob, soon cottoned on to a way of making money.

'I'd spoken to a couple of guys that I vaguely knew, Colin and a mate of his, Jonathan, and offered them the chance to go over to Bermuda and bring some of the stuff back. They were mad keen.

' "How much do we need to put in?" asked Colin.

' "The stake is fifteen grand."

'Colin whistled through his teeth. That was a lot of money back then but they knew they would be able to make ten times that when they got the stuff back. "OK," said Colin. "We'll do it."

'I didn't know Colin well and I didn't particularly like him. In fact, I thought he was a bit of a mug. But he liked the idea of making easy money and was more than eager to come out and get into the business.

'Colin and Jonathan were to head there first and settle into a hotel. The idea was that they would look like a couple of legitimate holiday makers having a week-long break rather than a couple of dodgy businessmen spending only a couple of days in the Caribbean. Doing it that way meant they were far less likely to be stopped on the way back.

'Bob and I flew out a couple of days later and got there late at night. It had been a long flight and we went straight to our hotel room and collapsed on the beds. A few minutes later there was a knock at the door and Colin and Jonathan came strolling in.

'They were both in the early stages of what would go on to become heavy tans, were wearing identical white towelling jackets with "MEMBERS ONLY" stitched on them and sea captain hats. They were grinning like Cheshire cats and sipping from oversized cocktails complete with little umbrellas.

' "Hello boys," said Colin. "Nice to you see you. It's lovely here. We're having the time of our lives. Is everything all right for . . . for our little bit of business?"

'Bob nodded weakly – we were both exhausted. "Yeah, everything's sweet, no problem. Tell you what, we're going to have a quick bite to eat and then get our heads down. Why don't we all meet down by the pool tomorrow morning, say 10 a.m.?"

'The following morning we woke up feeling refreshed and, after a light breakfast, got ready for our meeting. Bob dressed up in a smart but casual linen suit while I just pulled on a few old bits and pieces and told him I'm meet them all downstairs.

'From the foyer of the hotel I could see Bob, Colin and Jonathan lying on some sun loungers catching a few rays and discussing the day's business. I came out looking like a typical Brit abroad. I had black trousers pulled up halfway up my calves, boots with no socks, braces and a white vest. I flopped down in the nearest sun lounger. All my tattoos were showing and the only thing missing was the knotted handkerchief on my head.

'The Yank looked over at me. "Hey Joey, I don't think you should have come down here dressed like that."

' "Why not?"

'He nodded towards the far end of the pool, where a couple of men in suits were sitting at the end of the bar sipping mineral water and glancing around. "You see those two guys there, I think they're FBI. I think they're watching us."

' "Well fuck them," I said. "We ain't doing nothing wrong. So what if I'm sitting here dressed like this. There ain't no law against it. What are they gonna do? Arrest me? Fuck them, I ain't doing nothing."

'At the first mention of the FBI Colin's ears had pricked up, and by now he was sitting up on his lounger trying to signal to me to keep my voice down. His sense of ease and relaxation had completely vanished and he was on the edge of a full-blown panic.

' "Joey, Joey I think he's right. You stick out like a sore thumb dressed like that. Everyone's staring at you. We won't be able to get away with nothing. Go on, go and get changed."

' "Get changed? How am I supposed to get changed? This is all I brought with me."

' "Jesus Joe," said Colin. "You're gonna get us all nicked." He reached into his jacket pocket, pulled out his wallet and counted out a handful of notes. "For fuck's sake go down the shop and get yourself some new gear."

'I came back half an hour later with my own MEMBERS ONLY jacket and sea captain's hat like the others. We looked like some kind of cabaret act.

'We headed off to make the deal and the first order of business was for Colin to hand over the money. Being a British Colony the island had branches of Barclays, and Bob took the cash and made a deposit then called his brother back in England. Half an hour later the money was taken out of a branch in Notting Hill and Bob was given the go ahead to hand over the drugs.

'He left the three of us sitting in a little café – any excuse to get out of the heat of the noonday sun – and went off to meet his dealer. He came back half an hour later with a smile on his face, tapping the pocket of his jacket. We shifted to a corner of the café and turned our chairs into the corner so that none of the other customers could see what we were doing.

'Bob then pulled out a little plastic envelope stuffed with fine white powder and handed it to Colin. He examined it closely and passed it to Jonathan who did the same.

'"Should we test it or something?" asked Colin.

'Bob shook his head. "I'm telling you, my supplier is first rate. This is absolute top quality; you won't find anything better than this, not even in fucking Columbia."

'"But shouldn't we test it? I could have a line and still make more than my money back."

'Bob reached for the packet and ran his finger along the heat sealed end. "Take some if you want but I wouldn't advise it. You see that seal, if you break that then you reduce the value by half. People ain't gonna pay top dollar if they think it's been tampered with. That seal is the guarantee of quality."

'Colin scratched his head then looked at Jonathan, then at me then back at Jonathan. "I think we'll take it back as it is."

'We then had an early lunch and headed back over to the hotel to check out and get back to England. Bob was keeping hold of the powder in his bag and the plan was that he would hand it over on the plane. That way if there were any problems leaving the country, Colin wouldn't be caught up in them.

'We ordered a cab and sat in the lobby of the hotel enjoying the air conditioning and one last cocktail. My back was to the entrance and all of a sudden, I noticed Colin start to tense up. I slowly glanced back over my shoulder and saw that a police car had pulled up outside. I looked back at Colin. "Relax, I don't know what they're doing here, but it ain't gonna be anything to do with us." Bob nodded in agreement. "Just stay cool, everything is going to be fine."

'There were two policemen in the car, both well over six feet tall with large handlebar moustaches. They came into the lobby and started looking around. It was pretty clear that they were searching for someone.

'"Jesus," gasped Colin.

'Now I was getting worried. "For fuck's sake don't look at 'em. Just relax."

'We all tried to stay cool but I could see that even Bob was on the verge of breaking into a sweat as the two officers started striding in our direction and tapped Bob on the shoulder.

'"Excuse me sir," said the first policeman. "We need to see you down at the station." Bob's mouth was so dry he was having trouble swallowing as he tried to ask what they wanted to see him about. The copper was in no mood to give out any details. "Sir if you don't come with us voluntarily, I am afraid that I will have to arrest you."

'Bob shot up onto his feet like a rocket. "No, that's OK. I'll come. I'm coming right now."

'The bag with the drugs was sitting on the coffee table right in front of us. I could see Colin eyeing it nervously. Then the policeman saw it. "Is that your bag sir?" he said to Bob.

'"Er." Bob looked around at the three of us, hoping perhaps that one of us might claim it as our own and keep him out of even more trouble. "Er . . . yeah, it is."

'"Then you'd best bring it with you."

'It was all too much for Colin who suddenly jumped to his feet. "Now look here officer, what do you want this man for?"

'The policeman looked round. "Do you know him Sir? Is he a friend of yours?"

Colin slowly sat back down again. "Oh no, no, I was just having a drink with him. I don't know him at all. I . . ."

'The first copper looked over at his colleague. "Take their names." Then he pushed his face closer to Colin's. "This man is wanted in connection with a very serious offence – a very bad traffic accident that took place last month. Were you in the vehicle at the time of the accident?"

'The expression that suddenly developed on Colin's face was a strange mixture of relief and concern. Relief that the arrest was nothing to do with the drugs, but deep concern about what was going to happen to his investment.

'A few minutes later, Bob was being frogmarched to the waiting police car and the three of us were watching him and his bag of precious cargo being taken away.

'As the car vanished into the distance, Colin turned to me. His eyes were starting to water. "Joey, what are we going to do?"

'"Well I don't know about you two but I'm getting out of here like fucking greased lightning."

'"What about our money?"

'"Fuck your money. That man's going to get twenty years when they find that stuff in his bag. And if we're still on the island then we're going to be right up shit creek."

'Colin and Jonathan were shitting themselves all the way to the airport, and didn't dare so much as draw a breath until the plane had landed safely back in London.

'Two days later I gave Colin a call. I explained that Bob's bag had been searched and – surprise surprise – they had found the drugs. Bob had managed to get himself released on bail and was certain that he could get the charges dropped if he could put out a few bribes.

'At the other end of the line I could hear Colin start to choke. "You what? He doesn't expect to get any more money off us does he, you must be kidding."

'"Well where else is he going to get it from? He said he's going to call your office at two o'clock tomorrow. He needs another ten grand to sweeten everyone up. He reckons we owe him because he kept stumm about the deal. I'm gonna send him three grand but it's not going to do much unless you two put up the same amount."

'"No way," said Colin. "There's no way he's getting any more money from us."

'"Well, I don't know what to say. He's going to phone anyway so I guess I'd better come over to your office and take the call."

'The next afternoon I get to their office in plenty of time. Colin and Jonathan are as adamant as ever that they are not going to pay any money. But Colin doesn't want a confrontation. Colin tells me that when Bob calls I should say that he got called away on business and that only Jonathan, who had little say in what was going on, was around.

'Bang on two o'clock the phone goes and it's Bob. I put the phone on speaker and tell him that only Jonathan is around but that Colin has refused to put up any more money.

'"Listen Joey," says Bob. "I guess I don't expect any less from those two stinking motherfuckers, those two lousy stinking motherfuckers, but you Joey, you are a man of your word. You're not like those two dirty stinking motherfuckers. I can't believe you're doing this to me."

'"I ain't doing nothing, Bob. I'm sending you the money. I'll send you three grand as soon as I put the phone down. You mark my word, you'll get the money from me no problem. Never mind what the other two do, I'll do my bit."

'"Will you Joey?"

'"Yeah, as sure as eggs is eggs, I'll send you mine."

'"Hey thanks Joey. You're a real pal. And somehow I'll get the rest of the money. I'll get it from somewhere else if those two lousy stinking dirty motherfuckers ain't gonna help me. You wait till I get my hands on those stinking lousy dirty motherfuckers. God help them . . ."

'I put the phone down and turned to Colin and Jonathan. "Well there you are. You do what you want to do but I'm gonna send him the money. And when he gets back he will come and see you and I guess you'll have some explaining to do."

'Colin and Jonathan moved into a corner of the room and started whispering to each other. I couldn't hear what they were saying but a few minutes later they turned back to me. Colin's face was grey and pallid. He looked like he had been given the worst news in the world. He couldn't bring himself to speak so Jonathan did the talking for him. "Joey. We've had a talk about it and we feel bad. We want to help Bob. We're going to give you another six grand."

'It was Colin who had come up with the idea of trying it again. The only way he could see of making his money back was to go out and bring back an even larger consignment of cocaine. And if he was willing to put the money up, then we were more than willing to take it off him.

'But this time was going to be different. The main change was that I would not be able to go out to the island. Colin explained that me dressing so badly on that first day had brought them bad luck during the whole trip. "I know Bob is your friend," Colin explained, "but the only way I'll do this is if you don't go anywhere near it."

'Colin was determined that nothing would go wrong second time around. He arrived on the island and told Bob that he would have to accompany him to meet his supplier. Colin wanted to get his hands on the drugs as quickly as possible and then ensure they remained in his possession the whole time.

'The two of them drove to a remote farmhouse in the middle of nowhere and Bob took Colin's cash and then got out to collect the goods. He arrived back a few minutes later and handed Colin a small parcel. As Bob started driving away Colin found it hard to hide his glee. He held the parcel out in front of him, staring at it intently, saying to himself: "I've got it, I've got it now."

'They're shooting along the main road, heading towards the hotel and everything is going brilliantly. The next second, a police car appears behind them and switches on its sirens. Bob, still playing his part to perfection, starts to panic. Colin freezes with fear and doesn't know what to do. Then Bob grabs the parcel and throws it out of the window of the car. Colin is speechless with shock but doesn't have time to react – the police car is right up their arse and Bob has to pull over.

'The coppers get them out of the car at gunpoint and after a few minutes, one of them comes up with the parcel. "We saw you throw this out," he says. "We think it contains drugs." Colin is almost fainting as the coppers tell him to hand over his passport and copy down all the details. The cops then take a note of where the pair are staying and tell them not to leave island for a couple of days while they carry out an investigation.

'When they get back to the hotel, Colin is ranting and raving. "Well that's just fucking wonderful ain't it? We're fucking skint now and we're going to spend the rest of our lives in some fucking jail."

'Bob tries to calm him down. "Look, don't worry. We're gonna be fine. I got out of this before and I'll get out of it again. All we need to do is get some more money together. How much do you have on you?"

'Colin hands over everything that is left in his wallet and Bob tells him to stay put while he tries to sort things out. He goes out of the window and slips down the fire escape and off into the night.

'Five hours later there is still no sign of Bob and Colin is getting decidedly restless. He has his passport and a ticket, which he knows he can change, so he decides to get out while the going is good. He spends a couple of hours sleeping rough in a local park and, because he can't afford money for the taxi, he has to walk to the airport. He gets to the airport in the early hours of the morning and sees Bob walking through into the first class section. Bob is all loaded down with presents and duty free and looking as fresh as a daisy. He's obviously spent the night at some other hotel using the last of Colin's money.

'Colin starts screaming "You bastard, you fucking bastard", and runs over, planning to get his hands around Bob's neck. Only Bob is going into first class and Colin only has an economy ticket so they won't let him through.

'He's ranting and raving all through the flight and all the way home.

'The whole thing was, of course, a massive con trick. Bob and I had set the whole thing up to relieve Colin and Jonathan of as much money as possible. The plastic envelope – the one they daren't open because it would lower the value – contained nothing other than ordinary household baking powder. And the policemen who came to arrest Bob on the motoring offence were friends of his who were happy to join in on the con for a few quid.

'There had been no arrest and no need for bail or bribes. All we were doing was taking advantage of the naïveté and greed of people in the early days of the drug trade. The con worked so well that we actually did it several times and it worked like a dream. But in the case of Colin, he was such a good mark that we couldn't resist the temptation to do it all over again.

'Colin got back to London just as furious as ever and called me up. "Joey, I need to see you. We've been ripped off."

'I go around to his big house in Surrey and he tells me the whole story: the farmhouse, the packet of drugs, the chase and seeing Bob at the airport. "We've been conned. The first time was a con and this second time just proves it."

'"No, can't be. It's just bad luck."

'"I'm telling you Joey, he's had us over."

'"I can't believe it."

' "It's true. We've been had. He's taken my money and he's taken your money too."

' "Well if that's the case, then he's gonna pay for what he's done." And with that, I leave.

'Bob came over to my place the next day and we talked about the best way to get out of it all. In the end I told Bob to ring Colin there and then and tell a story. "What you need to say to him is that you were walking down Putney High Street with your wife and all of a sudden you see me. I come running over, ranting and raving, and hit you on the chin. Your wife starts screaming, there's shopping all over the place and you're well pissed off. Tell him that you're not standing for it.

' "Then this last bit is the most important. Say to him: 'If that's your attitude, if you gonna put the boys on me, then just remember one thing. I know where you live but you don't know where I live.' And make sure those are your last words to him before you hang up."

'So Bob picks up the phone and dials Colin's number:

' "What's your idea getting fucking Joey to come after me?"

' "Well you conned me out of my money, you deserve it, I want my fucking money back."

' "And that's why you've put a heavy on me?"

' "That's right."

' "Well Joey chinned me in Putney High Street earlier."

' "Fucking good job. Give me my money or it will get worse."

' "Well I'm going to tell you something now –"

' "What's that then?"

' "I know where you live, but you don't know where I live."

There was a pause.

' "What do you mean by that?"

' "You know what I fucking mean by that." And Bob slammed the phone down.

'Two minutes later my phone rings. It's Colin.

' "Hello Joey, er . . . I hear you whacked Bob."

' "Yeah, down the high street. Gave him one on the chin."

' "Oh right. Well he's just called and said that he knows where I live but I don't know where he lives. What do you think he means by that?"

' "Oooh. You be careful. What he's saying is he could do you and you'd never be able to get him back."

'For a moment or two there was silence on the other end of the line. I could almost hear Colin thinking through the implications. Finally he spoke. "I'll tell you what Joey, leave him alone for a while; keep away from him. Will you do that for me?"

' "If that's what you want Colin, that's what I'll do."

'And that was the end of it. From that day on, it was all forgotten.'

11. 'HE NEVER SAID ANYTHING, BUT BEFORE THE FIGHT, I COULD TELL HE WAS COMPLETELY GONE'

In the history of professional boxing, there has never been a more complete fighter than Joe Louis, the Brown Bomber. His punching power with either fist was easily equal to that of Jack Dempsey or Mike Tyson, his hand speed was right up there alongside Ali and Patterson while his left jabs, left hooks and right crosses were as devastating as those of Sonny Liston, Lennox Lewis and Joe Frazier.

'No one could put their punches together as beautifully as did Louis,' says renowned sports writer Monte Cox. 'He threw every punch in the book with textbook perfection, the jab, the hook, the cross, and the uppercut. He placed his punches with waste-less accuracy to vital points; to the heart, across the liver, behind the ear, under the floating rib, to the chin. His punches were short, often travelling only inches, yet they landed with jolting power.'

In a record 25 title defences, 21 were won by knockout, and 17 of those were 10 counts! He also knocked out five men who held the Heavyweight Championship of the World. From 1934 to 1949, when he first retired as champion, his record was 60-1, with 51 KOs. He held the World Heavyweight Championship for a record twelve years.

Hype Igoe, a boxing writer and historian, in the 1941 February issue of *Ring* magazine, stated: 'It has been my contention that had Louis always fought with a rush (as he did against Schmeling), none of his opponents would have gotten out of the first round.' Louis was indeed a devastating puncher with either hand. Commenting on Louis's power, Jimmy Braddock said, 'It ain't like getting hit with a punch. It's like someone nailed you with a crowbar!'

Pyle recalls, 'Joe Louis has always been my idol right from when I was a little kid. In fact when I was young I didn't think he was a real person. To me he was like Superman. All I ever saw were pictures of him and bits of film. When I realised I was actually going to meet him and shake him by the hand, well, it was one of the most exciting moments of my life.

'It happened in the late 60s and a man called Robbie Margolis, who was running the Pigalle club, had brought him over to be the handshaker and greeter. The Pigalle was one of the clubs Johnny Nash and I were looking after so we were in there on a regular basis and got quite pally with him.

'We spent a lot of time talking about all his old fights. I'd seen most of them on the telly and old bits of newsreel but it was incredible hearing about them right from the horse's mouth. He told me about the fight he had with the Englishman Tommy Farr and how easily he had beaten him, and about his fight with Billy Conn where he'd hit the guy on the chin so hard that he'd lifted him off the floor.

'There were no such things as video recorders back in those days, but Joe had brought over a load of old cine films of his fights. I had a couple of mates who were locked up in Broadmoor – Roy Shaw and Mad Ronnie Fryer – and I knew they were having a hard time because I used to go in and visit them regular. When I got to know Joe well enough I asked if he would come along and show some of this films. He said he'd do it willingly.

'I let the governor at Broadmoor know and they got really excited about the idea of a genuine celebrity coming to visit. The day came and I drove over to Joe's hotel to pick him up. He was in the shower so I sat in his suite with Robbie Margolis while we waited for him to get ready.

'Robbie started telling me that, even though Joe was well into his sixties he still had a massive sexual appetite, and also the biggest cock he'd ever seen. We were laughing about it, then Robbie called out: "Hey Joe, who was the best lay, Lana Turner or Ava Gardner?" Louis had had affairs with them both and got into massive trouble as a result. America in the 1940s was not too happy about the idea of mixed-race relationships.

'Louis came out of the shower with a towel wrapped around him and a huge grin on his face. "Gee man, that Lana Turner, she had a wild body I'm telling you." Then Robbie grabbed the towel away and there was this big thing hanging down, almost touching the ground. We all just fell about laughing.

'We left for Broadmoor and on the way down, Joe was asking me for the names of my friends who were inside. He wasn't very good with names and didn't want to get it wrong. "Just remember Roy and Ronnie," I told him. "There's no point in trying to remember their last names as well. Just go for Roy and Ronnie."

'We arrived to find the place had been turned into a media circus. There were television cameras and press photographers everywhere. The governor, a bloke called Tom Sands, was over the moon to be making the headlines for all the right reasons, and posed for his picture with Joe at every opportunity. It took ages before we finally got inside and we were lead into a large room where they had a set up a projector specially.

'All the chairs had already been lined up. In the first two rows there were all the prison guards, doctors and home office officials. Behind them were all the male patients and behind them all the female ones. They called Joe up to give a speech and introduce the films and everyone started clapping.

'"Ladies and gentlemen, before I go ahead, I'd like you to put your hands together for the people responsible for having me here today . . ." and as he spoke you could see all the people in the front two rows all puffing their chests out, getting ready to take the credit. Then Joe continued. "Let's hear it for Roy and Ronnie, let's all give Roy and Ronnie a big hand. Stand up Roy and Ronnie."

'Of course Joe didn't know them from Adam, but Roy and Ronnie stood up and all the officials had to turn around and start clapping them. And the governor and all the invited guests. And they didn't like that at all.

'Then Joe said a few words before showing the first film. I will always remember what he said and so will everyone in Broadmoor, because the governor found it so moving, he wrote it down and made it into a little plaque which he then hung on the wall. Joe said: "When I was boxing I had a trainer called Artie Blackburn and when I reached the championship of the world he took me to one side and said Joe, I have taught you all I know, the rest is up to you. So all you people in here, the doctors have helped you as much as they can, the rest is up to you."

'When the films were over Tom Sands took me and Joe down to his local pub, mainly so he could show him off to all his mates. The day was a big success and I knew that Roy and Ronnie, as well as the others, really appreciated what Joe had done for them.

'A couple of weeks later Tom Sands turned up at the Astor club with a couple of Assistant Commissioners from the prison service. Sands was making out that he and Joe Louis were really good mates and he was keen to prove it by introducing him to his colleagues.

'I sat him down and had a quick chat, asked if they wanted a couple of girls sitting down with them because we had a whole bunch of girls working in the place that night. But Sands was all "oh no, no, no" and very straight because he was supposed to still be on duty. But that didn't stop them wanting a drink so I got them a bottle of scotch and had a couple of glasses with them.

'In the meantime, I had called Joe and got him to come over from the Pigalle to say hello to Tom and the others. By the time Joe had to leave, Tom was half pissed. "Where are these girls you promised us then?" He was starting to loosen up pretty quick and I realised the time was right to find out the truth about how my friends were doing.

'"Mad Ronnie is all right, I can help him," Sands told me. "But Roy Shaw is a different kettle of fish. The man is a rebel.

He's got to learn to calm down a bit, to cool down otherwise he's not going to make it."

'I asked what kind of things Roy was getting up to, and Sands elaborated. "Well if a screw tells Roy to walk up the wall, he's got to walk up that wall. He can't keep rebelling and fighting all the time. I'm telling you Joe, they have got him down on the punishment block the whole time and they are pumping him full of drugs. They are giving him injections of the strongest drug there is every four hours because it's the only way we can control him, the only way we can stop the violence. But if he carries on the way he is going, he is going to die. The drugs are going to end up killing him. If something doesn't change, he'll be dead in a month."

'I knew that if I could get to see Roy, I could talk some sense into him, tell him how desperate the situation was and get him to clean up his act. Prisoners who are being held on the punishment block – at Broadmoor they call them the Dungeons – are not normally allowed visitors but Sands, feeling that he owed me something of a favour, agreed to make an exception.

'The only way to do it, he explained, would be for the visit to take place well outside normal visiting hours, where there would be only a skeleton staff on the premises. And whoever it was would have to be personally escorted by Sands. The idea was that it would look as if Sands was giving a close friend a tour of the facilities.

'The only problem with that was that I was far too well known. If any of the staff or other inmates saw me – a well-known face – wandering around Broadmoor in the middle of the night, it would lead to a huge scandal. Instead I decided to send Sulky, a little Jewish fellow who was the owner of the Astor.

'Sulky arrived at Broadmoor just after 11 p.m. and was taken right to the Dungeons. When he got there Roy was sitting in total darkness. It had become his habit that every time the door to his cell was opened, he would rush out and attack any screws he could find. When the door popped open Roy started charging but thankfully, even in his drugged-up state of mind, he recognised Sulky. The confusion made him stop in his tracks and almost immediately he started to calm down. Sulky explained that I had sent him and that if he wanted to get out of prison, I could help but only if he started to behave himself.

'Incredibly, that one visit did the trick. The next morning Roy had cleaned up his act as best he could and started behaving a little better. Within the space of a few days he had been let of the block and back into the main part of the prison. Within the space of a few weeks, he was off the drugs completely, and eventually got himself transferred out of Broadmoor altogether. Roy always says that I saved his life and in many ways I think I probably did. We had always been good friends but the whole Broadmoor incident meant there was a special bond between us that could never be broken.'

'In the early part of 1975 Roy was finally released from prison and I decided to surprise him by driving up to Long Lartin jail in Worcestershire, where he was being held, and picking him up. Only, when I got there, I'd missed him. It turns out they'd let him go half an hour earlier than they were supposed to and he had made his own way back to London.

'I knew he'd turn up eventually and, sure enough, the following day, he came over to the car site in Peckham which I was running with my brother. I gave him an old Jag to drive about in and asked him what money he had and how he was going to live. He told me he had a little flat in East Ham which he had been letting out to his sister and that he'd be moving back in there. He had a couple of grand stashed away but that was it and he knew it wasn't going to last long.

'"So what are you gong to do with yourself Roy?"

'"Well Joey, the only thing I knew how to do is fight, so I'm gonna fight. I'm gonna get back in the ring."

'This was nowhere near as simple as it sounded. Roy had always been one of the chaps but had never been on any of the firms. He had made his living as a thief on the pavement and it was while doing a blag that he had got caught and sent to prison for eighteen years. He was a hard man and very well respected. He even became friendly with the Krays.

'Before he had got put away, he had been fighting as a middleweight, weighing in at around eleven stone. He was being managed by Mickey Duff and fought under the name of Roy West because he could not get a licence from the British Boxing Board of Control in his real name because he had a couple of earlier convictions.

'Second time round he couldn't get a licence in any name because his age was against him. He was as still as strong as an ox and in prime condition. While inside he had broken down two prison doors from the inside and that takes some real doing. But Roy was 41, and that was simply too old for the legitimate fight game to allow him to take part.

'I was keen to help out if I could and we tried to find ways to get around the age limitation, but to no avail. Then, before I knew what was happening, Roy told me he was going up to a gypsy horse fair in Barnet, close to where he lived, because he knew they usually had bare-knuckle matches on there. He explained that he was going to challenge them to fight him and win a few quid by betting on himself.

'Roy got to the fair and had a couple of quick little scraps that netted him around three grand in winnings, but after that, just when he was getting warmed up, none of the others were up for it. They had realised who he really was and after that, they all said that there was only one man who would take him on – Donny "The Bull" Adams, the so-called King of the Gypsies.

'Adams was no mug. A teetotal, non-smoking, hard-faced mauler, he was a powerful fucker who had a top reputation among the gypsies. He was going around scrap metal yards challenging people to fights and coming away with stacks of cash every time. He had fought his way right across England, Scotland and Wales and in 48 bare-knuckle bouts he had never once been defeated.

'Roy had heard of Adams and came back to me after the fair to ask if I could get hold of him to make a match. Although I'd never met Adams myself I knew of his reputation and through my contacts it didn't take long to track him down. Adams was well up for fighting Roy but as I was setting things up, it suddenly occurred to me that if Roy was only really doing it for the cash, there might be a way that both he and I could make some serious money.

'Instead of just putting the fight on in a caravan site or scrap metal yard with a crowd of people gathered around, I decided to make the whole thing much more professional and make a real event of it. I booked a field on a farm and set the whole thing up so there would be beer tents, pony trek racing and the fight would be the highlight of the day, all for ten quid a ticket.

'Although we were going to have a proper ring set up, that was more about making sure everyone was going to have a good view of the action. The fight would still be bare knuckle and Roy and Donny were to fight stripped to the waist wearing army boots and long trousers. Kicks, head butts and elbows would all be allowed. There were to be no rules, no rounds and no referee – it was simply a fight to the finish. And that's just how both men wanted it. Within a couple of weeks, the first thousand tickets had sold out and I had another batch printed up, which were proving every bit as popular.

'But then the law got involved and fucked it all up. I knew they would be getting wind of the fight and would try to stop it, but I thought I'd allowed for that. We'd had hundreds of tickets printed which had on the address of a farm but the fight was actually going to be taking place somewhere else. We were going to have a group of lads standing on the corner of the road that led down to the farm and every time a car showed up, they would stop them and give them direction to the real venue. But the police had got wise to the plan.

'A few days before the fight was due to take place we were called in to see the Chief Constable of Essex. He told me in no uncertain terms that he didn't give a fuck where the fight took place as long as it wasn't anywhere in his jurisdiction. He knew about both the real and the fake venue and said that both would be flooded with officers who would come down so heavily on everyone there that I'd never make a penny.

'There was no time to find another venue so I told Roy we had no choice but to call the whole thing off, at least for the time being. We spent the next few days telling as many people as we could that the fight had been postponed, but on the day hundreds of gypsies still turned up at the old venue. ITN news were there too and they filmed all these blokes going mad, ranting and raving and screaming about they money they'd spent on their tickets and wondering what the hell was going on. At first I was worried but then I realised that all the publicity was making the fight seem even more important. The build-up was huge and more people than ever wanted to be a part of it. It made finding a new, bigger venue more crucial than ever.

'Everywhere I tried I heard the exact same thing. We can't put on the fight unless it is governed by the British Boxing Board of Control. And of course there was no way that was ever going to happen because of Roy's age. The buzz about the fight continued to build and in the end the police decided to take some pre-emptive action to kill the whole thing dead. They arrested Roy and Donny Adams and charged them with breach of the peace.

'It turned out to be a huge mistake. In October 1975 the two men appeared before a magistrate at Hereford court. Donny Adams stood up and told the magistrate that whatever he did, he could not stop him and Roy Shaw having a fight. "This fight will take place," he explained. "It might take place in a park where innocent people might get hurt but it will take place. We had hoped that by staging it in a ring we might be able to make it safer but now that has been denied to us."

'Then it was Roy's turn to speak. He explained that when he was in Borstal and had the needle with someone, he was told the best way to sort it out was to get into a boxing ring and have a fight with the other person. Then the police stood up and said that they had no choice but to act because it was illegal for any fighter not to wear gloves or to fight without a time limit.

'I guess the magistrate must have been an old soldier-type because, though he bound them over to keep the peace for a year, he said that as long as they wore gloves, had proper rounds and a referee, then they could fight each other and, although it would be unlicensed, it would definitely not be illegal.

'That was just what we wanted – an official sanction that with a few minor adjustments, the fight could take place. I got hold of Billy Smart, explained the situation and soon had his agreement to put the fight on at his Big Top in Windsor, the winter quarters for his circus.

'The Press had been covering the case ever since the first venue had been abandoned. I was quick to recognise the value of free publicity and was more than happy to talk to journalists about the preparations for the bout. Roy preferred not to talk – he just wanted to concentrate on his training – but he was more than happy for the press to come and watch him work out. Donny had also been busy, giving interviews to different tabloids about how he was going to do this and that to Roy. None of it ever bothered me – Donny was a game fucker but my Roy was gamer.

'The only thing Roy had missing was a nickname. Donny was "The Bull" but Roy was nothing. In the end it was down to a journalist, who noted that Roy was a bit of a handsome fellow, to come up with the tag that would stick with him for the rest of his life: Pretty Boy.

'Officially, there was going to be a referee, the fight was to be split into ten rounds and both fighters would be wearing gloves and observing the Queensbury Rules. Privately, I had other plans. I knew the police would be there in force, but they had already agreed to stand right at the back of the tent rather than take seats away from paying customers. The idea I came up with was to have all my mates – big lads each and every one – down at ringside and, on my signal, for them to stand up and link elbows. Once that had been done, two or three rounds into the match, Roy and Donny would take their gloves off and finish the fight bare-knuckle style. By the time the police got down to the ring and managed to break through, the whole thing would have been over. Not only was I going to make good money and put on a great fight, I was going to have one over the Old Bill as well.

'The day of the fight finally arrived and the atmosphere in the Big Top was absolutely electric. The place was packed to the rafters with thousands of top faces and gypsies, who had all paid up to thirty pounds for their tickets.

'The place was filling up nicely when I came across my first crisis. The bloke I had asked to be the referee had not showed up. Without him, the police would step in and stop the fight right away. Then I saw a friend of mine, an ex-boxer called Ray, who was making his way to his seat.

'"Ray, Ray, come here, I want you to be the ref."

'"The ref? But I've paid thirty quid for my fucking ticket."

'"That don't matter. You can be the ref. You'll see it better from inside the ring anyway."'

In his dressing room, Roy 'Pretty Boy' Shaw was raring to go. Like a finely tuned racing car waiting for the green light, he was fitter and stronger than ever and more than ready to unleash his awesome power the second he stepped into the ring.

'Roy had stopped training three days before the fight to concentrate on building up his anger and aggression. It had clearly worked and as we stepped out into the Big Top and made our way down the steps to the centre the crowd went wild and began baying for blood. But Roy stayed completely focused on the task in hand.

'The moment the bell rang, The Bull rushed at Roy, snarling and full of hatred. Roy saw the attack from a mile off and smashed his right fist into The Bull's chin, full force. The blow knocked the gypsy down to one knee and Roy followed up with lefts and rights.

'Donny slumped to the floor and Roy kicked him in the ribs then lifted him up so he could hit him some more. He dragged him to his feet, laid him over the top rope and hit him again and again and again. By now The Bull was out cold, but you could see from the look in Roy's eyes that he wasn't going to stop until he had killed him. Jumped on The Bull's head a couple of times until the referee and the marshals managed to drag him away.

'My elaborate plans to turn the event into a good old bare-knuckle scrap had all been for nothing. The fight had been over in a matter of seconds.

'The whole place was going crazy. All of Roy's fans were standing on their seats, clapping and cheering, while The Bull's mob was screaming at him to get out. All the gypsies had put their money on Adams and now they were out of pocket. It was only a matter of minutes before the first challenges started coming in. Having seen off The Bull, all the hard men wanted to have a go at Roy themselves.

'In the days after the fight I must have had half a dozen people coming forward but we had to be careful. The purse for the fight with Adams had been split evenly because they had support on both sides and were seen as an even match. If we let just anyone fight Roy then all we'd be doing is giving them a good pay day. They would make far more money fighting Roy than they would anyone else.

'In the end we decided to set out terms. Any fight that took place would be on a winner-takes-all basis and the challenger would have to guarantee to sell a certain number of tickets. And that's just what happened. The next two or three fights were all with gypsies and Roy just knocked them all over, no trouble at all.

'At first, I hadn't seen anything beyond a single opportunity to earn some money by matching up Donny and Roy, but it quickly turned into something far bigger. Before that fight, there was no such thing as unlicensed boxing or unaffiliated bouts. If you weren't with the British Boxing Board of Control, your only option was to go and fight gypsies at horse fairs. But then the thing really took off and everyone wanted to be part of it. From former boxing stars that had had their licences taken away to wannabe sporting heroes after their fifteen minutes of fame in the ring, the scene flourished.

'Pretty soon it wasn't just Roy fighting; there were dozens of others wanting to have a go too. Roy would be top of the bill and his bout would be the highlight of the evening's entertainment, but there would be a whole programme of unlicensed fights to precede it. Along with Roy and Alex Steen, a businessman with whom I had started promoting fights, I'd gone and invented a whole new sport.

'During those first few contests there had been hardly any rules, but as the business grew so we brought out a few regulations, mainly to ensure we stayed on the right side of the law. Fighters were under strict instructions to wear their gloves at all times and to start or stop boxing every time the bell rang. There were proper referees, trainers, seconds and timekeepers. It became a good way of earning a living, though never a licence to print money. At the end of the day you had to sell seats and fill the places otherwise you were gonna be fucked.

'Roy fought a few more gypsies and other fighters before I lined up the match that all London had been waiting for: Roy against Lenny McClean. Back then McClean was a young lad, some twenty years younger that Shaw, and had been travelling up and down the country and having bare-knuckle fights at horse fairs.

'Lenny had been eager to get involved in the unlicensed side of things ever since he saw a poster advertising Shaw vs Adams. He apparently pointed at the pictures of the two men and boasted to a friend: "I could do both of them in one night."

'Lenny was originally out of Hoxton and mentioned to Roy Nash that he wanted to make a fight with Shaw. Roy mentioned it to me but I'd never heard of McClean and thought nothing more of it until a young fella called Frank Warren and his brother Bobby turned up at the office me and Alex Steen had in Piccadilly.

'Frank was mad keen to get a foothold in the world of boxing and saw fixing up a fight between his man and Shaw as the way to do it. He sat down and explained that McClean – he called him Lenny Boy – wanted to challenge Shaw and asked if we were interested.

'I almost had to laugh. I told him I'd never heard of his fighter and that I had all sorts of people – boxers, bouncers and doormen – lined up all the way to Glasgow wanting to fight Roy because of the money they could make. "If Lenny was a professional boxer he would have to work his way up the ranks," I told him. "He'd have to prove himself and have twenty or thirty fights before he was ready for the big time and big money. Just because this is unlicensed, it doesn't make that part of it any different."

'But Frank insisted he could sell heaps of tickets and that McLean had more than enough of a following and reputation to make it a fight to remember. In the end I agreed on one condition: the bout would be winner-takes-all. Frank agreed and the fight was on.

'As I arrived at the venue in Croydon a couple of months later with Roy and his entourage, I could see that Warren had kept to his part of the bargain. Virtually every seat in the place was filled and, having seen a few fights from lower down the bill, the crowd were eager to see the main event.

'There had been masses of publicity in the run-up to the match. McLean had been telling the papers that he was going to rip Roy Shaw's head off and that the old man was past his best – no match for his youth and strength. The tale of the tape certainly looked to put things in McLean's favour: he was twelve years younger, four stone heavier and six inches taller. But, as always, I had total faith in Roy.

'Now, if you read Lenny's book, *The Guv'nor*, he says that I stitched him up by making him wear a pair of gloves that were too small. That's not true. To make sure no fighter can claim his opponent has any kind of advantage, boxers always wear identical gloves. The gloves Lenny wore were small on him, but then Lenny had hands like bunches of bananas. The same gloves fitted Roy perfectly and even though Lenny was still complaining just before the fight started, there was nothing I could do. It just wouldn't have been right to give Lenny bigger gloves and that's just the way things go.'

'The bell sounded and both men rushed towards each other. McLean smashed Roy right on the chin but Roy didn't even blink, he just started pounding McLean in the belly, trying to make him double up. Then McLean started playing up to the crowd, calling Roy names and laughing at his punches: "Look, he can't hurt me." But Roy kept up the onslaught and by the end of the first round, McLean was puffing hard and staggered back to his corner.

'In the second round, Roy managed to wedge McLean into a corner and landed punch after punch on the big man's chin and belly. Roy put him under so much pressure that McLean didn't land a decent punch during the whole three minutes. But, to give him his due, he soaked up the punishment while Roy was in danger of wearing himself out.

'But when Roy is in the ring, there is only one way he can go – forward. So when the bell went for round three Roy was all over McLean like a rash, connecting with solid lefts and rights that eventually started having an effect.

'McLean's face opened up, blood all over the place, then Roy hit him with a right to the head that made him stagger back onto the ropes. Roy followed up with a wide left and a right. McLean was now exhausted and demoralised. The only thing keeping him up were the ropes and he knew if he went on, he'd end up being knocked out for the first time. "I've had enough," he mumbled, and the referee raised Roy's hand in victory.'

Despite his complaints about the gloves, Lenny admits that Roy was simply the better man on the night. In his own words: 'I don't want to make excuses and I don't want to take anything away from Roy . . . I've got to hold my hand up. I wasn't fit – I was used to the damage I could inflict with my bare knuckles inside the first minute. The gloves didn't help but I let myself down by not being ready.'

'As the unlicensed scene got bigger and bigger, so we started to attract even bigger names. There was an American boxer by the name of Ron Stander, who had built up an incredibly impressive track record culminating in a World Heavyweight Title bout against Joe Frazier. Stander had little respect for British heavyweights – at the time the best known were the likes of Henry Cooper and Joe Bugner, good fighters but no match for the top Americans of the day like Ali. He had heard about the unlicensed scene and decided that a trip over here would be a chance to pick up some easy money.

'The match took place at Ally Pally and everyone thought Roy had bitten off more than he could chew. In the first round, Roy hit Stander with some hefty shots right to the chin but Stander didn't even budge – this was a man who could really take a punch.'

As Roy himself said later: 'I punched Roy Stander harder than I have ever hit anyone in my life . . . It didn't matter what I threw at him, I couldn't hurt him. He just laughed.' It was only when Roy started working the body that he managed to get a reaction. By the third round, the end was near. Stander went down for two counts of three, and then Roy got him with a hard right in the stomach which sent him reeling back onto the ropes. Ten seconds later the referee waved his hand and Stander was out.

'As soon as the fight was over, Lenny McLean jumped into the ring from nowhere and challenged Roy to a return match.

He'd had a few more fights since the pair had last met and won them with impressive form. It was the match every fight fan in the country wanted to see and it didn't take long for us to make the deal.

'Roy had nothing to prove by fighting McLean a second time but just couldn't resist it. The problem was he didn't take it seriously enough. He didn't do his usual amount of preparation and didn't even do any extra training. He had been making more money that he knew what to do with and success after success had made him over-confident and lazy. On the way to the bout he had picked up a bottle of liquid ginseng and knocked it back, thinking it would give him an energy boost. In fact it did the opposite, making him sluggish and lethargic, as weak as a kitten.

'I remember being there in the dressing room and thinking that Roy didn't look his usual self. He never said anything to me about having taken anything, and he wouldn't have done because he knew I would have been annoyed. But before the fight, I could tell he was completely gone.

'You can see it on the video. The fight starts and Roy goes out in the middle of the ring but when McLean comes towards him, he just sort of falls forward. And then bang, McLean sticks his left jab out, boxing him very smartly, very neatly. Roy gets caught on the chin and that was it. Game over.

'When Roy came round, he wanted to carry on. He didn't think he had been counted out, just that the ref had decided to stop it and he was saying "no, no, let me carry on". But we had to break it to him that the fight was finished. Roy hadn't been hurt physically, but his pride had been dented and he had lost the title of "Guv'nor of London".

'When I saw Roy go over that night, the first fight I ever saw him lose, I felt sick inside. But that's how the boxing game is, it's just one of those things and you have to accept it. In all there were three fights. After the last one Roy was keen to face McLean again but for a whole host of reasons, it never came off.

'Years later I got to know Lenny properly. He turned out to be a really decent bloke and even jumped through all kinds of hoops in order to come and visit me even though I was an AA category prisoner. Another time when I was inside he gave my ex some money to make sure she would be all right over Christmas.

'At the time I was promoting the fights, he was the enemy but it was never personal, that was just business. At the end of the day you are always going to get differences between two boxers and, like Roy and Lenny, they are always going to end up running each other down. But Lenny McLean was a decent man right until the end. I never found any wrong in him. His kids should be proud of their dad.'

12. 'WHAT'S ALL THIS YOU'VE BEEN SAYING ABOUT ME?'

In the early months of 1967, the renowned film director Ken Loach had just begun casting his next project, *Poor Cow*, a gritty story of working-class London life, when he walked into a pub and spotted a tall, powerfully built man with a menacing but charismatic grin.

The man was John Bindon, a taxi-driver's son born in pre-gentrified Fulham and in and out of trouble all his life. During his infancy his mother used to force him to crawl under the kitchen table so he would be out of the way while she went about her business. With little love and affection in those early days, it was little wonder that Bindon developed a vast propensity for violence and destruction. 'Ever since I was a kid, I've had this overwhelming urge to smash things up,' he once said.

At the age of eleven, he was charged with malicious damage. A few years later he was sent to Borstal for possession of live ammunition and stealing a car. Still in his teens he served two more terms – one for car theft and another for living off immoral earnings. After leaving school he found undemanding and unsatisfying work laying asphalt and plucking pheasants and in the antiques trade until the chance of a better life walked into one of his regular drinking dens. Ken Loach, noted both for his use of amateurs and his ability to elicit stunning performances from them, spotted Bindon and immediately decided that he was 'absolutely right' for the film.

Bindon had only recently been released from a 21-month sentence, which he had served at Maidstone prison for attacking three Scots with a broken bottle. While there he had become friendly with none other than 'Mad Axeman' Frank

Mitchell who, in turn, had introduced Bindon to his good friends the Kray twins.

Loach's instincts proved spot on and *Poor Cow* was a huge critical and commercial success. Bindon soon won other film roles – alongside Michael Caine in *Get Carter*, as a drug dealer in *Quadrophenia* and in the company of James Fox and Mick Jagger in *Performance*.

During the 1960s the worlds of show business and crime were closely linked. The Kray twins, who would soon become friends with Bindon, were partying with the likes of Judy Garland and actor Roger Moore. Bindon sought out more work as an actor but maintained close contact with his underworld friends. He went on to appear in *Z Cars*, *Softly Softly*, *The Sweeney* and the slick private-eye crime drama *Hazell*, always as a bad guy. Being typecast never bothered him, though he often expressed a whimsical desire to 'play a priest sometime'. His new-found notoriety also brought him into contact with an ever wider circle of acquaintances.

'I'd heard that John Bindon had been bad-mouthing me. It was never clear exactly what he was supposed to have been saying but it was something along the lines of "who the fuck does that Joey Pyle think he is?" – something like that. Something that seemed to suggest I was getting too big for my boots.

'I sent out a message for him to come and see me. I figured if he had something to say he should say it to my face. At the time I had a nightclub that I was looking after in Garratt Lane. I got a message back telling me that Bindon didn't want to come down the club because he "didn't know if he'd ever get out again". But that didn't satisfy me at all, so one night I went out looking for him.

'I eventually found him in a club called the Britannia which was close to the Chelsea football ground. I went over to him and pulled him over to one side of the room.

' "What's all this you've been fucking saying about me?"

' "No Joey, I don't know what you mean. I ain't been saying nothing. The only thing I've ever said is that I'd like to be your pal."

'And from that day on, that's just what he became. John and I respected each other. I knew that he could handle himself and he knew the same about me. From my point of view, he was a lovely bloke. I never saw no wrong in him.'

Joey wasn't the only high-profile gangster to become friends with Bindon. The Kray twins became great admirers of his, as did the likes of Flash Harry Hayward, of Mr Smiths fame.

'The Twins had a lot of respect for John. One time there was a fella in Fulham who had pulled a bit of a stroke on the Twins. They got in touch with John and he did what he had to do in order to resolve the matter. That was the kind of relationship he had with the Twins.'

But there was another side to the new social circles Bindon was moving in. While acting in *Performance* he met the Honourable Victoria Hodge, daughter of the baronet Sir John Hodge, who was then working as a model. At the time she was dating the highly suitable Ian Heath, son of a glass magnate, but this did not stop her plunging headfirst into a passionate affair.

Five months later, Heath proposed and Hodge accepted. She spent her pre-wedding night with Bindon, who even attended the service, walking along by the Bentley that carried her away through the King's Road traffic.

The marriage did nothing to halt the affair but slowly, a darker side of John Bindon began to emerge. His deep-rooted propensity for violence and voracious appetite for other women began to override his charm. By the mid-70s Hodge had begun to fear for her life. Once, when she accused Bindon of being afraid of his father, he picked her up by her ankles and held her over the balcony of a five-storey building. He would regularly beat her up, although he was always careful never to damage her face, and once he even held a knife to her throat and threatened to kill her.

It was a reality far at odds with his public persona or anything experienced by Joey and his other friends. 'The only thing out of character,' said Bindon of his role in *Poor Cow*, 'is that I have to hit Carol White in one scene – and I never hit women.'

Making the most of his menacing physique and considerable charm, Bindon was a gregarious self-publicist. Casual acquaintances were often frightened of him, but recall him as 'screamingly funny'. When Lord Longford was engaged in his celebrated investigation into pornography, Bindon 'flashed' at him outside the Chelsea Potter pub.

In the early 1970s Bindon dominated many Chelsea and Fulham pubs, where he was rumoured to run protection rackets. He could be gallant, but a close relationship was precarious. On one occasion a young man who offended him was reputedly driven in a car boot to Putney Common, where Bindon made him dig his own grave before relenting. Bindon's innate anger was apparently only checked by the liberal consumption of cannabis.

Bindon had a voracious sexual appetite and was remarkably well endowed. His most famous party trick was to loop five of six half pint beer glasses (the old fashioned kind with handles) around his erect penis and support the weight of them all. He would stick it through letterboxes, put it in women's handbags and expose it without the slightest provocation. It was little wonder that, before too long, the baronet's daughter was no longer enough for him.

Two years into his relationship with Hodge, he began to tell her about the other women he was sleeping with. He boasted that he often had sex with as many as six women a day, many of them glamorous women in the public eye. He claimed he had a one-night stand with Barbara Windsor, then at the height of her fame as a star of the Carry On films and Christine Keeler, the woman responsible for the Profumo scandal that almost brought down the government.

In 1974 Hodge left her husband and moved into a Fulham flat with Bindon. At the same time, Bindon became increasingly drawn back into the darker side of his existence. He would often work as an enforcer, hired by gangsters to go and beat up their enemies, often for large sums of money. At the same time he developed a powerful cocaine habit, which only fuelled his violent rages.

It was, Hodge remembers, only the beginning. 'He routinely broke down the door of our flat in fury. Once he ripped off my car door and in the ensuing struggle, the tops of three of my fingers were torn off. John started screaming how sorry he was, blood was everywhere. We went to hospital where my fingers were sewn back on. Then we went home and made passionate love. One night, a former girlfriend, Sheila, with whom John had a child, rang at two in the morning, in floods of tears. Someone had beaten her up. John took a great big kitchen knife and made me drive to Elephant and Castle in south London.

'He told me to turn the lights off but keep the engine running, and left me in the car. Eight minutes later, he was back, covered in blood. He said he had cut off the arm of Sheila's attacker. I then knew I was living with an extremely dangerous man.'

The following year the couple went to Mustique on holiday and while there, had an encounter that would push Bindon's celebrity status into new stratospheric heights. Hodge takes up the story.

'We were having lunch on Macaroni Beach with Princess Margaret, Colin Tennant [now Lord Glenconner] and others. John had been there the previous year – sporting a shirt bearing the legend "Enjoy Cocaine" – playing court jester to the Princess who, like most women, was captivated by his Cockney rhyming slang and macho character.

'We sat around the table overlooking the beach, while a butler served us lobster and topped up our glasses with chilled white wine. Princess Margaret, cigarette holder in one hand, gin and tonic in the other, sat next to John, laughing at his off-colour jokes.

Then Colin Tennant leaned towards him and said something which took my breath away: "Ma'am knows about your advantage in life and would really like to see it." John didn't think twice. He jumped up and, with Princess Margaret and her lady-in-waiting in tow, walked along the beach. Then he took out his appendage. The Princess examined it rather like a fossil. We all gasped.

'After a few moments, they all came back to the table. "I've seen bigger," the lady-in-waiting said. "You may have seen bigger," John replied, "but you don't know how well I use it." '

The story, along with pictures of Bindon and the Princess together sparked rumours of an affair. Bindon, eager for the kudos, did little to quell the suspicions that something might well have happened between the two. Officially, however, Her Royal Highness denied ever meeting Bindon.

Joey comments, 'I know John had been offered a lot of money to tell what had happened when he was out on the island with Princess Margaret but he never would. He thought she was a lovely person and he said he'd never do that to her because he had too much respect for her.'

Back in London the violence was escalating and so was Bindon's cocaine habit. He was losing work because of his uncontrollable behaviour. He was given a part in *Man In The Wilderness*, with Richard Harris, but lost his temper on set and found himself promptly fired.

His personal life also started to collapse. Hodge caught him in bed with Serena Williams, a former playboy bunny. Before storming out of their home she threw Bindon's dirty clothes at the pair. 'If you are fucking him then you can do his fucking laundry as well.'

Then, in November 1978, Hodge received a phone call in the early hours of the morning. 'This is it babe,' Bindon gasped. 'I'm dying.' When Hodge saw him she almost fainted. He had been stabbed in the chest, in the back, in the eye, in the throat and in the testicles. Every time his heart beat, blood gushed out of his shirt.

Hodge tore up her own clothes to make bandages, then called a friendly doctor who was willing to attend to Bindon without informing the police. Desperate to escape, the badly injured Bindon persuaded Hodge to drive him to Heathrow airport, throwing a bloodstained knife out of the window on the way. At the check-in desk, Hodge told the clerk that her boyfriend had been injured in a rugby game and had to get home to Dublin. She had wrapped Bindon up in a red blanket to hide the blood, which was still pouring out of him. Remarkably, he was allowed to board the plane.

At five o'clock the following morning, a dozen police officers burst into Hodge's home. By then she had burned Bindon's bloodstained boots and clothes in her fireplace. Her lambskin rugs, covered in blood, were soaking in the bath. The police piled into the flat asking for Bindon but Hodge told them she had not seen him. They left without finding any of the evidence that would have pointed to him having been there just a few hours earlier. It was only as they were leaving that Hodge found out that Johnny Darke, the man Bindon had been fighting with, had died as a result of his injuries and that Bindon was now wanted for murder.

To this day, exactly how Bindon had come to receive his terrible injuries remains unclear. What is certain is that on the night in question, Bindon was at the Ranelagh Yacht Club in Fulham, a small drinking club and known hang-out for local villains. Also there was Johnny Darke, a small-time thief.

Darke was said to be the leader of a south London gang known as the Wild Bunch and had been a police informer for some years. He had been paid £850 for information about men arrested for armed robbery in 1977. The previous year he had been accused of murder but acquitted after a lengthy trial. In 1978 there had been a contract of £5,000 on his life after he had spirited away a consignment of marijuana. The sort of man who would 'carry a knife to church', Darke was believed to be planning to rip off another drug dealer when he died.

The fight had started when Roy Dennis, a friend of Bindon who also had a beef with Drake, threw the first punch. 'I hit the guy and put him on the floor, but he got up again. I didn't realise he had a blade. He did me twice in the face and then in the back a couple of times.'

According to his police statement, Bindon tried to break the fight up. 'I grabbed him and told him to leave it otherwise he was going to kill the guy. Then I felt a sharp pain in my back. Then Darke got on top of me and pinned me down. He pushed the knife down into my chest. I could feel the pain and the coldness. I could see the handle of the knife sticking out of my chest. He then circles the knife around my face as if he was trying to decide where to put it. He jabbed it at my left eye. I managed to jerk my face out of the way. I was literally screaming for help. It made me realise that this man was mad, that he was going to keep on stabbing me until he killed me.'

His friend Lenny Osborne tried to help. He grabbed the knife by the blade but Darke pulled it away, virtually severing four of Osborne's fingers. Darke resumed his attack on Bindon, drawing the knife across his throat. As he did so Osborne returned and slashed Darke across the back with a machete. Bindon knew it as his last chance. He pulled a knife out of his snakeskin boot, a knife which Serena Williams had given him as a present, and threw himself at Darke. 'I may have stabbed him more than once,' he told them. 'I just can't remember.'

When it was all over, Darke had nine stab wounds. His body was dragged into the street by two members of his Wild Bunch gang, who then fled before the police arrived. Back at the club, staff cleaned all the glasses and wiped the whole place down leaving no trace of what had occurred a short while earlier. Having found Darke's body in the street, the police took time to make the link to the club and by the time they did, most of the forensic evidence had been destroyed.

'If it had been my club I would have done the same,' says Joey. 'They took away the membership book, got rid of every fingerprint and every drop of blood. They would have been idiots if they had not done that.'

Over in Ireland Bindon lay low for three days. Friends and acquaintances did what they could for him but it was clear that he needed professional help. His heart had been injured – the chest wound had been so deep that it had nicked it – and his lung collapsed during the flight, so he gave himself up. As armed guards stood outside his room at St Vincent's Hospital, Dublin, he said: 'I want to come home of my own free will and tell my side of the story.'

Remanded in custody at Brixton prison, doctors said the 34-year-old ex-docker was lucky to be alive at all. At the same time police began rounding up those whom, they said, had helped Bindon to escape and evade capture, and also had some link to Darke's murder. Among them was none other than Joey Pyle.

'The whole thing is a bit of a blur – I never really knew what was going on or what I was supposed to have done. It was a dawn swoop and they just came and took me down the nick without ever saying what it was about.

'I remember being taken into a room at Limehouse police station and seeing a row of cabinets along the wall of this office. Every single cabinet was packed with files and every single file had my name on it. I soon found out that I had been picked up as part of some big swoop – there had been more than ninety arrests in all and every single person they pulled in had been asked the same question: what do you know about Joey Pyle.

'They were desperate to get me on something. First they questioned me about a million dollars' worth of American Express travellers' cheques that had been stolen from Heathrow Airport and said I had been observed being shown one of the cheques while I was at the Peacock Club in Streatham. That charge was complete bollocks and I told them so.

'Then they asked me whether I had travelled over to Holland to give money to Lenny Osborne, the man who had helped Bindon escape to Ireland. I denied making any such trip but this time, I was the one lying. I had gone to

Amsterdam after visiting John Bindon when he was being held at Brixton. He told me that Lenny was still on the run in Amsterdam and worried that Bindon might be giving evidence against him. John wanted me to go over, give him a few quid and tell him not to worry.

'I'd made the trip with a friend, a guy called Tony Oliver. I'd met Osborne in a casino, gave him the money and come straight back to London. When they were asking me about it at Limehouse, I denied ever having gone, but what I didn't know was that they had been to see Tony Oliver the day before and he'd made a statement saying that I had and that he had seen me hand over the cash to Osborne.

'Because Osborne was wanted in connection with the murder, me giving him money made me an accessory after the fact in murder. I went from visiting John in Brixton to being banged up in a cell just down the corridor from him.'

The murder trial took place in November 1979, with Bindon claming that he had stabbed Darke in self-defence.

The prosecution maintained that Darke's death was, in fact, a contract killing for which Bindon had been paid a fee of £10,000. The principal source of this was a supposed confession that Bindon made to a fellow prisoner, William Murphy. Asked why he grassed Murphy, who was also on trial for murder, justified it by saying: 'I just don't think it's right that people should go around killing other people and getting paid for it.'

The actor Bob Hoskins appeared as a character witness: 'When Bob walked in,' Bindon later recalled, 'the jury knew I was OK.' Hoskins was asked how Bindon had acquired the nickname 'Biffo' and whether it was anything to do with his habit of hitting people on a regular basis. Hoskins shook his head and said it was short for Biffo the Bear because Bindon was so big and cuddly and comical. He was rebuked by the trial judge, who ordered the jury to ignore the remark. Renowned film director John Mackenzie also made an appearance on behalf of Bindon, saying he was a 'serious, dedicated actor'.

Finally it was Bindon's turn in the box. He described in graphic detail how he had been pinned to the ground by Darke and had had to strike back to avoid being killed himself. He told a fascinated jury how his life had changed from being an ex-Borstal boy and bad lad to a fêted actor.

His reputation as an essentially decent man was further enhanced by the revelation that he had been given the Queen's Award for Bravery in 1968. He got it for diving into the Thames in a vain attempt to rescue a drowning man – although Bindon later boasted that he had been fighting with the man on Putney Bridge, had pushed him in and had dived in to save him only when he saw a policeman approaching. Many say that the performance Bindon gave in the witness box was the best of his life. He was acquitted and the champagne flowed.

The acquittal also marked the end of seven months on remand for Joey Pyle. If no murder had taken place, then Pyle could not have been an accessory. Although he still had the charges relating to the travellers' cheques hanging over him, he was now allowed out on bail.

As soon as he recovered Bindon was back to his old tricks. He resumed his glittering life with the showbiz and society friends he'd acquired through his TV success, but at parties he would get down on all fours, thump the floor and yell: 'What's it like down there, Darkey? Is it hot enough for you?'

Unable to manage his money, he went bankrupt in 1980. The work dried up as ex-con actors became less of a novelty. He drew unemployment benefit and drifted from the papers' diary pages.

In 1981 Bindon began a new career as a director of a company manufacturing hand-made shoes, but his impetuous personality continued to land him in trouble.

It didn't help that Johnny Darke had many friends and the threat of gangland revenge haunted him. There was a series of unhappy court appearances, often resulting in acquittal, for criminal damage and threatening behaviour. In 1982 he pleaded guilty to possession of an offensive weapon – a piece of concrete – following a fight with a 'short and weedy' young man who had bumped into Bindon as he was celebrating his birthday. He was fined £100 and magistrate Eric Crowther remarked: 'I regret that I have not had the pleasure of seeing you act to my knowledge – except here.'

In 1983 he was again declared bankrupt. In July 1984, Bindon was having dinner at a restaurant in Kensington when he grabbed a carving knife and held it up to the throat of a man on a nearby table, telling him: 'Get out or you'll get this.' The man turned out to be off duty policeman DC Neville Sprague, and Bindon was promptly arrested.

During the subsequent trial for possessing an offensive weapon and threatening behaviour, Bindon claimed that the officer had looked like a friend of John Darke who, along with others, had been stalking and threatening him and his family ever since the murder. 'There's a little gang of them,' he told the jury. 'I've had threatening phone calls. I am afraid of them.' He was originally given a two-month jail term but had this overturned on appeal.

In 1985 he was cleared of causing criminal damage to a restaurant in Earls Court. Two years later he was charged with possessing an offensive weapon, and soon afterwards cleared of threatening to petrol-bomb the home of a mother of three. His final days were spent in some privation and loneliness in the tiny Belgravia flat he had purchased in more prosperous times. But by the time he died in 1993, the glamorous crowd had deserted him – unlike his old friends the Krays, who still wrote fondly from their prison cells.

Bindon had begun an affair with a teenage heroin addict and it would be this that would eventually kill him. In 1993 he was very ill with what was described as cancer. Close friends, however, believe he had contracted Aids through his outrageous lifestyle.

Hodge was one of the last people to see him alive. 'He begged me to remember the good times.' 'I've lived the life of ten men in my one life,' he told her.

* * *

With the accessory charge dropped, Pyle still had to face court in connection with the stolen travellers' cheques.

'During the big swoop, where they had arrested ninety people, thirty-odd people ended up being charged and quite a few of them were in Brixton on remand with me before I got bail. One of them was a bloke called Mickey Francis who had been hanging around with the crowd I moved in. He was sharing a cell with a man called Mickey Savage who was also a pal of mine.

'One evening I was unlocked and on my way to collect some hot water when I walked past Savage's cell and noticed that he was on his own.

'"Where's Francis gone?" I asked.

'"Oh, he's gone off for a meeting with his solicitor."

'I glanced at my watch and frowned. "What, at this time."

'"That's what he told me Joey."

'"Well why didn't they call me out as well? He and I have got the same solicitor. What the fuck is going on?"

'I was still puzzling over it the following morning when I bumped into Francis in the queue for breakfast.

'"What was going on last night then? Did you see our solicitor?"

'"Oh no," Francis replied. "That was about my divorce, a different solicitor."

'"What, and he came in at seven o'clock?"

'"Yeah, he couldn't get in any earlier."

'I had too many other things to worry about to pay it too much mind and I'd forgotten all about it by the time we went to court the following week. Normally you try to travel as lightly as possible when you are going to court but prison rules state that if you are trying to get bail, then you have to take all your stuff with you in case you don't come back.

'When I got to the holding cell, waiting to get on the coach, I noticed that Francis had all his stuff with him. Now you have to bear in mind that this is a man with the worst possible form. He had got seven years for resisting arrest by putting his foot down when a copper tried to stop his car. The bloke ended up being dragged along the ground. After that he got another five years for shooting a security guard.

'"Why have you got that lot with you?"

'"I'm gonna try for bail."

'"Bail? You haven't got a hope in hell. No fucking chance."

'"Yeah, well, you still have to try don't you."

'Of course Francis did get bail. It turned out that rather than meeting his solicitor he had actually been meeting the police. He had made a statement saying that he had seen the travellers' cheques and that I had told him that we were going to be making big money out of them. It was totally made up and Francis knew it – he had done it purely to get himself out of prison, taking advantage of just how badly the cops wanted me.

'He bumped into my brother as he was leaving court and told him not to worry because he had a plan. He would retract the statement that he made and then there would be no evidence against me.

'He went along to my solicitor, along with my brother, and made out an affidavit in which he said the police had come to see him in Brixton prison one night and presented him with a pre-written statement which they told him to sign.

'The next time I was in court, I had the affidavit with me and expected to be freed straight away, but what happened then was that the police threatened to send Francis back to prison unless he kept to his original story. After that, he retracted his affidavit and reinstated the original statement.

'It was a stupid legal merry-go-round and I couldn't be arsed fighting it any more. I waited until the case came to trail and left it to my barrister to pull him to pieces in court.

'"Mr Francis, in 1982 you appeared in court on a charge connected to pulling a policeman along in your car. Is that true?"

'"Yes."

'"And how long a sentence did you get?"

' "Seven years."

' "Did you plead not guilty?"

' "Yes I did."

' "And did you give evidence in the witness box?"

' "Yes I did."

' "But the jury found you guilty."

' "Yes."

' "So that's twelve people who found you to be a liar."

' "Well . . . I wouldn't put it exactly like that."

' "But they did didn't they Mr Francis? They didn't believe you were telling the truth. They believed you were lying."

'Francis said nothing. The barrister continued going through the same set of questions for Mickey's other conviction – attempted murder.

' "So that's twenty-four people who found you to be a liar, proving that when you appear under oath you cannot be trusted to tell the truth." Then he pointed to the jury. "But you expect these people to believe you today?"

'That swung it for me and once again, I walked out of court a free man. But I was only too well aware that, next time around, I might not be quite so lucky.'

13. 'I'VE JUST GOT MARRIED. I WANT MY MONEY'

The Kray twins may not have had much of an empire when they were sent to prison in 1969, but within a few short years they had made far more money from behind bars than they ever did when they were free.

The countless books, film deals and memorabilia sales were only part of it. There were also scams like a phoney charity ball, where all the proceeds went straight to the Twins; then there were legitimate businesses like clubs, pubs, betting offices and snooker halls from which they continued to receive a 'pension'.

Their notoriety never faded and there was little they would not do to ensure they remained in the public eye. Both received regular visitors and both received hundreds of letters, many of them from female admirers.

Ronnie, in particular, had any army of female fans. Many sent photographs of themselves along with the letters and those that Ronnie liked the look of would receive an invitation to come and visit him at Broadmoor.

It was during visits like this that Ron formed a particular friendship with 29-year-old divorced mother-of-two, Elaine Mildener. Having learned that the government had recently introduced special dispensation allowing inmates to marry while in prison, he came up with the idea for the ultimate publicity stunt: Ronnie Kray, now claiming to be bisexual rather than simply gay, was going to get married.

'Ron told me all about it when I went to see him on a visit and he asked if I'd be his best man. The wedding was set to take place in the summer and the arrangements were still at an early stage when I got sidetracked into something else.

'My old pal Tony Baldessare had got himself into a spot of bother. We had stayed in touch ever since we were young and running around with Jack the Hat, but for most of our adult lives I had only ever seen him across a prison table when I went in to visit.

'He'd not been out long when he staged a robbery on a bank in south London. He and a mate called Murray burst in with their guns and forced two security guards to hand over some bags of cash. But it just so happened that one of the customers in the bank was a police dog handler who was there with this massive German Shepherd called Yerba. The copper told his dog to attack and it started charging across the room. Tony lowered his gun and shot the dog, hit it three times, before it stopped coming and then he and his mate got out of there sharpish.

'They caught Murray at Gatwick airport, trying to fly off to Tenerife, but Tony had managed to get away. It turned out that it was all for nothing – the guards had given them bags of dummy cash and Tony was as desperate for cash as ever. A couple of months later, around the same time that they had a posthumous award ceremony where the dead dog was presented with a medal for bravery, Tony was part of a team that tried to rob a Knightsbridge department store.

'The gang managed to snatch about £60,000 but the whole thing went horribly wrong when an Embassy policeman, one of those who are allowed to carry guns all the time, intervened and fired a couple of shots. One of the kids involved, guy called Art, was hit and died. Again Tony got away – the police didn't even know he'd been involved – but he knew that he couldn't stay on the run for ever.

'Tony used to come and see me when he was on the run but after a while it started to get to me. I knew he always had a gun with him and, what with my little boy running around the place, I didn't want my house being turned into the scene of some massive shoot out with the police. I knew I had to say something but I didn't want to hurt his feelings or make him feel that I didn't want to be his friend any more. In the end, when I told him that he just couldn't come round to the house any more, he was fine about it.

'Instead we would meet up at the Windmill pub on Clapham Common. He'd ring me using the name Toby and we'd talk in a special code that we had developed so that I would know what time he was getting there. Then one early one morning while I was still in bed, the phone rang.

' "Hello Joe, it's Toby."

' "Hello Toby. How's the operation? Feeling any better?"

I could hear him grinning on the other end of the line.

' "Yeah, I'm feeling a lot better. Much better. It's a big fucking operation though. They are all outside the house right now. They want me to come out with my hands held out in front of me as if I'm sleepwalking."

'He didn't need to say any more. It was obvious that the place was surrounded and that armed officers had trained their guns on him. I was gutted for him but also relieved. I knew the stress of being on the run was getting to him and in some ways it would be a relief to have it over with, even though he was looking at a serious bit of bird.

' "Is there anything I can do for you?" I asked.

' "Yeah, I want you to get in touch with my boy. He'll be at work in a couple of hours. Have a word with him, explain what's happened and tell him to come over. Will you do that for me Joey?"

' "No problem mate, I'll do that for you."

'When Tony had gone I flicked on the radio in time for the 9 a.m. news. Top of the bulletin was a story about a siege in south London. Dozen of armed officers had surrounded a flat in Gleneldon Road, Streatham, where a man wanted in connection with an armed robbery was holed up. The reports said that about thirty people had been evacuated from nearby houses and that they were being put up in local hotels.

'An hour later I phoned St Thomas's Hospital where Tony's son, Frank worked.

' "Did you hear about that siege on the news earlier?"

' "Yeah, I did."

' "Well, that's your dad."

' "Oh fuck . . ."

' "Listen, he wants you to go and see him. Can you do that?"

'By the middle of the day dozens of television cameras had plotted up outside Tony's flat and were giving a minute-by-minute account of what was going on inside. I was still watching the coverage when Tony rang again.

' "Did you speak to my boy?"

' "Yeah, but I have to tell you something Tony, I don't think he's going to be able to get anywhere near you. The road is all taped off and they've evacuated all the neighbours. I'm watching it on the TV right now."

' "Don't worry, Joey, it's OK. The police have been on the phone. They were listening in while I was talking to you and they said when he gets here, they will let him through."

'I was momentarily shocked and a little annoyed that I was now part of the siege, that the police might think I was somehow involved and might even start tapping my phone, but let it go. "Well that's all right then isn't it?"

' "Nah Joey, I'm not going to see him now."

' "Why not?"

' "Because that's just what they want. They want me to lower my guard and they'll use my boy to get to me. I'm not going to let them do that. I've got plenty of ammunition, plenty of guns and they're all loaded up. If they come in here, they're gonna get it."

'A chill ran down my spine. Tony knew only too well that the police were listening. He wanted them to know he meant business.

'The siege went on and on, two full days and two full nights, and the phone calls kept coming. Most of the time we talked about anything other than what was really going on. We talked about Muhammad Ali fights and people that we knew and even the fucking weather. Anything to try to take our minds off of it all. Then on the third morning Tony told me that he had his £40,000 share from the last robbery in the room with him.

' "What are you going to do with it?"

' "Well, I wish my missus was here because then I could throw it out of the window to her. But that's not going to happen. I'm not going to let anyone else get it. I'm going to get the fire going and burn the lot."

' "Tony," I said softly. "You've got to come out of the house, mate. It's the only way. You've got to give yourself up and come out."

' "I can't Joey. I just can't do it. After what I've done, after what's happened in the last couple of days, they are going to give me so much bird that I'll never be free again."

' "So what are you going to do? Don't think you can just walk out there with a gun in your hand and get away. I've seen in on the telly. There are dozens of them, all with rifles pointed at all the doors and windows. The minute you walk out they are going to blow you to pieces."

' "Ain't gonna happen, I'm not walking out."

' "Then what are you gonna do?"

' "I'm gonna let them come in here and get me, then I'm going to take a few of the bastards with me."

' "Jesus Tony, why don't you come out?"

'There was a long pause, then Tony sighed. "Listen Joey, the only way I'll come out is if my missus tells me she wants me to come out. If she asks, then I'll come. Otherwise I'm staying put."

'I glanced at my watch. It was close to midnight but I knew there was no time to waste. I told Tony to stay put, jumped into my car and raced over to Pollards Hill where Tony's wife lived.

'When I arrived, a lone police panda car was parked outside, and as I approached the pathway an officer climbed out and held up his hand.

' "I'm sorry Sir, you can't go in there."

' "You can't stop me."

' "Yes I can. And I will."

' "But she hasn't done anything wrong. Maybe her husband has, but she ain't. What right have you go to stop me going in there?"

That stumped him for a second, then he asked for my name.

'"Joey Pyle, I'm a friend of the family."

'The officer pushed the button of his radio and reported back to his commanding officers. I heard the radio crackle to life a few seconds later and a tinny voice said: "It's all right, let him in."

'Inside, Louise was in a bit of a state, desperately trying to hold it all together.

'"Look Lou," I said. "You've got to tell him to come out. You've seen what's going on out there. It's the only way. You've got to tell him to come out."

'She looked away; I could see tears welling up in the corners of her eyes.

'"I can't do that Joe," she said softly.

'"Why not?"

'"Because when Tony did his last bit of time he said to me that if he ever gets into this sort of position that I shouldn't interfere. He said I should let him do things his own way. So that's what I'm doing. I'm not interfering."

'"Lou, do you want him dead? Do you want to be following him out of this house in a box?"

'"No, of course not."

'"Then you have to do something. You can't just let it go on. You know how it's gonna end. The police are talking about storming the place."

'Louise told me she had to talk things over with Frank. I went out of the living room and sat in the kitchen while Frank and his mother had a good long talk together. Forty-five minutes later, Louise called me back inside.

'"OK Joey, I'll do it. I'll tell him to come out."

'I went outside and went up to the copper who was guarding the house. "Quick, get hold of your guv'nor right away. I need to talk to him. It's very, very important." I handed over a scrap of paper with Louise's phone number and said I'd be waiting for the call.

'About ten minutes later the phone went.

'"Is this Mr Pyle?"

'"Yes."

'"What can we do for you?"

'"I need you to speak to Tony. Get him to ring his wife. It's really important."

'"No can do Mr Pyle. Mr Baldessare has taken his telephone off the hook so he can get some sleep. He said we were calling him too often and he needs a bit of kip."

'"But if you tell him to put the phone back on and ring his wife, then she'll tell him to come out peacefully."

'"Mr Pyle, it's after one in the morning and the shop is closed. Open shop tomorrow morning."

'I gasped in disbelief. "Listen, you could save lives this way. You can save his life and maybe the lives of a few policemen."

'"I can't do anything. I told you, the phone is off the hook. The shop is closed."

'"All you need to do is get one of those loudhailer things, you must have one of them, get it and shout through the window for him to put the phone back on."

'"I can't do anything until tomorrow morning. I am under strict instructions."

'I continued pleading with him but he just wasn't having any of it and in the end I had to give up and go home. As soon as I got up the next day, I called Louise.

'"Has he rung you yet?" I asked.

'"Yeah, I just finished speaking to him."

'"Great. Did you tell him to come out?"

'"No."

'"Shit. Why not?"

'"I changed my mind Joey. I know what he's like. I don't want to see him go back to prison for thirty-odd years. He was right. I shouldn't interfere. I have to let him sort this out in his own way."

'All I could think was what a bunch of soppy bastard the cops in charge of the siege were. If they had only done what

I'd asked the night before, Louise would have made the call and told him to quit. Giving her the time to think it over had robbed them of their only chance to end it all peacefully.

'Four hours later Tony rang me. "Hello Joe, how are things?" It was just the usual conversation that we had been having for the past few days, but this time there was something in his voice that I didn't recognise. After a while we ran out of things to say and the conversation ground to a halt. Then Tony said: "Anyway Joe, you look after yourself and your family."

'For the second time in three days, a chill ran down my spine. "What you talking like that for? What's going on? Don't you start talking like that." Tony started laughing, a great big belly laugh like he'd been playing some kind of joke on me, winding me up. He knew exactly what I was thinking. "Don't be silly mate, I wouldn't do anything like that."

'But he did. Two hours after we'd spoken Tony sat down on the floor of the living room with his back to the settee, put the same gun he had used to kill the police dog against his chest and pulled the trigger. The shot blew his heart to pieces. He died instantly. The siege of Gleneldon Road was over.

'First Jack the Hat and then Tony. Two of my closest school friends who, like me, had chosen a life of crime and had ended up dying violently. It was certainly food for thought.'

'Three months after I delivered the eulogy at Tony's funeral, I was best man at Ronnie Kray's wedding.

'It all took place in a little room in Broadmoor. Elaine was there in her dress, sitting at the table opposite the registrar and then Ron came in, all suited up, and sat down next to her.

'The registrar started reading all this stuff out about what marriage meant, that kind of thing, and Ronnie just sat there looking around the room. To him it was just a big joke. He opened up a packet of cigarettes and lit one up while the registrar was halfway through the vows. Then he turned around and started giggling and winking at me in between drags.

'Half a minute later, he realised the registrar was trying to get his attention and he turned back. "What did you say?" he asked.

'"I said you are now man and wife. You may kiss the bride."

'"Oh, right," said Ron. He gave Elaine a little kiss on the cheek and then left her at the table to walk over to the corner where I was standing with his older brother, Charlie.

'"So," said Ron. "Where's the money?"

'He'd struck a deal with the *Sun* newspaper for exclusive coverage of the marriage and he was supposed to be getting paid £15,000. It turned out that this was his main reason for going ahead with the whole thing.

'"Steady on," said Charlie. "You've only just . . ."

'"I've just fucking got married. I want me money."

'"Tomorrow," I said. "We'll get the money tomorrow."

'"OK," said Ron. "But there's something I must tell you. You see that woman?" he nodded towards his new bride. "You know she's got a couple of kids. Well you ain't gonna believe this – they call me Dad!" Ronnie didn't stop laughing for almost ten minutes after that.

'For the next year or so he milked the marriage as much as he could, selling stories to the papers including one about wanting to become the father of twins and trying to obtain special permission to be allowed to consummate his marriage.

'The final story was the one giving details of the divorce. After three years of being in the public eye, the new Mrs Kray decided she'd had enough of it all, stopped visiting and had it on her toes. I guess she had decided that the best thing all round would be if she vanished for a while.

'A few months later, I found myself in exactly the same situation.'

14. 'THEY'RE THE MILANO BROTHERS. THEY RUN LOS ANGELES'

When little-known East End villain Archie Davis got pulled in on drugs charges, he knew two magic words which had the power to ensure the time he spent behind bars was kept to an absolute minimum. 'I'm just the middle man in this,' he told the officers who arrested them. 'But I know exactly who is behind it all: Joey Pyle.'

'Everything Archie said the day he got arrested was absolute bollocks,' Joey retorts. 'The only reason I knew him was because he owed me money, and the only reason he named me as the top man was in order to get some leverage in his case. None of that mattered to the law, all they saw was another shot at putting me away. A couple of days after they picked Archie up, they asked to interview me down at Dulwich nick.

'It was two or three days before Christmas and I just sat there while they asked a whole bunch of questions about Archie, about Australia where the drugs had been intercepted, and about whether I had been to this or that place and knew this or that person. I can honestly say that for the most part, I had no clue what they were talking about. I answered "no comment" to each and every one of the questions and when it was all over, they said they had to make a report to the DPP before deciding whether they were going to charge me.

'I was appalled. The only evidence they had against me were the things Archie had been saying. Apart from that there was nothing. I wouldn't have been worried but for the fact that a similar thing had happened a few years earlier and I had ended up spending a couple of months behind bars.

'That time it turned out that some drug smuggler had used my name to make it seem they were a big player, and reduce the chance of them getting ripped off. In fact the people behind that shipment had originally approached me and I'd told them to fuck off, but when they had approached others, they had decided to make it seem as though I was involved.

'I was arrested along with a bunch of others, including Howard Marks, author of *Mr Nice* about his career in the drugs trade, and I ended up spending two months in Brixton, all of it on AA Category. Then one day I was in the yard and they called out my name. They had finally realised there was no evidence against me and let me go. I was absolutely fucking livid. The whole thing had nothing to do with me – just like Archie's case – but I still ended up paying a heavy price.

'I was going back over the whole experience in my mind as I made my way out of Dulwich nick. Then I remember one of the detectives telling me that they might want to interview me again.

'"Do you think that will be before Christmas?"

'"Oh no, if we talk to you again it won't be until the New Year."

'That suited me fine. I knew the whole thing with Archie was going to blow over, I just didn't fancy having to wait it out in some pokey little prison cell. I had a nice relaxing Christmas with my boy and a few close friends, and then on New Year's Eve I decided to have it on my toes.'

'I'd been to New York for the first time a couple of years earlier as part of a trip to raise funds for the film about the Kray twins. I'd gone over there with Wilf Pine, a big name in the music industry, who I'd got to know after Reggie Kray had introduced us. Reggie had known that I was interested in moving into the music business myself and Wilf was a useful man to know. He had once managed Black Sabbath and organised massive tours that criss-crossed the States for dozens of other leading artists.

'I've never been much into music – I think I'm fucking tone deaf – but ever since the days when I was promoting boxing events, I've known I had a talent for putting on a show. I had the ability to get acts organised for charity events and the like, get people together and make sure everything went smoothly. At the end of the day, boxing is entertainment, and the skills you need for one form are the same as you need for another. It seemed to be a short step to take from managing fighters to managing singers – so that was what I did.

'Wilf and I soon became good pals and, knowing everything there was to know about my background and the kind of things I'd been involved in before, Wilf said he would introduce me to the right sort of people once we arrived in the Big Apple.

'First on the list was Joe Pagano, one of the top men in the Genovese organised crime family – the biggest and most powerful of New York's five Mafia families. Wilf knew Joe through his son Danny, who worked as a record producer. The two were virtually best friends and Danny had actually been best man at Wilf's wedding.

'In the world of American organised crime, reputation is everything and recommendation is the key. It's easy enough to find a way to meet people and say hello to them, but unless you come to them by way of introduction, they will never be anything more than simply polite. The better the introduction, the warmer the greeting you receive. I don't know exactly what Wilf told Joe Pagano about me, but when we met, Pagano put his arms out to me as if I were some long-lost friend.

'I saw Pagano a few times during that first trip and when I returned to New York a couple of years later I had no hesitation in calling him up again, and soon found myself sitting down to dinner with some of the most powerful criminals in the western world.

'I got on with them all so well that it was all to easy to forget that they were major mobsters involved in a lot of really big stuff. But at the end of the day they were really just ordinary people. They don't have "Mafia" printed on their foreheads or anything. It's not like they are from another planet. For most of them their lives were a lot like mine – they had little bits of business here and there and they made a bit of money.

'There were killings of course, some of them quite spectacular in the way they would be carried out in broad daylight in front of dozens of potential witnesses, but anyone who got involved with the Mob knew exactly what they were getting into. If you crossed them, then you were going to get it. And if there was a war between rival factions or rival gangs, then someone was going to get it too. But it wasn't like *The Godfather*; it wasn't like they were going around killing people every day or anything like that.

'There were little rows and incidents and bits and pieces going off the whole time I was in New York, but none of them directly affected me and none of them had anything to do with my decision to turn down Joe Pagano's kind offer to "run" with the Genovese family.

'A lot of it was the weather. It was January and New York was absolutely freezing. I knew the West Coast was going to be a hell of a lot warmer and thought if I was going to be on the run for a while, I might as well make the best of it.

'But more than that was the thought that if I did accept, that would be the end of it – I'd never get to go home. A lot of people spend their whole lives wanting to join the Mob – it's their ultimate ambition – and once they do, they know they are set for life. You have an international support network, real financial and legal muscle and genuine power. But there are disadvantages too. Rows that might not involve you personally but affect your family suddenly become your row too. Your loyalty has to be to the family, regardless of whether that is in your best interests.

'And while I'd never want to take anything away from any of the guys that I met, I found the code of honour was a lot stronger back in London than it was over in the States. I met people over there whose attitude was if they got pulled in by the police, they would talk. "You gotta tell them something ain't you," they would say. They couldn't get their head around the idea of going no comment. I think the problem was that a lot of the top people had never been pulled in, never done any time in prison or anything. Getting that confidence that enables you to look a copper in the eye and tell him to go fuck himself comes from knowing the worst that can happen and not being intimidated by it. A lot of these guys didn't have that – they left everything to their lawyers instead.

'A month or so after Joe Pagano asked me to become a part of the Genovese family, I moved down to the West Coast. I spent a couple of weeks in LA and then, on the suggestion of my friend, Jack O'Halloran, I moved out to Palm Springs. Jack was a former professional boxer who had moved into acting and carved out a niche for himself playing arch villains. He stood six feet six, was powerfully built and managed to land big roles in the first two Superman films.

'Jack was increasingly moving in Hollywood showbiz circles and told me that Palm Springs was the place to be and be seen. It didn't take long for me to see exactly what he meant.

'As soon as I set eyes on the place it was love at first sight. Built around an oasis in the middle of the desert, where the temperature rarely drops below 70 degrees, Palm Springs is a playground for millionaires with fine restaurants, great bars and every creature comfort you could ever wish for.

'Although it's only 100 miles away from the City of Angels, the high mountains that surround the place mean permanently blue skies because the rain – and most importantly the Los Angeles smog – cannot get through. The scenery is stunning, with massive canyons, deserts and parks all around. There are also massive hotels, each one the size of a small town, bustling with bars and shows and the most incredible nightlife you have ever seen.

'I'd been in the Springs for a couple of weeks and was drinking with a pal in the bar of the Riviera Hotel when a group of about twelve Italians came in and sat down on the other side of the room. "They're the Milano brothers," my friend whispered. "They run Los Angeles." '

Throughout California, anyone who knew the Milanos knew better than to mess with them. The brothers had originally been brought up in Cleveland, Ohio, where their father Anthony 'The Old Man' Milano had been consigliere of the local Mafia clan.

Once they came of age the brothers decided to seek their fortunes amid the bright lights of the West Coast, hitting the area with a tidal wave of crime in the early 70s.

In 1974 one of the brothers was convicted of operating a rigged craps table and blackjack game. At first it seemed he would be going away for a long time but the case against him was suddenly severely weakened when two key witnesses, Johnny and Frances DuBeck, were shot dead the week before they were due to give evidence.

A decade later the brothers were arrested for trying to muscle in on a $1 million-a-week bookmaking operation, but charges were not brought because of a lack of evidence. As their empire grew they expanded their operations into Las Vegas, taking over topless bars, late night restaurants and a storefront social clubs.

Of the brothers the most remarkable was Bobby, a talented singer and actor. He performed his Sinatra-style act in nightclubs throughout the West Coast and had an army of loyal fans. He also appeared in films like *The Untouchables*, *The Gangster Chronicles* and *The FBI* – roles in which his mobster looks were a distinct advantage.

'When Joe Pagano heard I was going out to LA he told me to look out for the Milanos as they were good friends of his. He told me to be sure to say hello and that he had told me to speak to them. I gave them a few minutes to settle down and get their drinks then I went over and introduced myself.

'"Hello, I'm Joey Pyle, I've just come from New York and Joe Pagano told me to say hello to you."

'Bobby Milano looked at me rather cock-eyed, completely uncertain what to make of me. I also think the English accent and the reference to Pagano threw him for a bit. I'd expected him to be cautious – a lot of people claim to have Mob connections or friends in high places to help grease the wheels. Before any of the Milanos cut me any slack, they were going to have to be sure I was legit.

'Bobby spoke slowly, deliberately, and with a complete lack of emotion. It was almost as if he was giving me one last chance to change my mind. "You know Joe Pagano? Oh great, great. And what did he say to you? OK, we'll check that out." That was my signal to go back and join my friend. Even before I'd turned away Bobby was back in conversation with the man sitting next to him. I didn't take offence. I'd gotten to know enough Mob guys since arriving in the States to know that, with strangers, that is just their way.

'After that I didn't go back to the Riviera for a few days. When I did the Milanos were there again. Bobby spotted me right away but this time it was as if I was meeting a completely different person. He stood up and came strolling over to me, his arms wide open. "Joey, where you been? We've been looking for you. We checked you out with Joe Pagano, he says you're a great guy, come on over to our table, join us."

'From that day on they couldn't do enough for me. They were buying me drinks, taking me out to shows and basically painting the town red. As the weeks went on I found myself getting friendly with more and more members of the Milano clan.

'It was while I was having lunch with a guy by the name of Two Fingers Tony that I got my first little up-close taste of Mob violence. Tony had been arguing with a couple of brothers who were linked to the Gambino family.

'As we were eating, one of the brothers suddenly rushed into the restaurant wielding a baseball bat. Before I could say a word he had smashed Two Fingers across the back of the head. His face slammed forward into the plate of spaghetti and meatballs that he was eating, sending them splashing all over me. I was absolutely covered in the stuff.'

What Joey had witnessed was a relatively minor incident but brewing under the surface was something much more serious. Within the space of a few years most of the Milano gang would be behind bars, caught out in a massive FBI investigation that would include more than 1,700 audio and video tapes, dozens of confidential informants and one defendant who committed the ultimate sin by breaking the code and giving evidence against the others.

Before then the considered thinking was that the West Coast Mafia had tended to shun the violence associated with the gangs from the East, but all that was about to change. Sixty-three-year-old Herbert 'Fat Herbie' Blitzstein, one of the last remnants of the wise-guy era captured in the movie *Casino*, was found shot dead in his living room, a single bullet in his head. Blitzstein was a former right-hand-man to Chicago Mob enforcer Anthony Spilotro, who himself had been murdered a few years earlier.

More than sixteen members of the Milano family and their associates were charged with the murder. In many cases the accused were so old and feeble that the idea of them being top gangsters seemed almost laughable. One attorney said of his client: 'He's sixty-nine years old. He lives off Social Security, he gets food stamps and Medicaid pays his medical for his three heart attacks. If this is organised crime, then it's the most unorganised and poorest paying outfit that I've ever seen.'

But the prosecution went ahead and the reign of the Milanos in California effectively came to an end. According to the FBI, the Milano clan had demanded a piece of Blitzstein's loan-sharking action. 'Rather than compete, they went the old fashioned 1930s way and decided to kill him.' But long before that, Joey Pyle had already moved into pastures new.

* * *

In California during the late 1980s, you were nobody unless you knew somebody, and the one somebody that everybody wanted to know was a man by the name of Joe Isgro.

Born in Philadelphia, Isgro had joined the marines and then started his career proper working for a small record company in his home town. He soon outgrew these humble roots and moved to the West Coast, where he started up a record promotion business. No one quite knew how, but in a very short space of time he became an incredibly wealthy man, and he was not shy about flaunting it.

First he took over the Hollywood club Bar One, where regulars included the likes of Jack Nicholson, Sylvester Stallone, Charlie Sheen and Sean Penn. Then he took over Stefaninos, the largest bar-cum-nightclub-cum-restaurant in all of Los Angeles and a venue once co-owned by Frank Sinatra. Isgro could be found holding court there almost every night and as well as being a favourite of the biggest names in Hollywood, Stefaninos also attracted some of the biggest names in American organised crime.

Isgro made no secret of the fact that he regularly associated with top figures from the Mob. In particular he enjoyed a long and close friendship with Joe 'Piney' Armone, the underboss of the Gambino family. 'He's like family to me and always will be,' said Isgro of his friend. 'If I go to New York tomorrow I will meet Joe Armone and his wife and children and have a plate of linguine with them like I always do.'

Isgro cruised around town in a chauffer-driven Rolls Royce, enjoyed the company of beautiful women and invested heavily in lavish property across the country. Within Hollywood circles, he was far more famous and alluring than any actor.

'While I was living in Palm Springs Joey Isgro came into town and I was introduced to him. He immediately reminded me of the Great Gatsby. He was very smart, immaculate, with not an ounce of fat on him. He wore black and white shoes and a really smart outfit, a real Dapper Dan type. He was a good-looking bloke and very popular among the entertainment set but everyone was mystified about exactly how he made all his money.

'Isgro had these two big security guards that would shadow him wherever he went. As I was being introduced to him, one of the guards leaned over and started speaking with a strong London accent. "Hello Joey, how you doing? Do you remember me?"

'I looked at this bloke. His face didn't ring any bells and I didn't know him from Adam but, wary of the company I was in, the last thing I wanted was to come across as being rude.

'"Yeah, I think I remember you," I said slowly.

The man smiled at me. "I'm Dave. Dave Smith. I used to box and I was on the bill of a tournament you put together a good few years ago. Roy Shaw was on that night and I was fighting under the name of Dave Strong. Do you remember me now?"

'I smiled back and told him that I did. The truth was that I remembered the name Dave Strong but didn't remember him at all.

'I soon got back to talking to Isgro and we really hit it off, especially when he found out about my interest in music management and the recording industry. He invited me over to Stefaninos and when I turned up a week later, he sat me down to one of the most lavish meals I have ever had in my entire life. Everything was free – Isgro insisted that I didn't pay a penny – and we were soon on our way to becoming good pals.

'I started helping out in Isgro's business, going round his office and getting involved in little bits and pieces, and it didn't take long for me to find out just how he had gotten to be so rich.'

The American singles charts are notoriously slow-moving, and were even more so in pre-MTV days: the sheer size of the market means that it takes longer for a song to excite sales coast-to-coast in the US than in Britain, and chart-orientated stations are cautious about their programming policy, preferring to reflect public taste than to lead it. The Billboard charts are calculated using a complicated formula that combines sales and airplay. Unless a record scores highly on both counts, it has little chance of making it. Airplay is seen as the key to increasing more sales.

A decade earlier it would have cost around $100 per week to hire a freelance promoter to hype records around local radio stations, but Isgro had made things far more efficient and reliable – as well as developing a stranglehold on the industry. Once he had reached the position where everyone knew that unless they paid him, a record would never get played, competition for the service pushed up the asking price until it was sky high. When CBS Records installed a new deputy president and asked him to cut costs, he was shocked to discover that after staff salaries, 'independent promotion' was the single biggest drain on CBS resources.

CBS attempted to buck the trend in 1980 by refusing to pay to promote the single 'Another Brick in the Wall' by Pink Floyd. The band had just finished a five-night residency at a major Los Angeles arena where tickets for the event had sold out in hours. The spectacular show had guaranteed column upon column of newspaper coverage and masses of airtime on television. Yet despite this incredible public profile not a single West Coast radio station had the single on their playlist. CBS eventually gave in and paid; the record was then heard dozens of times per day and stormed up the Billboard charts.

As the price for the service continued to rise, Isgro effectively forced small labels out of the singles charts; by the start of the 80s, only the biggest and richest record labels could afford proper promotion. By 1985 the US record industry was spending at least 30 per cent of its pre-tax profits in this way, an estimated 60 to 80 million dollars each year. Spending on an individual single might reach as much as $300,000, a dangerously high and inefficient amount on a medium often regarded as a loss-leader designed to trigger album sales.

'It was big business and it was all completely legal. Joe had almost $500 million going through his books each year. He was powerful because even the biggest stars still needed to have airplay because without it, none of their records would count as hits. Joe would give the record companies a menu – the more they paid the more times they would get the record played on prime time radio during the course of a single day.

'Isgro then decided to expand the business into Europe and asked me to look after that end of things. The big record companies were paying Isgro fortunes to get their records played, and if any English bands truly wanted to make it in America, they were going to have to do the same.'

But then it all started to go horribly wrong. Isgro became the subject of a massive FBI investigation. He was suspected of inducing radio stations to play records he was plugging by giving them illegal payments and plying them with cocaine. Dozens of his close associates were subpoenaed to testify about his activities before a grand jury.

'Isgro wasn't too concerned but had worries over what Dave Smith might say. Smith had been more than just a minder: he had been around when several key deals had been done and had regularly rubbed shoulders with the likes of Joe Armone. Isgro asked Dave to leave, but he wouldn't go; I guess he'd considered all the options and figured that the best thing was to get Dave to go back to England voluntarily. But Dave was having none of it. Then Isgro asked me to try and talk Dave into leaving so I went to see him.

'The second I clapped eyes on him I knew it wasn't going to be easy: he was driving around in a big fucking Rolls Royce, one of Isgro's old cars, he was getting all the cash he wanted, usually a thousand dollars at a time, there were loads of beautiful women and loads of other stuff going up his nose. He was living the life of an absolute playboy and had little reason to go back to England where it was cold and miserable.

'Eventually I managed to convince Dave that going back was only going to be a temporary thing, not a permanent move. After that his main objection was that he would not have anything to do once he got back, nothing to occupy him. That was when I arranged for Dave to go and work for my old business partner Alex Steen, doing a bit of touting.

'Once that was sorted, Dave went back and Alex fixed him up with a bit of work with a bloke called Ron Fairbrother who was also doing a bit of work for him. After that I had little to do with him and focused exclusively on my business activities in America.'

In the meantime, back in England, the case of Archie Davis had finally come to trial.

'Although he had originally made a statement against me, I wasn't mentioned at his trial. He realised that because I wasn't around, he had nothing to gain by pretending that I had any involvement in what was going on.

'He got eight years, and once he'd been sentenced I knew that the danger was over, as he no longer had anything to gain by dragging me into the case.

'I'd enjoyed my time in America and met a lot of good people, many of whom remain firm friends to this very day. But I missed London. Despite the great weather, the good times and the amazing lifestyle I had out in Palm Springs, I couldn't wait to get back.

'Soon after I got back to England I got a call from Joe Isgro saying he was going to send some money over to me to pass on to Dave Smith. I met up with a guy called Tommy Sallo, who I knew well from New York, and he said he'd been given three grand by Isgro to pass on to Smith. A meeting had been arranged outside Morden tube station, of all places.

'I was standing around like a prat for a bit then, all of a sudden, I saw Dave coming down the street. "Hi Joe, how you doing?" We had a little chat about this and that but then I had a sudden fear that the money I was handing over was some kind of blackmail demand. If that was the case, then I didn't want to have anything to do with it.

' "I need to ask you something Dave. You're not putting the fucking blackmail on Joe Isgro are you?"

' "Nah Joe, on my life, I swear I'm not."

' "Because if you are, if you're telling him that unless he keeps giving you money you're going to go back and testify, then I don't want to give it to you, you can go somewhere else and get it."

'Dave swore on his mother's life, on his father's life, he took every oath under the sun to reassure me and eventually I accepted what he was saying. "OK," I said, handing over the envelope, "here's your money."

'It was a bright summer evening and Dave was wearing a T-shirt and light denim jacket. As I handed over the money, I noticed that his T-shirt was away from his chest – something about it didn't look right. It took me a few seconds to realise that he was wearing a bullet-proof jacket, and by that time I'd also seen the handle of a gun sticking out from his waistband, only barely covered by the denim jacket.

' "You no good fucking bastard, what are you playing at, coming here to meet me with a fucking piece on you?"

' "Nah Joey, it's not like that."

' "Well what is it like then?"

' "Er . . . well, I've got a bit of work to do right after this meeting, I need it for that. It's nothing to do with you."

'I wasn't happy but there was nothing much I could do. I gave him the money and got out of there. Then a few days later I read a piece in the *Sunday Times* all about Joe Isgro being embroiled in a Mafia trial and how the police over here were looking for Dave Smith and couldn't find him. The story quoted his aunt: "The last I saw of my David was when he went to meet a well-known criminal." My heart sank.

'Then the next thing I knew there was a knock at my door. I expected it to be the police but it was a couple of reporters.

' "Mr Pyle, we want to ask you about Dave Smith."

' "I don't have anything to say about him."

' "Do you know him?"

' "Yeah I know him, but that's all and I haven't got any more to say." Then I slammed the door in their faces.'

For a while there were rumours that Dave Smith had been murdered, but then he turned up in the States, giving evidence against Isgro. He claimed that he had been not only Isgro's minder but also his main bagman, collecting the laundered proceeds of the Payola.

Despite Smith's testimony the case collapsed and Isgro was allowed to go free. The investigation had taken ten years and cost millions of dollars but had got nowhere.

This was not the case on the other side of the Atlantic. For Joey Pyle, the man who had not been convicted of a crime since the Pen Club case some thirty-odd years earlier, a series of equally dubious and lengthy investigations were about to bear bitter fruit.

15. 'I WILL NOT BE DICTATED TO BY MEMBERS OF THE CRIMINAL FRATERNITY. THIS TRIAL WILL NOT BE ABORTED. WE WILL CARRY ON'

During the mid-1980s, Joey Pyle had developed yet another string to his bow: loan sharking.

'It wasn't a big thing for me and I didn't exactly advertise, but I was lending out quite a lot of money in bits and pieces, charging different rates of interest depending on how much the person wanted to borrow.

'I got approached by some friends of friends who said they knew someone who was looking for a loan of £20,000 and willing to pay good interest. I didn't know this guy from Adam so I decided to go and check him out. They said he had owned a club in Eastbourne. When I got down there I was amazed. It wasn't so much a club, more like a holiday camp. There were chalets out the back, swimming pools, carousels and all sorts. He had loads of top-rate performers going down there and doing shows and as far as I could see, the place was a really big success. I met up with the owner, Richard Ledingham he was, and I laid out the deal. He said he wanted to borrow £20,000 and would give me £500 a week until the debt was repaid.

'"That's fine," I told him, "but you still owe the £20,000. If you pay it back in one week, then it'll only cost you £500 in interest, if you pay it back in a month, then it'll cost you £2,000. That's the deal." Then I looked around the gaff. In a corner were about half a dozen slot machines and they all seemed to be doing pretty good business.

'I leaned forward, my elbows on the table. "And if you don't pay, then I'm gonna come down here and empty your slots. They look like they're taking at least £500 a week."

'We shook hands on it and I told him I'd arrange to send the money down in the next couple of days. I left Eastbourne feeling pretty good about things.

'The man was a stranger to me but it wasn't as if he didn't have a pot to piss in. I mean, this club was massive, and he was the owner – there was no way he was going to walk away and leave it. But that's just what he did.

'At the end of the first week, he paid up right on time. And the same thing happened the second week. But after that, I didn't hear from him. I went back down to Eastbourne to find out what was going on. When I arrived there were loads of coaches outside and a big commotion going on. It turned out that Freddie Starr was supposed to be appearing but that something had gone wrong and the show had been cancelled. People were milling about all over the place and getting their ticket money back. I found a couple of people who seemed to be in charge and asked them what was going on. They said the whole place had been shut down and that Ledingham had left the country.

'That was it. The club never, ever reopened; Ledingham just skipped with my money. In fact, I think the reason he'd taken the loan was to get enough cash together to do a runner. I had to swallow it. I never gave any of his family any hassle or anything because I just couldn't blame them for it. It was all my own fault. I had made a bad business decision based on the fact that no one in their right mind would leave a thriving business like the club Ledingham had. But appearances can be deceptive and I didn't realise just how much debt the man had behind him.

'All this happened back in 1985 and after that I didn't hear anything. About three years later I got a call from some bloke who told me he was a born-again Christian. He explained that Richard Ledingham had also become born again, was feeling terrible about never having paid back my money, and now wanted to settle the debt.

'He was worried that I might cause trouble but I told him that as long as I got the money back, there would be no problem. I even told him to forget all about the interest. Within a couple of weeks, I had met Ledingham and been repaid the £20,000. As far as I was concerned it was like Christmas and my birthday all at once. I may not have made any more, but I was no worse off than I had been, and in my book that was a good thing.

'I supposed I thought that because he had done that, Ledingham couldn't be all bad. We became friends of a kind and I considered him to be someone I could trust. I didn't know just how wrong I was.'

In October 1990 Ledingham was arrested for conspiring to steal more than £5 million from Barclays Bank. He had also presented a series of stolen cheques worth around £600,000 to the London branch of an Italian bank, trying to get them credited to an account that he controlled.

With his trial due to open at Knightsbridge Crown Court in June the following year, Ledingham knew the evidence against him was so overwhelming that he could do little apart from plead guilty. The only way he could possibly avoid spending the best part of the next decade behind bars was to find something to bargain with. And that was where Joey Pyle came in.

Soon after his arrest by officers from the City of London Police, Ledingham told them that Pyle was in possession of a large amount of heroin and had asked him to come up with a buyer. Ledingham was promptly handed over to Scotland Yard's Criminal Intelligence Branch, SO11, and massive resources were suddenly diverted into what many officers saw as their best chance in years to finally take Pyle out of the game.

It turned out that the police had been watching Pyle for years, logging his every move. They were convinced he was tied to the drugs trade but had no evidence to support this. There were two possibilities. Either Pyle was not involved in the drugs trade, or he was so clever and so cautious about his dealings with his suppliers and sellers that he had so far managed to avoid detection. As far as the police were concerned, they believed only the latter scenario.

As a result, Ledingham would soon find himself at the hub of one of the biggest and most elaborate sting operations Scotland Yard had ever launched.

By now Pyle had moved on again and was running his own film company, Touchdown, out of an office at Pinewood Studios.

'The film thing just grew out of the music management and was just another form of entertainment. We did some good work including a hard-hitting documentary about politics in the Seychelles, where there had been a series of attempted coups.

'As far as the rest of the world was concerned, the coups had been bloodless. But the truth was far from that. People had been tortured, dozens had been badly hurt, and there had been soldiers goose-stepping their way down the high streets. The former president, James Mancham, had ended up living in exile in Putney and wanted a film made about what had really happened in order to help him get back into power.

'It was a big project and it all had to be carried out undercover. We couldn't tell them what we were really doing because they would never have let us into the country. Instead we claimed we were making a film about flora and fauna. Once there we went to interview several dissidents and got loads of evidence that backed up the torture claims – shackles on walls, bloodstains and all sorts of compelling stuff.

'The final film was incredibly powerful and we had strong interest from the ITV documentary strand, First Tuesday, who wanted to buy and screen it. But then Ledingham came along, and everything fell apart.'

In May 1991 Richard Ledingham again approached Joey Pyle for a loan, this time on behalf of his son-in law who was after £10,000. Pyle eventually agreed to stump up £3,000, feeling there was less risk attached to giving out the smaller amount. This time the money was due to be repaid in four weeks with interest of £600.

When the time was up, Ledingham said he was having problems finding the money but was selling a consignment of drugs and would use the profits to repay the debt. 'I met up with him at a hotel in Epson. When I got there Ledingham was drinking with another man. He came over and told me the bloke he was with was called Dave, a dealer from Manchester and the man who was buying the drugs that he was selling. Only the drugs had not turned up, so Dave had not paid him, so he wouldn't be able to pay me. Once he told me that, there was nothing more to discuss. So I left.

'A couple of days later Ledingham told me that Dave was messing him about, worried that he might get ripped off. He explained that he had told Dave that I would be supplying the drugs and wanted me to reassure him that it was all above board. Looking back I know it was stupid, but the only reason I went ahead with it was because I wanted to get my money back. I went to see Dave, meeting him at a hotel near Heathrow, and made out that I was this big drug supplier and would be sending him loads of heroin in the near future.'

Dave was, of course, an undercover policeman and all his meetings and conversations with Pyle were duly recorded. But Dave wasn't the only undercover cop working on the case. Over in Joey Pyle's Pinewood offices, a pretty, young secretary called Lucy had started work in an office a little way down the corridor.

She had placed a bug directly inside Pyle's office and in the course of six months recorded 160 45-minute tapes of his conversations and phone calls. Of these, only a single six-minute conversation between Pyle and Ledingham was believed to have any connection to drug dealing.

'A month or so before I'd had the meeting with Dave, Ledingham had come in out of the blue and asked if I had any drugs. I asked him why he was asking and he explained that he knew someone who had around £200,000 going spare and wanted to invest it in a shipment. I told him that I wasn't into that – that I was only involved with the film business, but he asked if I knew anyone. That's when the wheeler-dealer in me came out. Instead of saying no I asked him how much the guy wanted to pay per kilo and how many kilos he wanted.

'What was annoying was that it was clear that Ledingham knew the office was bugged. He could never admit that in court, however, because if he had, it would have made him an agent provocateur and the case would have collapsed. But as far as I am concerned, that is just what he was. I guess it was that conversation that convinced them to go ahead and bring in Dave, the other undercover officer.

'But the whole time I was talking, just like when I spoke to Dave a few weeks later, I knew there was no heroin, because I've never dealt in the stuff. The first time I was just on autopilot, the second I was desperate to get my money back.'

Pyle's account certainly seems to make far more sense that the theory put forward by the police. They had, after all, considered Pyle to be a villain of first class order, one clever enough never to get his hands dirty and a man who had managed to evade capture for decades. The reality was that Pyle was right in there, getting his hands dirty and putting himself right in the picture. The only possible answer is that he really was bluffing. But then the bluff came to an end.

It was around this time that Pyle first met the other man who would unwittingly be responsible for his downfall.

'Pete Gillette had come to me via Reggie Kray, who told me he was a singer and asked if I could do anything with him. Gillette turned up in my office and brought some tapes with him and I listened to them. At first I thought it was a joke. The boy could hardly sing a note, there was nothing, no talent at all. But Reggie wasn't having any of it. He thought Pete was beautiful, a great singer and a real talent in the making. The only other person who thought Pete was talented was Pete himself. He was alright, harmless I suppose, but he was also a bit soft in the head.'

Gillette had been formally adopted by Reggie and soon set about trading on the Kray name.

'He came to me one day and produced a small glass vial from a matchbox and placed it gently on the desk in front of me.

'"Do you know what this stuff is?"

'"I ain't got a clue."

'"It's Omnipom."

'"You what?"

'"Omnipom. It's a drug. Athletes and bodybuilders use it."

'"I've never heard of it."

'"Well, I've got about two grand's worth and I wondered if you knew anyone who might want to buy it."'

Gillette went on to explain that Omnipom was turning out to be the latest thing in the clubs, that kids were going crazy for it. What neither of them was aware of was that because it contains opiates, Omnipom counts as a Class A drug, and trafficking or selling it attracts the same penalties as the trade in heroin or cocaine.

'Now I've never heard of this stuff in my life, and I've never ever heard of anyone actually taking it, but straight away a potential buyer, someone mug enough to buy anything I might put their way, came into mind – Dave. We arranged a deal and Dave agreed to pay two quid per tab, fourteen grand in total. It was way more than I had expected to get and just confirmed my view that Dave was a bit of a dummy.'

As far as the police were concerned, Pyle was merely offering the Omnipom as a tester, a carrot to prove they were bona fide buyers. Dave kept asking for heroin but Pyle only had Omnipom. In the end, desperate to ensure the deal went through, Pyle found himself promising to supply heroin in the future if Dave would take the Omnipom.

'I met up with Dave at the Sheraton in Heathrow. I can honestly say that I really didn't think the stuff I was selling was any good – I thought my luck was in and that I'd found some right mug who was going to buy it off me.

'Of course, I'd been giving it loads of shit about just how much kids love Omnipom and that it was really big on the streets, but I wasn't even convinced it was a proper drug. I'd never heard of anyone taking it then and I've never met anyone who ever has.

'I got up to his hotel room and as soon as I got in I told him to turn on the television. One of the first rules is that if you have to talk business in a hotel, you always turn the telly on, just in case the Old Bill have bugged the place. But when I flicked the switch nothing happened. He was wandering around the room, out on the balcony and back, while I was trying to work out what was wrong with it. Then I realised it hadn't been plugged in.

'"Leave it Joey," said Dave. "We don't need that on. Don't bother, there's only tennis on and it gets on my nerves. Let's just get on with it."

'I didn't warm to Dave at all. There was something about him that put me right off from the start. I didn't like the look of him or the way he spoke. He was chatting away and said something about using the money he'd make to take his mum on holiday and I remember thinking I don't care, I don't give a fuck. As long as you buy the stuff I don't give a toss what you do.

'He seemed a bit reluctant so I went into the spiel again about how great this stuff was, how popular it was on the streets and how he'd have no trouble selling it. In the end he finally handed over the money and, with a loud "Seeya Joey", waved me out of the door.

'I got about three steps down the passageway when I heard someone shouting: "Stop where you are!" Then bosh, some-one hit me on the back of the head with what I later found out was the butt of a rifle. I went down hard. I was seeing stars and there was blood everywhere. And as I was lying on the ground, I felt people crouching over me, a knee in the small of my back, slipping my wrists into handcuffs and that was it. I'd been nicked.

'The room had been bugged, of course, and what they had on tape was me and my big mouth bragging about how great Omnipom was and how I'd be able to supply him with all the heroin he'd ever need. That part was bullshit but I couldn't deny that I'd said it. Having kept one step ahead of the law for years, I'd gone and done myself up like a kipper.'

Joey Pyle's trial for charges of trafficking in Class A drugs took place at Southwark Crown Court in early 1992. As in the case of the Pen Club murder more than thirty years earlier the issue of jury protection would be a key factor.

'All I can say is that I was in prison, so, personally, I could not have had anything to do with it. People will always imagine that if something happens to a jury, then it is down to the defendant but that's not the case. If my friends or associates did something, that was down to them, not me.

'I've never been involved in jury nobbling myself but I know that years ago, there were people who used to make a full time living from it. They would spend days and days following each juror home, finding out where they all lived and then work out which ones to approach based on the ones who were most likely to go a certain way, either for money or through threat of violence.

'It was different then because juries weren't protected the way they are today. Now they have armed guards and they get escorted to and from the court. Nowadays I'd have to say it is almost impossible. Almost.'

At pre-trial hearings, Pyle was described as a gangster of the very highest order, a man with connections to the American Mafia and well known and respected throughout the British underworld. On that basis it was agreed that the jury at the trial would have 24-hour protection. They would be taken to and from the court by armed officers, who would also remain outside their homes at night to ensure there was no possibility of anyone being approached.

On the first day of the trial proper, Pyle was told there would be a delay before he was allowed to go into court. Once he was allowed into the dock Pyle noticed that the jury were absent. It didn't take long to find out why: one of them had been threatened. The judge, Mr Justice Butler, was furious and admonished the police for failing in their duty. Assured that it could not possibly happen again, the judge decided to continue the trial with eleven jurors.

'The next day we were late going in again. Another juror had been approached. The judge decided to carry on with ten. The next day, it happened again. Now the judge was getting really furious. He banged his fist down on the bench. "I don't believe it," he said. "I will not be bullied into aborting this trial. We will carry on with nine."

'On the fourth day he absolutely flipped his lid; went ape when he found out there had been yet another one. "I will not be dictated to by members of the criminal fraternity," he said. "This trial will not be aborted. We will carry on."

'The defence said that would be fine but that they needed to ensure that the juror had not mentioned being threatened to her colleagues, otherwise they would be biased. In the previous cases, the jurors had told no one apart from the police officers protecting them about what had happened. The remaining members of the jury had no clue as to why the others had been discharged.

'The judge ordered the juror – a middle-aged woman – to be brought before him. As soon as she appeared in court you could tell she was terrified, especially being made to walk up the middle and approach the judge's bench.

' "I can see these people have frightened you haven't they."

' "Yes your honour."

' "Well you needn't worry any more. You can go home now. We are discharging you from the trial. You will be well protected day and night and I want you to know that we are very proud and very grateful that you have come forward about this. You should not trouble yourself to worry about it any further. You may go."

'The woman thanked the judge and turned to walk out of the court. Then one of the barristers stood up and reminded the judge that he needed to ensure the integrity of the remaining jurors. The judge called the woman back.

'"I just need to check something. There is no one you have told about this is there?"

'"Oh no your honour," said the woman. "No one."

'"Thank you. You may go."

The woman headed for the door once more, then stopped and turned back to the judge, her finger resting on her lower lip. "The other jurors don't count do they?"'

The retrial took place in October at court number two of the Old Bailey. This was chosen partly because the jury sit beneath the public gallery, frustrating the work of nobblers who might attempt to follow them from court.

Normally, the name of each juror is read out loud as they are sworn in and as the date of the retrial approached, police expressed concerns that even this might make it possible for the jurors to be identified. Although the jurors themselves might be protected, people could still get to their families or friends and exert pressure that way.

To combat this the court agreed to take an unprecedented step. Each member of the jury would wear a number on their lapel. Rather than calling out their names, they would be sworn in by number. Only the court officials, the judge and the police would know their true identities. The nobblers didn't stand a chance.

And so it was that Joey Pyle, the enduring face of the underworld, the man who, despite being arrested more than fifty times during the preceding thirty years had always managed to walk free from court, whose last sentence had been eighteen months for GBH after the Pen Club murder, was finally found guilty once more.

Convicted of making an offer to supply heroin and opium, the then 59-year-old Pyle was sentenced to fourteen years.

Pyle appealed against his conviction and the Court of Appeal ordered a retrial. On 13 April 1995, at Woolwich Crown Court, Pyle was again convicted, but his sentence was reduced to nine years. Finally released from the restrictions of the AA category, he saw out the end of his sentence as a Category C prisoner at Coldingley prison, Surrey.

EPILOGUE

'I got out of prison for the last time in 1997 and ever since then I've kept myself busy and kept my nose clean.

Working closely with my son, Joe Jr, I have moved into the behind-the-scenes side of the music industry. I act as an agent for the likes of Oliver Cheatham, Jocelyn Brown and Wyclef Jean and I manage stars like Mark Morrison and Brian Harvey, formerly of E-17.

'I'm still tone deaf but I know enough about the music business to make my way through and keep my artists happy. The main thing I know is that there are a hundred pence in the pound and I know just how many pounds each of my people should get paid. When it comes to talking, especially when I'm at a meeting with all these fancy lawyers, I hold my own. When it comes to talking, I can talk with the best of them.

'The thrill of securing a good deal is never going to compete with the thrill of dividing up a bag of cash after you've done a job across the pavement, but you have to move on and I got used to the idea a very long time ago that those days were long behind me.

'The memories live on – I still keep in touch with all the chaps and every now and then we sit around and tell our war stories, but that's as far as it goes.

'In 2002 I married Julie, a beautiful woman in a beautiful ceremony out in Las Vegas attended by good friends and a few of the acts I look after. I know how lucky I have been to find someone like her and I now arrange my life around spending as much time with her as I possibly can.

'I know the law are still interested in me, but that's their own concern. The only times I see a prison now are when I go to visit some of my old mates. And that's just the way I'm going to keep it.'

INDEX